Nigeria and the Millennium Development Goals

Assessing the Implementation of the United Nations Development Agenda

“Diplomacy and Strategy”
English Series

Directors: Fouad Nohra and Michael J. Strauss

Diplomacy and Strategy is a collection initiated by the academic directorate of the Centre d’Etudes Diplomatiques et Stratégiques to promote the outstanding scientific work presented by Ph.D. graduates, professors and researchers. The scope of subjects covered is as wide as international relations itself, encompassing disciplines such as political science, economic science, international law and sociology.

OTHER TITLES

ZARE Kambiz, *The Gulf Cooperation Council Project. 1981-2016. The elusive potential for economic gain through regional integration*, 2018.
ZERMOUNI Hakim, *Smart Power in Barack Obama’s Foreign Policy. A Systemic Approach to Diplomacy with the Gulf Cooperation Council*, 2016.
CARTA Gianni, *Berlusconi and the Power of Television: 2008-11*, 2016.
SADIA Antoine, *Democratic Governance and Foreign Aid in Sub-Saharan Africa*, 2013.
DOUHAN Alena F., *Regional Mechanisms of Collective Security. The New Face of Chapter VIII of the UN Charter?*, 2013.
SOLVIT Samuel, *Dimensions of War. Understanding War as a Complex Adaptive System*, 2012.
DUQUESNE Isabelle, *Nepal, Zone of Peace. A Revised Concept for the Constitution*, 2011.
STRAUSS Michael J., *The Viability of Territorial Leases in Resolving International Sovereignty Disputes*, 2010.

Chukwuebuka Dominic Onyechi

Nigeria and the Millennium Development Goals

Assessing the Implementation of the United Nations Development Agenda

L'Harmattan

5-7, rue de l'Ecole-Polytechnique, 75005 Paris

http://www.editions-harmattan.fr

ISBN : 978-2-343-17020-6
EAN : 9782343170206

TABLE OF CONTENTS

ACKNOWLEDGEMENTS

Firstly, I would like to thank God Almighty for granting me the strength of character and perseverance to stay the course on what has been a challenging yet enlightening experience of mine.

I want to specially thank my supervisor, Dr. Michael Strauss, whose invaluable guidance, patience and support proved critical to producing this body of work. Your helpful inputs created the structure of this work, including guiding the direction of discussions herein.

I would also like to appreciate my parents, Barr. and Mrs. Dom Onyechi, for their moral and financial support throughout the duration of my studies. They have always been my role models and all I try to do is to make them proud. I hope to one day repay them for all they have sacrificed for me to be here today. Also, my sincere appreciation goes to my sister, Odera Onyechi, for her moral support and prayers.

My sincere thanks also goes to the UN Women Nigeria country office, Ms. Adjaratou Ndiaye and Mr. Desmond Osemhenjie for providing me with an internship which gave me valuable insight into development work in Nigeria.

Last but not least, I would like to show gratitude to my family and friends: Elizabeth Onyechi, Onyeka Iwobi, Yemi Esan and Damilare Adewole, for the kind words and encouragement through the course of this program.

INTRODUCTION

This book examines the United Nations development agenda from the perspective of the Millennium Development Goals (MDGs). It discusses these goals and examines the degree to which Nigeria has achieved them in relation to its peers in Sub-Saharan Africa (SSA), with the primary aim of understanding the degree to which Nigeria is prepared to meet the demands of the Sustainable Development Goals (SDGs).

The book consists of three main sections. The first provides a contextual analysis of development in Nigeria, particularly human development, and it builds on human development conditions in the country prior to the launch of the MDGs. This section also identifies and discusses some critical development challenges in Nigeria, the majority of which were supposed to be addressed by the MDGs. The key actors of the development agenda in Nigeria are also identified.

The second section discusses each Millennium Development Goal and the degree to which Nigeria has achieved it. Poverty reduction, for example, is one MDG that is especially relevant, considering that poverty is one of the main factors militating against Nigeria's socio-economic development. The level of poverty is very high and difficult to explain given the abundance of human and material resources in the country. With every new administration in Nigeria comes a new poverty eradication program, such as 'Operation Feed the Nation', 'Green Revolution', 'Better Life for Rural Women', 'Family Economic Advancement Program', etc. To date, these programs have failed in bringing about a significant reduction in the poverty level. Some of the factors responsible for this are discussed. In examining the degree to which the MDGs have been achieved, this section also entails comparative analyses with several other countries in Sub-Saharan Africa with a view to determining how Nigeria has fared in relation to them. The comparisons also cast a spotlight on development challenges plaguing the African continent more generally.

The third section discusses the shift from the MDGs to the Sustainable Development Goals. It examines Nigeria's preparedness for the demands of the SDGs from the standpoint of the roles of the public and private sectors in achieving them. Also considered are efforts to improve human development outcomes for Nigeria. Over the years, donor agencies – together with their service contractors and implementing partners – have committed significant amounts of money to address different thematic development challenges, yet human development indices for Nigeria, such as the maternal mortality ratio, remain dismal.

This book concludes with a presentation and discussion of key findings, with recommendations that suggest ways of positioning Nigeria to achieve the SDGs.

Background of the Study

The Millennium Development Goals were created to respond to the global development challenges as they appeared in 2000. At the time, the policy orthodoxy that had placed more attention on macroeconomic fundamentals as a basis for improving development outcomes had achieved insignificant results. The Asian financial crisis of 1997-98 had sent shockwaves around the world, and Latin America was recovering from its own series of economic crises. Most disconcertingly, Sub-Saharan Africa had suffered decades of negative economic growth while an HIV/AIDS pandemic infected 25 million people without a global intervention effort.[1]

The late 1990s and early 2000s also witnessed a deepening worldwide distrust of global economic institutions. This stemmed from widespread perceptions that globalization was a force that imposed the will of rich corporate interests against the needs of the disadvantaged poor. This was the reason why many developing countries rejected the OECD's Multilateral Agreement on Investment (MAI). The Asia crisis only deepened the reputational burdens of the World Bank and the International Monetary Fund (IMF) after ten years of 'structural adjustment' impositions on developing countries. Nigeria also experienced the debilitating effects of a Structural Adjustment Program (SAP) mandated by the World Bank and the IMF. The economic policy packages embodied in the SAP for Nigeria provided explicit encouragement to nurture an unregulated, dependent capitalist development model, while allowing only a supportive role for the government in a refurbished economic environment of highly decreased government ownership and control of enterprises.[2] The SAP left Nigeria worse off than it was before. SAP-induced inflation resulted in adverse income redistribution, leading to increased personal insecurity and less personal satisfaction, while heightening interpersonal and institutional tensions and deterring investment and consumer spending.[3] Other costs emanating from implementing the SAP

---

[1] MacArthur, J.W., "The origins of the Millennium Development Goals." *SAIS Review*, 2 (2014): 5-24. Accessed from: http://johnmcarthur.com/wp-content/uploads/2015/01/SAISreview2014mcarthur.pdf [4 January 2017].

[2] Anyanwu, J.C., "President Babangida's Structural Adjustment Programme and Inflation in Nigeria." *Journal of Social Development in Africa*, 7 (1992): 5-24.

[3] *Ibid.*

in Nigeria included a marked depletion of foreign exchange reserves, an inadequate balance of payments position and a significant decline in foreign direct investment (FDI) inflows.[4]

Global mistrust of development institutions and the negative effects of globalization resulted in calls for a new form of global partnership to address development challenges around the world. This new spirit of partnership is what informed the creation of the MDGs in 2000. The MDGs have since become the globe's central reference point for development cooperation. They took shape through a series of global political processes, agreements and proposals, intertwined with real-time international debates, led by the UN.

The MDGs are time-bound and quantified targets for addressing extreme poverty in its many dimensions – including hunger, disease, lack of adequate shelter and exclusion – while promoting gender equality, education and environmental sustainability. These dimensions represent fundamental human rights, *i.e.* the rights of each person on the planet to health, education, shelter and security. The MDGs were introduced and adopted at the UN Millennium Summit in September 2000 with nearly 190 countries, including Nigeria, as signatories to the agreement. The eight MDGs are as follows:[5]

1. Eradicate extreme poverty and hunger
2. Achieve universal primary education
3. Promote gender equality and empower women
4. Decrease child mortality
5. Improve maternal health
6. Combat HIV and AIDS, malaria and other diseases
7. Ensure environmental sustainability
8. Develop a global partnership for development

The aforementioned set of development goals serves as the globally shared framework for development actions at the global, regional and country levels. Besides these inter-linked development concerns and others that include employment, finance and governance, the goals also comprise systemic concerns such as the differential effect of globalization, inequalities among and within nations, and increased participation and involvement of developing countries in the governance of the global economy.[6]

---

[4] Philips, A.O., "A general overview of the Structural Adjustment Programme." In Philips, A.C. and Ndekwu, E.C. (eds.), *Structural Adjustment Programme in a Developing Economy: The Case of Nigeria* (Ibadan: NISER, 1987).

[5] United Nations, "Millennium Project: what they are" (2000). Accessed from: http://www.unmillenniumproject.org/goals/ [3 January 2017].

[6] United Nations, "The United Nations Development Agenda: Development for All" (2007). Accessed from: http://www.un.org/esa/devagenda/UNDA_BW5_Final.pdf [4 January 2017].

Rationale for the Study

Results from implementing the MDGs in Nigeria have been somewhat mixed, especially considering that Nigeria still has poor human development indicators. This comprehensive review will, in addition to examining the performance of Nigeria in the various MDGs, identify challenges that inhibited the country from realizing all the goals.

Nigeria's participation in the MDGs presents an opportunity for engagement with the government on development issues. The MDGs are intended to impact all strata of society from the government to the grassroots. It offers a veritable connection between local and international actors towards human-driven development. In Nigeria, significant financial and material resources have been committed by the government and donor agencies towards achieving the targets set for each of the goals. In addition to resources, government commitment to the MDGs has come by way of policy initiatives such as the National Economic Empowerment and Development Strategy (NEEDS). To ensure that public spending on the different sectors of the economy align to the MDG agenda, the Mid Term Sector Strategies (MTSS) were created to inform the drafting and implementation of the Medium Term Expenditure Framework (MTEF), with 57% of aggregate spending – especially at the national level – allocated for sectors related to the eight MDGs.[7] For example, the debt relief granted to Nigeria by the international community in 2005 was used by the government to create a 'Virtual Poverty Fund (VPF)' whose objective is to reduce the level of poverty in the country. To achieve this, funds from the VPF were channeled to grassroots development.

Furthermore, since 2006, the government has committed about US$1 billion, through the VPF, towards health, education, water and sanitation (WASH), environmental issues, housing, HIV/AIDS, women's empowerment (*i.e.* related gender equality concerns), social safety nets (*i.e.* conditional and unconditional cash transfers), etc. Given the problem of corruption and mismanagement of resources, the federal government, through the National Planning Commission (NPC), established a monitoring framework to track the expenditure and impact on target beneficiaries. Civil society organizations and non-governmental organizations (NGOs) are at the core of the framework, given the need for transparency and accountability.

The monitoring framework is critical to Nigeria's capacity to fulfil the MDGs. At this point, it is essential to note that effective monitoring of the utilization of financial resources committed to MDG-related sectors and projects determines the degree to which the MDGs are realized in the country.

---

[7] Kolawole, T.O., Adeigbe, Y.K., Zaggi, Y.H., and Owonibi, E., "Millennium Development Goals (MDGs) in Nigeria: Issues and Problems." *Global Journal of Human Social Science*, 14 (2014).

There have been many reported cases of dilapidated MDG projects littered across Nigeria's six geopolitical regions. One of the reasons for this is the limited involvement of communities or target beneficiaries in prioritizing MDG-related projects. These challenges also informed the decision to conduct this comprehensive review of Nigeria's performance on the MDGs.

Objectives of the Study

In accordance with the main aim of this study, some objectives have been developed to guide its focus:

1. To conduct a comprehensive review of the development challenges in Nigeria based on the thematic areas identified in the MDGs.
2. To critically examine Nigeria's performance under each MDG.
3. To conduct a comparative analysis of Nigeria's performance under the MDGs with other countries in Sub-Saharan Africa.
4. To use results from the review to ascertain Nigeria's preparedness to satisfy the demands of the SDGs.
5. To outline recommendations for positioning Nigeria to meet the demands and targets of the SDGs.

Scope of the Study

To fulfil these objectives, the study covers several topics that address critical aspects of the MDGs as they relate to Nigeria's development context:

- Development challenges in Nigeria
- Overview of the Millennium Development Goals
- Challenges and prospects of the MDGs in Nigeria
- Challenges and prospects of the SDGs in Nigeria
- The UN Development Agenda
- The Sustainable Development Goals
- Nigeria's Performance under each MDG
- Role of the public and private sectors in Nigeria's Development Agenda

Overview of the Methodology

The mixed methods approach is used in this study, *i.e.* qualitative and quantitative approaches are used to carry out the review of the MDGs in Nigeria. The qualitative approach entails non-numerical analysis of the scope of the review while the performance review component uses descriptive statistics to present how well Nigeria fared under each goal. Both qualitative and quantitative techniques were used to compare Nigeria's performance with those of some other countries in Sub-Saharan Africa.

The study uses the case study and comparative research designs. The case study design studies a phenomenon, situation or condition by placing it into its real-life context.[8] Essentially, it involves a real case as a basis for understanding the phenomenon being studied. Nigeria is the case study for conducting the contextual analysis of the MDGs in developing countries. On the other hand, the comparative research design involves making comparisons between different cultures or countries.[9] In this review, Nigeria's performance under each MDG is analyzed and discussed in relation to the performance of other countries in SSA.

Only secondary data is used in this study. It is gathered from a variety of sources, such as progress reports for donor-funded projects in Nigeria, reports from the MDGs office in Nigeria,[10] United Nations Development Programme (UNDP) assessment reports, the National Demographic Health Survey (NDHS), statistics from the National Bureau of Statistics (NBS), the World Bank, reports published by the Federal Ministry of Budget and National Planning, etc.

---

[8] Collis, J., and Hussey, R., *Business Research: A practical guide for undergraduate and postgraduate students.* 3rd ed. (London: Palgrave Macmillan, 2005).

[9] Saunders, M., Lewis, P., and Thornhill, A., *Research Methods for Business Students*, 3rd ed. (Harlow, Essex: Financial Times/Prentice Hall, 2005).

[10] The MDGs office was established by the Federal Government to coordinate projects and programs targeted at achieving the eight goals. This office is under the Presidency and receives budget allocations to implement projects and programs that complement those of donor agencies. The MDGs office – in collaboration with the Federal Ministry of Budget and National Planning – also liaises with federal ministries and parastatals to implement development projects that are supposed to bring about incremental progress in the realization of the MDGs in Nigeria.

SECTION 1

BACKGROUND

CHAPTER 1

NIGERIA: COUNTRY PROFILE

This chapter focuses on the contextual background for reviewing the MDGs in Nigeria. It presents an overview of the demographics of Nigeria's population and its development challenges. Most of the development challenges identified in this chapter were supposed to be addressed by the MDGs. The key actors of the development agenda are identified and their roles discussed.

Political Governance

After years of military dictatorship, Nigeria appears to have returned to civilian rule. Since 1999, it has enjoyed a relatively stable democratic governance process with certain inherent challenges, mostly involving poor leadership and low-quality service delivery. The three arms of government are the legislature, the judiciary and the executive. The country operates a bicameral legislature consisting of the House of Representatives and the Senate. There are three levels of government: federal, state and local. The federal government – the central government – is the most powerful, considering that it controls 41% of revenues that accrue to the Nigerian state while the remaining 59% is shared by the 36 states and 774 local governments.[11]

The origins of Nigeria's federalism lie not in the plurality of economic and geographic regions or of ethnic nationalities, but in the plurality of administrative traditions imposed by colonialism. These traditions generated regional rivalry and conflict that have, through nation-building and consolidation, become entrenched in the Nigerian political space. Following independence, the regional rivalry became the grounds for causing conflicts between economic and ethnic elements within Nigeria's federal system and for creating more states in an attempt to accommodate varying ethnic interests. In describing Nigeria's federal structure, one author notes that "Nigerian

[11] Lukpata, V.I., "Revenue Allocation Formulae in Nigeria: A Continuous Search." *International Journal of Public Administration and Management Research*, 2 (2013).

federalism is sick, unbalanced and lopsided especially considering the over-centralization of power."[12] Ethnic tension in Nigeria is the result of the impact of inequitable distribution of resources and functions.[13]

Despite its abundance of resources, successive military and civilian administrations have failed to deliver the dividends of good governance and improved standards of living to Nigerians. Efforts at building a democratic polity have been trapped in ethno-religious divisions.[14] Furthermore, the centralized political and economic structures made the military and civilian individuals who controlled key state positions excessively wealthy, while 70% of Nigerians continue to live in abject poverty.[15] These leaders and political appointees have shared a disregard for the rule of law, fostering the lack of an independent judiciary and legislature. Poor leadership has resulted in economic stagnation and alienation of the citizenry.

Corruption is equally responsible for Nigeria's economic stagnation and the high levels of poverty in the country.[16] Its economic and political landscape is pervaded by corruption and abuse of office. In fact, Transparency International ranked Nigeria 136th out of 176 countries sampled in its 2016 Corruption Perception Index (CPI). According to the National Planning Commission, "systemic corruption and low levels of transparency and accountability in governance have been the bane of development in Nigeria".[17] Corruption is widespread in Nigeria because the society or environment is conducive to it. Bureaucratic corruption and political corruption have thrived owing to the failure of governance systems and the lack of political will to implement policies that encourage good governance.

Economy

Nigeria is the most populated country in Africa with more than 180 million people.[18] Its economy, measured through the gross domestic product

---

[12] Majekodunmi, A., "Federalism in Nigeria: the past, current peril and future hopes." *Journal of Policy and Development Studies*, 9 (2015): 107-120.

[13] Uhunmwuangho, S.O., and Epelle, A., "Corruption and the Nigerian state: the relevance of ICPC and EFCC in the war against the scourge." *Babcock Journal of Management & Social Sciences*, 6 (2007).

[14] Joseph, R.A., "Democracy and prebendal politics in Nigeria," (Cambridge: Cambridge University Press, 2014).

[15] Sklar, R.L., Onwudiwe, E., and Kew, D., "Nigeria: Completing Obasanjo's Legacy." *Journal of Democracy*, 17 (2006): 100-115.

[16] Uhunmwuangho and Epelle, "Corruption and the Nigerian state".

[17] National Planning Commission, "Transparency and accountability in governance." *Vanguard* (22 March 2005).

[18] U.S. Central Intelligence Agency, "World Factbook: Nigeria" (2016). Accessed from: https://www.cia.gov/library/publications/resources/the-world-factbook/geos/ni.html [21 January 2017].

(GDP), became the largest in Africa and the 26th largest in the world following a change in the base year that caused Nigeria's GDP for 2013 to be revised from US$270 billion to US$510 billion.[19] This 89% increase is attributable to new sectors of the economy such as movies, telecommunications and online retail activity,[20] which were not captured previously. Nigeria also enjoys the reputation of being the trading hub of West Africa. This is because a considerable amount of West African economic activity is situated in Nigeria. Cross-border activities closely connect Southern Niger to the Hausa economy, while Benin and Togo also benefit from the major economic activity between Lagos and Ibadan. Nigeria plays a critical role in the economic situation in Africa, where it has increasingly been committing significant investments – especially in the banking sector – in different African countries. Moreover, the Lagos Stock Exchange is the only large-scale financial trading hub in the region.

While the growth in Nigeria's economy is seen as positive, the true size of Nigeria's economy is dwarfed by revenue leakages, *i.e.* weak tax revenue-generating capacity and poor accountability in the energy sector, especially the petroleum segment.[21] Prior to the economic recession that occurred in 2016,[22] Nigeria had recorded annual average economic growth of 7.1% between 2004 and 2014.[23] Ironically, the rate of poverty continued to increase over the same period owing to high levels of corruption and misplaced development priorities. There is growing agreement among development economists that high GDP growth rates do not necessarily translate into poverty reduction or alleviation. Some economists argue that widespread illiteracy, rising vulnerability to hunger and disease, and environmental deterioration, among other factors, affect human welfare independently of income.[24] GDP growth can only reduce poverty levels when it expands employment as well as productivity and wages of the poor,[25] and when public resources are spent on human development and infrastructure development.

---

[19] International Monetary Fund data. South Africa's GDP, previously the continent's largest, overtook Nigeria's again in 2016. See "South Africa regains Africa's 'biggest economy' title from Nigeria," BBC, 11 August 2016, https://www.bbc.com/news/world-africa-37045276.

[20] The growth of the retail sector has been largely driven by online shopping; a sign of the potential of the middle class in Nigeria.

[21] Adedeji, T.O., and Oboh, C.S., "An empirical analysis of tax leakages and economic growth in Nigeria." *European Journal of Economics, Finance & Administrative Sciences*, 48 (2012).

[22] Nigeria entered into recession in the third quarter of 2016, and the International Monetary Fund estimated that the economy contracted by 1.8% that year. Accessed from: https://www.ft.com/content/ab4f9ce6-4dc9-11e6-88c5-db83e98a590a [14 January 2017].

[23] International Development Corporation, "Economic Overview," November 2015.

[24] Fleurbaey, M., "Beyond GDP: the quest for a measure of social welfare." *Journal of Economic Literature*, 47 (2009): 1029-1075.

[25] World Bank, *Poverty: World Development Report* (Washington DC: World Bank, 2001).

Key Economic Data for Nigeria, 2016

Measure	*Result*	*Source*
Gross domestic product	US$404.7 billion	World Bank
GDP per capita	US$2,176	World Bank
Inflation rate	15.7%	World Bank
Foreign direct investment inflows	US$4.4 billion	UNCTAD
External debt stock at year-end	US$11.4 billion	Debt Management Office
Corruption Perception Index	136 (of 176 countries)	Transparency International
Doing Business Index	169 (of 189 countries)	World Bank
Human Development Index	157 (of 189 countries)	UNDP

The recession that began in 2016 had the potential to scale back any progress achieved from efforts to realize the MDGs, and placed doubts on Nigeria's ability to achieve the SDGs. The fall in prices of oil as well as other commodities on world markets had significantly reduced Nigeria's foreign exchange earnings. By late 2016, Brent crude was trading at between US$45 and US$50 per barrel, representing a major adjustment from the US$90-US$110 average price levels witnessed over the previous five years.[26]

Nigeria is the largest exporter of crude oil in Africa, with the largest natural gas reserves in Africa.[27] Oil is the main source of government financing, and the drop in crude oil prices had diminished growth expectations for the economy. Although the government has hinted at the need to diversify the economy away from dependence on crude oil exports, the foundations for achieving this are weak, as evidenced by the Doing Business index in the table above. Nigeria's physical infrastructure is in bad shape following decades of poor maintenance and investment. Another source of pressure that threatens the capacity of the government to achieve the SDGs is the poor political and security outlook. The Boko Haram insurgency in the North, coupled with high levels of kidnapping and armed robbery in the South, have hindered the administration's ability to attract sufficient FDI inflows needed to build resilience to the oil price shock. Nigeria's precarious economic position is further highlighted by waning investor sentiment. In fact, Nigeria's country

[26]PricewaterhouseCoopers, "What next for Nigeria's economy? Navigating the rocky road ahead," Technical Report (2016). Accessed from: http://www.pwc.com/ng/en/assets/pdf/economy-watch-may-2015.pdf [8 December 2016].
[27] *Ibid.*

risk premium (CRP)[28] has significantly increased, reducing foreign investors' interest in being exposed to the country.

People and Society

Nigeria's population is projected to grow from more than 180 million people currently to 390 million by 2050, making it the fourth most populous country in the world. According to the CIA World Factbook, "Nigeria's sustained high population growth rate will continue for the foreseeable future considering its population momentum and its high birth rate".[29] Nigeria has the largest youth population in Africa and this presents a number of challenges, one of which is the lack of viable economic opportunities.[30] The country must harness the potential of its youth if it is to improve economic development, decrease poverty and reduce crime and ethnic conflicts.[31]

Nigeria is made up of six geopolitical regions[32] and has more than 250 ethnic groups, of which there are three main ones: Hausa/Fulani, Yoruba and Igbo. Although English is Nigeria's official language, the Igbo, Hausa, Yoruba and Ijaw indigenous languages are also spoken.

In terms of religion, 50% of Nigerians are Muslim, 40% are Christian and 10% have indigenous beliefs.[33] The majority of Muslims reside in the North while the majority of Christians are in the South. This divide is often seen in violent conflicts across the country. The Boko Haram insurgency in the North East is an offshoot of it (Boko Haram translates as "Western Education is Evil"). The ethno-religious divide in Nigeria remains a clear and present threat to social cohesion and unity, especially as there are growing agitations from different parts of the country for political relevance.

Nigeria's population is spread between urban and rural areas, with the balance gradually changing as more people migrate from rural areas to urban areas in search of better economic opportunities.[34] Today, 48% of Nigeria's population is urban, while 52% is rural.[35]

---

[28] A high CRP increases the cost of borrowing. For Nigeria's CRP, see: http://financial.thomsonreuters.com/en/products/tools-applications/trading-investment-tools/datastream-macroeconomic-analysis.html.

[29] 37.3 births per 1,000 population, according to the NDHS (2013).

[30] About 60% of Nigeria's population is aged between 15 and 40 years.

[31] World Bank, "Nigeria: Economic Profile." Quarterly Report (July 2013). Accessed from: http://www.worlbank.org [17 July 2017].

[32] North East, North Central, North West, South East, South South and South West.

[33] National Bureau of Statistics, Annual Abstract of Statistics, 2012. Accessed from: http://www.nigerianstat.gov.ng [22 January 2017].

[34] U.S. Agency for International Development (2011).

[35] U.S. Central Intelligence Agency, "World Factbook: Nigeria."

Major Urban Areas of Nigeria

Urban Area	*Population*
Lagos	13 million
Kano	3.5 million
Ibadan	3 million
Port Harcourt	2.4 million
Abuja	2 million
Benin City	1.5 million

CIA World Factbook (2016)

High rural-urban migration in Nigeria has placed enormous strain on urban areas as existing infrastructure and public services are grossly inadequate to address growing needs. In 1974, the urban population in Nigeria was 25% of the total, but by 2001 it had grown to 45%, with a net rural-urban migration of 30% as at 2001.[36] The trend has continued as more and more young people move to urban areas in search of better economic prospects.[37] People tend to be attracted to areas of prosperity as migrants are usually concerned with the benefits they hope to gain there.[38] The burden of rural-urban migration is multifaceted. Congestion in housing and communities carries far-reaching implications for both the health and psychology of victims. Cities in Nigeria such as Lagos, Port Harcourt, Kano, and Onitsha have not only human congestion but also vehicular congestion, high levels of pollution (especially air and noise pollution) and uncontrolled physical expansion to accommodate the growing population.[39] The seventh MDG, which deals with environmental sustainability, is relevant to this rural-urban migration because a highly concentrated population places significant strains on the environment and natural resources.

---

[36] U.S. Agency for International Development, "Urban Profile: 'Nigeria' - Making cities work (2002). Available from: http//www.makingcitieswork.org/files/pdf/Africa/Nigeria.

[37] National Bureau of Statistics.

[38] Braunvan, J., "Towards a renewed focus on rural development." *Journal of Agriculture and Development,* 11 (2004): 4-6.

[39] Aworemi, J.R., Abdul-Azeez, I.A. and Opoola, N.A., "An appraisal of the factors influencing rural-urban migration in some selected local government areas of Lagos State." Nigeria. *Journal of Sustainable Development*, 4 (2011): 137-141.

CHAPTER 2

DEVELOPMENT CHALLENGES IN NIGERIA

This chapter identifies and discusses Nigeria's development challenges based on the following thematic areas as they relate to the MDGs: poverty, education, health, gender and environment. This material will form the basis for evaluating Nigeria's progress in each of the MDGs. Essentially, discussions in this chapter provide a contextual analysis of the development challenges in Nigeria.

Development is critical to a country's growth and sustenance. A country is seen as developed when it has the capacity to offer quality or improved standards of living to its citizens. Over the past five decades, Nigeria has been struggling with the challenges of development despite having an abundance of human and natural resources. Nigeria still falls within the 'developing countries' category. This is worrying, especially as the perceived gap between the developed and the developing countries appears to be constantly widening. Many developing countries – including Nigeria – struggle with a myriad of development problems such as growing urban populations, rural underdevelopment, high levels of youth unemployment, poor infrastructure and rising inequalities.

Before identifying and discussing Nigeria's development problems, it is necessary to provide a definition of what the concept of 'development' entails. Offering a useful definition for development is challenging, especially considering its pluralistic or multi-faceted attributes. Despite this, development can be viewed as an idea that encompasses all efforts to improve the conditions in which human beings live.[40] It implies improvement in the material well-being of all citizens, especially the poor and underprivileged. It also entails eliminating the barriers that encourage poverty and increase inequality. Another way of seeing development is that it is a form of societal advancement evidenced by the equitable distribution of resources and the provision of healthcare, education and other essential services.[41] One way to

---

[40] Gboyega, A., *Democracy and development: the imperative of local governance*, (Ibadan: University of Ibadan, 2003), 6-7.

[41] Naomi, O., "Towards an integrated view of human rights." *Hunger Teach Net*, 6 (1995): 6-7.

gauge where a country stands in its development trajectory is through the UN Human Development Index (HDI), developed by the UNDP as a tool for assessing human conditions in a country.[42]

At this point, it is necessary to draw a distinction between 'development' and 'growth'. Development here is viewed from the standpoint of human development. The relationship between development and growth is a mutually reinforcing one, as human development has a significant impact on economic growth.[43] Essentially, if the core attribute of economic growth is enabling economic agents to identify and apply their comparative advantage, a rise in the capabilities of individuals should support more of them in pursuing occupations or activities in which they are most productive. In this sense, human development can be viewed as the relaxing of constraints which may interfere with profit maximization.[44] Although human development is a broader concept, many of its attributes overlap to a significant extent with the traditional idea of human capital. Consequently, to the degree that human development has a positive relationship with human capital and human capital influences a country's economic growth, human development influences economic growth, *i.e.* development is the foundation for economic growth. This implies that the different mechanisms of human development are likely to have a distinct effect on growth, as, for instance, education has a strong impact on labour productivity.

As the basis for subsequent discussions in this chapter, it is essential to note that Nigeria ranks 157th out of 189 countries in the UNDP's 2016 human development report, *i.e.* a low level of human development; this captures Nigeria's development challenges.[45]

Poverty and Hunger

Despite having an abundance of human and natural resources, Nigeria still has high levels of poverty. The National Bureau of Statistics indicates that 61% of Nigerians were living in 'absolute poverty' in 2010, an increase from 55% in 2004. The problem was most apparent in the North of the country, with the North East region having a poverty rate of 86%.[46]

---

[42] The HDI is a summary measure of average achievement in critical dimensions of human development.

[43] Ranis, G., *Human Development and Economic Growth* (New Haven: Yale University Economic Growth Center, 2004).

[44] Birdsall, N., Ross, D., and Sabot, R., "Inequality and growth reconsidered: lessons from East Asia." *World Bank Economic Review*, 9 (1995).

[45] U.N. Development Programme, *Human Development Report 2016: Human Development for Everyone* (New York: UNDP, 2016).

[46] National Bureau of Statistics, "Nigerians living in poverty grows to 61%." Accessed from: http://www.bbc.com/news/world-africa-17015873 [14 December 2016].

Poverty in Nigeria, 1980-2010
(millions of people)

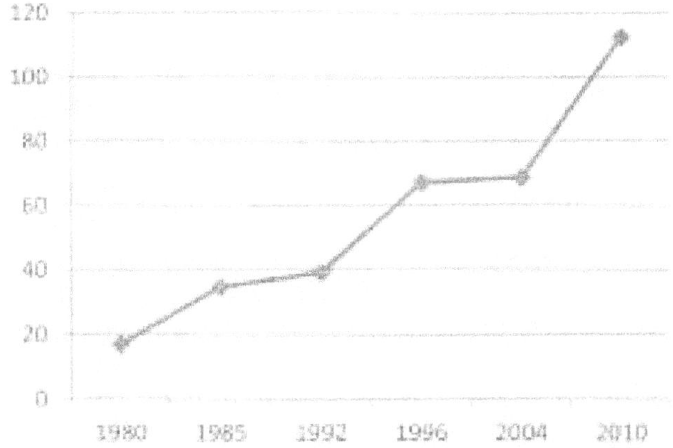

National Bureau of Statistics (2011)

For the purposes of this study, the definition of poverty is the one provided by the World Bank, in which poverty is perceived as living on less than US$1 per day, *i.e.* the amount deemed necessary for the fundamental needs of life such as food, clothing and shelter.

As noted above, the relationship between development and growth is a mutually reinforcing one. Nigeria's economic growth in recent years has yet to be translated into horizontal and vertical development. Indeed, the standard of living in the country has witnessed a continuous decline, as seen in the data for GDP per capita. This shows that economic growth has not led to a significant reduction in unemployment or the prevalence of poverty.

Although poverty in Nigeria can be described as pervasive, the country should not be among the poorest nations in the world with its vast human and material resources. Nigeria's inability to harness its economic potential will influence its performance as it relates to the MDGs and will also determine the degree to which it fulfils the SDGs.[47] Nigeria is ranked as one of the twenty-five poorest countries in the world.[48] Eradicating poverty is a critical objective in policy formulation and implementation, especially as it

[47] World Bank, "Nigeria: Poverty in the Midst of Plenty – The challenge of growth with inclusion." Report No. 14733-UNI. Accessed from: http://documents.worldbank.org/curated/en/582991468759320261/pdf/multi0page.pdf [11 January 2017].

[48] Odion, W.E., *Millennium Development Goals (MDGs) and the Poverty Questions in Nigeria* (Abuja: Panaf Publishing, 2009).

relates to human emancipation.[49] Consequently, it should be topmost in the plans and development agenda of the government.

Of the eight MDGs, the first deals with the need to reduce the number of people living on less than US$1 per day and to reduce hunger by 50% by 2015.[50] Nigeria is seen as one of the most of unequal societies in the world, with income distribution skewed so heavily that an increase in economic growth has little or no impact on living standards. The reason for this is that most Nigerians are income-poor. To put this into proper perspective, while the highest income bracket constituting only 10% of the population controls or receives 32% of the aggregate national income, the poorest 10% has access to only 2% of the national wealth. Approximately 50% of aggregate national income is owned by 18% of the highest income classification. By contrast, the poorest 20% of the populace has access to 4% of the national income.[51] Nigeria's Gini coefficient rose from 0.42 in 2004 to 0.45 in 2010, showing that inequality rose significantly during the period.[52]

Poverty Eradication Programs

Successive military regimes and civilian administrations in Nigeria have initiated different poverty alleviation programs as a way of addressing the challenge of poverty. As noted earlier, these programs have failed to achieve the objective of reducing poverty and hunger. Several of them are discussed here.

The Green Revolution

The Green Revolution was launched in April 1980. Its major goal was to revolutionize the agricultural sector with a view to achieving self-sufficiency in food production. Based on the strategy, several agriculture-centred projects were launched to increase food production. They included land-clearing schemes; moving towards mechanized farming, *e.g.* creating opportunities for leasing tractors; establishing agro-service centres to improve farming techniques; strengthening the value chains of agricultural commodities, especially cash crops; river basin development initiatives; providing low-interest loans to support agricultural activities; and accelerated food production schemes.

---

[49] United Nations, *The Millennium Development Goals Report, 2010* (New York: UN, 2010).

[50] United Nations, "Millennium Project: what they are".

[51] National Bureau of Statistics, Nigerian Poverty Profile Report, January 2010.

[52] A commonly used measure of the income or wealth distribution of a country's residents. A Gini coefficient of 0 represents equality and a coefficient of 1 represents extreme inequality. See Kanayo, O., "Poverty Incidence and Reduction Strategies in Nigeria: Challenges of Meeting 2015 MDG Targets." *Journal of Economics*, 5 (2014): 201-217.

The implementation strategy for the Green Revolution entailed the aggregate mobilization of resources. It included expertise in engineering the variables of food production and accurate monitoring of the institutions that supported different aspects of the agricultural value chain, *i.e.* processing, marketing, storage, seed marketing, soil erosion, development of grazing reserves, etc.

Directorate of Food, Roads, and Rural Infrastructure (DFRRI)

DFRRI was a domestic rural development agency established by the Babangida administration to complement other rural development efforts. Rural areas in Nigeria suffer from underdevelopment due to neglect by all levels of government. Most rural areas are marked by the following attributes: poor transportation networks, poor healthcare delivery, high levels of rural-urban migration, low levels of literacy, poor public service delivery and high levels of poverty. It is against the backdrop of these challenges that DFRRI was established to improve the living conditions of people living in rural areas.

DFRRI received allocations from the national budget to fund its rural development projects. Its policy development thrust involved social mobilization, infrastructure development and stimulating productive activities in rural communities (*i.e.* establishing agricultural output clusters).[53]

National Economic Empowerment and Development Strategy (NEEDS)

The main objective of NEEDS was to restore basic societal norms and values which had eroded over time. It was meant to promote poverty reduction through social cohesion, given Nigeria's status as a multi-ethnic and multi-religious nation. NEEDS was established to harness Nigeria's multi-cultural diversity as a channel for growth. The main attributes of this value system included respect for elders, honesty and accountability, cooperation, hard work, etc. NEEDS was designed to create a Nigeria where social justice and merit prevailed, but it failed to achieve its mandate of alleviating poverty.[54]

Failure of Poverty Alleviation/Eradication Programs in Nigeria

Several factors account for the failure of the poverty alleviation programs in Nigeria. These can be broadly categorized into two groups,

---

[53] Okunmadewa, F., "Nigeria Poverty Reduction, Growth, Strategies and Options in Nigeria: Prospects for Development," University of Ibadan (1996).

[54] Aidelunuoghene, O., "The Paradox of Poverty in Nigeria," *Research Journal of Finance and Accounting*, 5 (2014): 116-122.

namely: (1) reasons connected with the design and implementation of these policies, and (2) reasons connected with policy acceptability among the populace.[55] For the first group, there has been little dialogue or stakeholder engagement at the formulation stage of these policies. The policies were created without properly understanding the needs and expectations of the target beneficiaries. Furthermore, corruption and poor performance management hampered their effective implementation. For the second group of reasons, unacceptability and lack of ownership of the policies among target beneficiaries also contributed to their failure. When policy makers do not understand the needs of the target beneficiaries, they are likely to either overestimate or underestimate the challenges faced by them.[56]

Poverty alleviation programs in Nigeria also suffer from misplaced priorities associated with core development challenges. Many of these policies have been directed at the problem of 'unemployment' to the detriment of 'mass poverty' which is prevalent in rural areas.[57] Given the complexity of the problem in rural areas, targeted efforts are therefore needed to produce broad-based growth and deliver public services and basic infrastructure that decreases the severity of poverty in these areas.

Educational Development

Quality education and good governance are fundamental to the healthy development of a country. Quality education can be assessed from different perspectives, such as content relevance, access or outcome. Quality education is the foundation for good governance as people understand their individual rights and, as such, can demand quality governance from public officials. If children, who are the main beneficiaries, are properly processed through toward the main outputs, a country will no doubt produce the right people to manage its governance processes. Quality of education is determined by the performance of students. Education indicators for Nigeria are poor nationwide; the greatest need for assistance is in the predominantly Muslim North, where the primary school drop-out rate is the highest. Several factors account for this situation, such as financial costs, insufficient interest, a shortage of qualified teachers and poor school quality.

---

[55] Forae, O., and Benedict, A., "An appraisal of poverty alleviation programmes in Nigeria". *Journal of Research in Development*, 9 (2011): 296-304.

[56] Adeniyi, J.P., "Poor quality of rural life in Nigeria: implication for a policy." *Rural Development in Nigeria*, 1 (1984).

[57] Amis, P., and Rakodi, C., "Urban Poverty: Issues for Research and Policy." *Journal of International Development*, 6 (1994).

Education Statistics for Nigeria (2008-2012)

Education Indicators	*Results*
Youth (15-24 years) literacy rate (%) - Male	75.6
Youth (15-24 years) literacy rate (%) – Female	58
Primary school participation, net enrolment ratio (%) – Male	60
Primary school participation, net enrolment ratio (%) - Female	54
Primary school participation, Net attendance ratio (%) – Male	72
Primary school participation, Net attendance ratio (%) - Female	68
Secondary school participation, Net attendance ratio (%) - Male	54.2
Secondary school participation, Net attendance ratio (%) - Female	54.3

UNICEF, "At a Glance: Nigeria 2008-2012" (https://www.unicef.org/infobycountry/nigeria_statistics.html)

What is clear from the information in the preceding table are the gender disparities in education in Nigeria, as enrolment levels and outcomes for males are better than those of females. Additional light is cast on gender disparities in education when discussing the gender perspective of development challenges in Nigeria later in this chapter.

Factors Responsible for Primary School Dropouts in Nigeria

Reason for Dropping Out	*Proportion*
Monetary cost	30%
Lack of parental support	22%
Poor school quality	20%
Labour needed	16%
Insufficient interest	12%

UNESCO Fact Sheet, 2012

The challenges with education in Nigeria can be traced to a complex mix of socio-economic and socio-political factors. For one, the Civil War (1967-1970) and thirty years of political instability have contributed to the deteriorating state of education. Poorly planned programs and inadequate implementation of clearly articulated programs have also played roles.[58] In 2006, a ten-year national education development plan was developed by the Federal Ministry of Education to support reforms in the sector.[59] This plan was designed to address specific challenges at all levels of education, *i.e.* primary, secondary, and tertiary. Despite this initiative and other reform efforts, education in Nigeria is still plagued by problems such as low student achievement, low enrolment rates, inadequate infrastructure, unfit curriculum at all levels, poverty, poor parenting/guidance, poorly qualified teachers, inadequate funding, etc.[60] A key finding of a report on the MacArthur Foundation-funded 'Radio School' project was that poorly qualified teachers, poor parental support, poor interest in students' learning and inadequate funding were largely responsible for the disparities in student attainment between privileged urban and poor rural schools.[61] The report further indicated that a majority of the students had never used the internet.[62] These observations highlight the inherent challenges of education in Nigeria.

It was mentioned earlier that rural areas in Nigeria are marked by high levels of illiteracy. One of the programs that seeks to address this problem is the Universal Basic Education (UBE) scheme. The UBE scheme is a nine-year basic education program launched by the federal government to address illiteracy and ignorance with a view to stimulating national development and integration.[63] It is the government's strategy to increase access to education for all Nigerians, especially primary and secondary education. Following its launch in 1999, the Universal Basic Education Commission (UBEC) was created to oversee education projects in primary and secondary schools across the 36 states of the federation.[64] The UBE program is supposed to realize the second MDG, which concerns the need to "achieve universal basic education". Basic education is central to human and national development, and is the foundation for the other levels of education.

Prior to the launch of the UBE initiative, the government's education policy had entailed distortions, high dropout rates, inadequate curriculum, and poorly qualified and unemployable graduates. While the UBE initiative is a

---

[58] Jisse, S.R., "The dropout crisis in Nigeria's education". *Education Studies*, 5 (2010): 56-70.
[59] Federal Ministry of Education, National Education Development Plan.
[60] Ajaga, K.B., "Problems of evaluation in Nigeria's secondary school". *Education Studies*, 4 (2002): 70-79.
[61] The Radio School Project, implemented by the South Saharan Social Development Organization in Enugu and Adamawa states, runs from 2016 to 2018 and uses education as a learning and instructional tool to reach students in remote rural areas.
[62] Ogoko, G., Baseline Survey Report. (Enugu State: South Saharan Social Development Organization, 2016).
[63] UBEC, "Scope and mandate of the Universal Basic Education Commission." Accessed from: http://ubeconline.com/.
[64] *Ibid.*

positive development, it is not without its challenges. For one, inadequate funding has limited the ability of UBEC to fulfil its mandate as school buildings remain in bad shape and lack books and laboratory equipment.[65] Another challenge faced by the UBE program is incorrect data for planning. The politicization of data collection at the national and state levels has resulted in poor implementation of education development projects.[66] This jeopardizes the government's ability to fulfil MDG2.

Another problem facing the efficient and effective delivery of the UBE program is the lack of sufficiently qualified teachers, especially at the primary level. The teacher-student ratio in Nigeria is 1:40,[67] and some government-run primary schools have up to 70 pupils in one classroom. In addition, many teachers lack motivation as they are poorly paid. When the UBE program was launched, a curriculum for primary and secondary education was developed as part of measures to improve the quality of teaching and student performance.[68] Poor implementation of this curriculum has affected delivery of the UBE initiative. In fact, many teachers are ill-equipped to implement the curriculum. Finally, poor monitoring and evaluation (M&E) presents another challenge to the effectiveness of the UBE program.[69] Weak M&E systems make it difficult to track the performance of projects being implemented under the program across the country.

The problem of high levels of illiteracy in Nigeria can be studied and analysed at the national level. Student achievement provides a useful metric for understanding regional disparities. The ethnic factor in education development is seen as a critical consideration for appreciating the imbalance. Essentially, social stratification is a subject of the unequal system of educational distribution. The Southern part of Nigeria is known to have a higher literacy level than the North. The system of indirect rule in the North may be part of the explanation. Furthermore, there is a general dislike for the Western style of education among many Muslims in the North.

At this point, it is essential to note that Northern Nigeria has for the past five years been affected by the violent Islamist insurgency of Boko

---

[65] Anaduaka, U., "The Universal Basic Education (UBE) Programme in Nigeria: Problems and Prospects." *Journal of Research in Development*, 11 (2013): 152-157. Accessed from: http://www.transcampus.org/JORINDV11Jun2013/Jorind%20Vol11%20No1%20Jfun%20Chapter20.pdf [3 January 2017].

[66] Tahir, G., "The Universal Basic Education Programme: Issues and Challenges". Lecture delivered at the Federal College of Education in Kano State.

[67] Universal Basic Education Commission, *Standard Action Plan Based on the UBE Act.* (Abuja: UBEC, 2004).

[68] This curriculum is the Federal Ministry of Education-approved curriculum for primary and secondary schools. However, some private schools offer flexible curriculum.

[69] Obong, J.O., "The state of basic education in Nigeria: the way forward." Paper presented at the 47th annual conference of science teachers, Calabar, 13-19 August 2006.

Haram. The Almajiri system of education[70] is more common in this region and is partly responsible for poor education outcomes peculiar to the North. Non-school attendance is highest among states in the North East and North West zones. In fact, 72% of primary school age children in Borno state have never attended school. This compares with less than 4% in most states in the Southern part of Nigeria.[71] The Almajirai – itinerant children under Qur'anic instruction – represent the largest number of out-of-school children in Nigeria.[72] As described by Idris AbdulQadir,

> the Almajiri system of education as practiced presently in Northern Nigeria is a completely bastardized system compared to the form and conditions under which the system was operating and its output during the pre-colonial period. It is a scar on the face of Northern Nigeria.[73]

Distribution of Private Schools by Region

Period	*Northern Region*	*Eastern Region*	*Western Region*	*Mid-West Region*	*Total*
Up to 1959	2	9	9	5	25
1960-1969	0	10	24	15	49
Total	2	19	33	20	74

J.M. Kosemani, "The ethnic factor in educational disparity in Nigeria," in Educational Disparity: The Nigeria Situation *(Lagos State: Africa Heritage Research & Publications, 1992)*

The table above shows that the Northern region has the least number of private schools compared to the other regions of Nigeria. This provides useful insights as to why the North is the most educationally-deprived region in Nigeria.

---

70 The Almajiri education system is one where groups of children are sent for tutorship under an Islamic scholar; however, these children are often encouraged to engage in street begging by these tutors or guardians.

71 U.S. Embassy in Nigeria, "Nigeria Education Fact Sheet 2012." Accessed from: https://photos.state.gov/libraries/nigeria/487468/pdfs/JanuaryEducationFactSheet.pdf.

72 The National Council for the Welfare of the Destitute (NCWD) estimated the number of Almajirai in 2012 at 8 million. Accessed from: http://www.ncwd-youth.info/ [21 December 2016].

73 AbdulQadir, I., "The Almajiri system of education today." Lecture at Bayero University, Kano State, 2003. Accessed from: http://www.gamji.com/article5000/NEWS5956.htm [5 January 2017].

Health Situation

Based on the National Strategic Health Development Framework 2009-2015,[74] "the health indicators in Nigeria have remained below country targets and globally-determined benchmarks including the MDGs, which have registered limited progress over the years". Nigeria is among countries with the worst health status indicators in the world. Life expectancy at birth is 49 years while the disability-adjusted life expectancy at birth is 38 years.[75] Vaccine-preventable diseases and infectious and parasitic diseases continue to take their toll on the health and survival of Nigerians, remaining the main causes of morbidity and mortality. With an estimated 2.4% of the global population, Nigeria accounts for about 14% of global maternal deaths.[76] This observation is critical as it concerns MDG5.

Nigeria also has the highest number of HIV-infected people in Africa and the fourth highest tuberculosis burden in the world.[77] Non-communicable diseases are increasingly becoming a public health concern, especially among the well-to-do urban population. At present, the mortality rate for those under five years old remains high, and immunization rates are also low, with only 25% of children fully immunized by their first birthday. By contrast, a country like Ghana has 79% of children immunized by age one, according to the 2008 Ghana Demographic Health Survey (GDHS).

Significant disparities also exist in health indicators across Nigeria's six geopolitical regions. For instance, infant and child mortality in the North West and North East regions are twice the rate in South West Nigeria. Disparities also exist in these mortality rates when considered according to socio-economic status and rural-urban residence. These indicators do not converge towards the realization of 5th Millennium Development Goal.

Poor funding of the health sector is equally responsible for Nigeria's poor health indicators. Budgetary commitments to the health sector declined from 4.5% in 2009 to 3.5% in 2010,[78] and by the 2016 budget they fell to 3%. This is very low when considering the World Health Organization's (WHO)

---

74 Federal Ministry of Health, National Strategic Health Development Framework 2009-2015, available at http://www.internationalhealthpartnership.net/fileadmin/uploads/ihp/Documents/Country_Pages/Nigeria/Nigeria%20National%20Strategic%20Health%20Development%20Plan%20Framework%202009-2015.pdf [Accessed 3 January 2017].

75 World Health Organization, *Working Together for Health: The World Health Report 2006* (Geneva: WHO, 2006). Available at http://www.who.int/whr/2006/whr06_en.pdf [Accessed 1 January 2017].

76 According to the WHO, Nigeria's maternal mortality ratio is very high and highlights the health challenges in Nigeria.

77 World Health Organization, *Working Together for Health.*

78 http://www.nigerianstat.gov.ng/nada/index.php/catalog/30 [15 January 2017].

recommendation of a minimum budgetary allocation of 11% to the health sector. The dilapidated state of Nigeria's health sector, stemming from a lack of medical equipment, poor power supplies and an insufficient number of qualified medical workers, has resulted to a broad loss of confidence in it. Over the past 20 years, medical tourism has become very popular as government officials[79] and wealthy individuals travel abroad for treatment while the rest of the population continues to suffer from preventable diseases such as malaria, cholera, diarrhoea, cardio-vascular diseases, etc. It is estimated that 4,000 Nigerians travel to India to receive medical attention monthly and spend the equivalent of 20% of Nigeria's aggregate budgetary commitment to the health sector.[80]

The weak health system also contributes to the challenges bedeviling the sector. Only 50% of Nigerians have access to modern healthcare but only 9% of them use this service, mostly because it is of sub-standard quality. The healthcare delivery system in Nigeria is pluralistic in nature with orthodox and traditional delivery systems working side-by-side. Nigeria's orthodox health system consists of three levels: primary, secondary and tertiary. The primary level is the foundation for the other two levels and thus of the country's overall level of healthcare delivery. At the primary level, the local government is responsible for providing essential and preventive care. Secondary healthcare is the responsibility of the state governments, while tertiary healthcare is under the purview of the federal government. The Federal Ministry of Health estimates that there are about 23,600 health facilities in Nigeria.

The Revised National Health Policy [81] outlines the objectives, structure and strategic policy thrusts for effective healthcare delivery in Nigeria. It provides a comprehensive roadmap for addressing the challenges in the health sector. Its main objective is to strengthen the national healthcare system in a way that offers effective, efficient, quality, accessible and affordable healthcare services that will improve citizens' health status through the realization of the health-related MDG indicators for Nigeria. However, the effective implementation of this policy has been plagued by problems. One is that communities have played a limited part in the planning and implementation of health programs initiated by the Federal Ministry of Health.[82] Another problem area is the mismanagement and wastage of public resources. This is the main explanation for the continuation of Nigeria's poor

---

[79] Ciuti Consulting, "Outbound Medical Tourism, result of a bad medical system". Available at www.ciuci.us/wp content/uploads/.../Outbound-Medical-Tourism.pdf [4 January 2017].

[80] http://www.nigerianstat.gov.ng/nada/index.php/catalog/30 [15 January 2017]

[81] Federal Ministry of Health, *Revised National Policy* (Abuja: Federal Ministry of Health, 2012).

[82] Omoluabi, E., *Needs assessment of the health sector* (Abuja: International Organization for Migration, 2013).

health outcomes despite significant investments since the launch of the policy.[83]

Gender Equality Situation

Promoting gender equality is MDG3. Gender equality is a condition that emerges when males and females have equal opportunity to fulfil their aspirations, and are able to contribute to socio-economic and socio-political development.[84] This only happens when systemic causes of discrimination are identified and eliminated. Gender equality in Nigeria is far from meeting global expectations and standards. Cultural constraints, such as the masculine nature of its society, reinforce gender disparities in the country. Although Nigeria has taken steps to recognise the challenges faced by women, such as the passage into law of the National Policy on Women,[85] gender disparities remain rife. In the political sphere, Nigerian women have a negligible role and this affects their level of involvement in governance. From an economic perspective, women form the majority of the peasant workforce in the agricultural sector, while a majority of other women occupy the bottom of the occupational ladder.[86]

Political, religious and cultural sentiments regarding the role of the woman limit female participation in politics. Few women are registered members of political parties, and for them institutional bias restricts the extent of their integration into the operational structure of the parties.[87] Women comprise half the population of Nigeria, however, they have never exceeded 15% of elective offices.

Nigerian politics tends to be widely viewed as a 'dirty enterprise' and, as such, that it is not meant for women. This perception limits the opportunities allowed to women to express themselves and potentially find sustainable solutions to Nigeria's development challenges. Moreover, engaging in politics is an expensive enterprise and this situation creates entry barriers for women in the political scene.[88]

---

[83] Obi, P., "Nigeria: Health Sector's Hidden Crisis." *This Day*, June 2013. Accessed from: http://www.allafrica.com/stories/201309260109.html?viewall=1 [2 January 2017].

[84] Legal Defense and Assistance Project (LEDAP), *Gender Issues*, 2 (2003).

[85] This policy is guided by the Global Instrument on the Convention on the Elimination of All Forms of Discrimination Against Women (CEDAW).

[86] Awe, B., "Women's political participation: Why the barrier?" *Daily Times*, 31 October 1995.

[87] Canada International Development Agency (CIDA), *Gender and Politics in Nigeria*. (Ottawa: Policy Department, 1996).

[88] Omonubi, M.M., *Gender inequality in Nigeria*, (Ibadan: Spectrum Books, 2002).

Women's Representation in the 2003 and 2007 General Elections

Position	*Available Seats*	*Women Elected, 2003*	*Women Elected, 2007*
Presidency	1	0	0
Senate	109	2 (2.27%)	9 (8.26%)
House of Representatives	360	21 (5.83%)	25 (6.98%)
Governorship	36	0	0
State House of Assembly	990	38 (3.84%)	54 (5.45%)

Gender Audit and IPU PARLINE Database

Economically, women are deprived as they do not possess the same resources as their male counterparts. At the rural level, they suffer limited access to land for economic activities, thus restricting their financial well-being. A key observation in the 2012 Gender in Nigeria Report is that women were paid less than their male counterparts alongside disparities in access to finance, land and property. In many parts of Nigeria, people frown at women owning and engaging in meaningful investments.[89] At the urban level, women still face work discrimination as they are paid significantly less than men and struggle with the glass ceiling that prevents them from advancing their career prospects.

Socially, women in Nigeria are treated poorly and seen as less than men. Women are socially excluded across most parts of Nigeria and this affects their collective lives.[90] In the corporate world, even the most qualified women are made to operate on the margins and, as such, they cannot express their leadership potential and know-how.

Status of the Natural Environment

Nigeria has an aggregate land area of 983,213 square kilometres. Urbanization, deforestation, oil pollution and desertification have left their marks on the landscape. The Federal Environmental Protection Agency (FEPA) was established to manage the natural environment, including natural resources and exploitation activities. What is worrying is that environmental

---

[89] British Council, *Gender in Nigeria Report: Improving the Lives of Girls*, 2nd ed. (Abuja: British Council Nigeria, 2012).

[90] "Women, gender equality in Nigeria: A critical analysis of socio-economic and political gender issues." *Journal of Research in Peace, Gender and Development*, 4 (2014): 15-20. Accessed from: http://www.interesjournals.org/full-articles/women-gender-equality-in-nigeria-a-critical-analysis-of-socio-economic-and-political-gender-issues.pdf?view=inline [11 January 2017].

degradation has continued at a rate significantly worse than before the establishment of FEPA.

One of the main environmental problems is urbanization. A high population growth rate and significant rural-urban migration have taken their toll on the environment. In Nigeria, urbanization is characterised by city slums with a far-reaching impact on the natural environment as existing infrastructure and resources are insufficient in coping with the increase in human activities. Rapid urbanization – accompanied by low investment in strengthening urban infrastructure – has brought with it refuse and sewage disposal challenges alongside increased production of non-biodegradable materials, such as plastics. A connected problem is overpopulation, which places significant strain on public resources, including natural resources, and existing infrastructure. Overcrowding is largely responsible for the spread of city slums, which are a blight on the urban landscape in Nigeria.

As the largest and fastest growing city in Africa, Lagos' urban slums have attracted the attention of the Lagos state government, environment-focused NGOs and development agencies. These slums are characterised by poor sanitary conditions, dilapidated structures, high occupancy rates, a lack of social amenities and public facilities, etc. The conversion of environmentally fragile areas to slum dwellings by poor migrants exemplifies the connection between poverty and environmental degradation. Essentially, environmental degradation is both a cause and effect of the problem of poverty.[91] According to a UNDP survey conducted in 2004, "51% of male residents and 54% of female residents of the Lagos metropolis are classified as poor".[92] Due to poverty, people are forced to participate in unsustainable and ecologically-damaging practices to survive. Under the MDGs, Nigeria is committed to policies and practices that promote environmental sustainability; however, the situation leaves much to be desired.

About 15 slum areas are scattered across Lagos state, making the Lagos metropolis an environmental nightmare. A 2002 survey indicated that approximately 70% of the built-up area metropolis is blighted.[93] These slums are also characterized by public health issues, land disputes and ethnic clashes.

Discussion of the environmental situation in Nigeria would be incomplete without considering the problem of oil pollution in the Niger Delta region. The Niger Delta is situated in the Atlantic coast of the Southern region

---

[91] Aina T. "The Shanty Town Economy". In Datta.,S (ed.), *Third World Industrialization: Reappraisals and Perspectives* (Uppsala: Ord & Form, 1990).

[92] United Nations Development Programme, Human Development Report 2004. Accessed from: www.hdr.undp.org [3 January 2017].

[93] Lagos State Government/United Nations Centre for Human Settlements, "Identification of Urban Renewal Areas in Metropolitan Lagos", UNDP document UNCHS Habitat N1R 82/00/Implementation, 1984.

of Nigeria and is the world's second largest delta, with an estimated coastline of 450 kilometers. About 2,350 square kilometers of the region is made up of rivers, creeks and estuaries, and stagnant swamps cover about 8,000 sq km.[94] The Delta mangrove swamp spans an estimated 1,900 sq km, making it the largest mangrove swamp in Africa. Spills from crude oil exploitation are a global issue and nowhere more so than in the oil-rich Niger Delta region of Nigeria.[95] Aggregate spillage of crude oil into the natural habitat of the region is estimated to range between 0.7 and 1.7 million tonnes per year.[96] This situation poses a significant threat to the natural environment.

To put this into proper perspective, it is essential to note that crude oil exploration activities have already severely damaged the ecosystem in the Niger Delta. A report by the Federal Ministry of Education indicates that the quantity of oil spilled over the past five decades was at least 13 million barrels, which is equivalent to 50 Exxon Valdez-type spills.[97] Between 1976 and 1996, an estimated 4,647 oil spills from the complex system of pipelines spread across the region released about 2.3 million barrels of oil.[98] The majority of these oil spills affected land, water and swamps in the area. Some of the causes of these oil spills were ground erosion, vandalism, facility failures, corrosion, poor surveillance and inadequate maintenance.[99]

Ogoni, a community in the Niger Delta, is at the epicentre of environmental degradation from inadequately regulated oil exploitation activities in the region. Ogoni is characterized by oil fields and installations that stayed dormant following civil unrest that occurred in response to the damage done to the environment and livelihoods. From the latter perspective, the damage to the ecosystem from oil spills has increased the level of poverty in the region as traditional occupations such as farming and fishing have been severely affected. This is responsible for the high levels of youth restiveness

---

[94] Civil Liberties Organization (CLO), "Blood trail: repression and resistance in the Niger Delta". Country Analysis Brief (2002), 4. Accessed from: http://www.eia.doe.gov/cab/index.html.pds [15 January 2017].

[95] As at 2006, the Niger Delta region had an estimated 606 oil fields with 355 onshore and 250 offshore. There were about 5,200 drilled oil wells and 7,000 km of oil and gas pipelines, according to the Niger Delta Regional Development Masterplan.

[96] http://www.science.irank.org [11 January 2017].

[97] Federal Ministry of Environment, Nigerian Conservation Foundation, WWF UK and CEESP-IUCN Commission on Environmental, Economic, and Social Policy, "Niger Delta Resource Damage Assessment and Restoration Project" (2006).

[98] United Nations Development Program, *Niger Delta Human Development Report* (Abuja: UNDP, 2006).

[99] Ndubuisi, A.L., and Asia, I.O., "Environmental pollution in oil producing areas of the Niger Delta Basin, Nigeria: Empirical assessment of trends and people's perception." *Environmental Research Journal* (2007): 18-26. Accessed from: https://www.scholar.google.com [12 January 2017].

and crime in the region, as some youths have resorted to kidnapping and crude oil theft to survive.[100]

UNDP

Oil pollution in the Niger Delta.

A report by the United Nations Environment Programme was commissioned by the federal government to address the environmental degradation in Ogoni following five decades of pollution.[101] Its operational, technical and public health recommendations for environmental remediation in the area have been adopted by the government and are currently being implemented by the present All Progressives Congress (APC) administration. One of its main recommendations is to establish mini-treatment sites close to contaminated sites to minimize transportation and facilitate the return of the treated soil to the original trenches. Furthermore, local communities should

[100] Ayuba, K.A., "Environmental impacts of oil exploration and exploitation in the Niger Delta region of Nigeria". *Global Journal of Science Frontier Research in Environment & Earth Sciences*, 12 (2012): 18-28.
[101] United Nations Environmental Programme, *Environmental Assessment of Ogoniland* (Nairobi: UNEP, 2011).

be involved in the operation of these treatment centres, thus offering job opportunities for youth in the region.[102]

Another problem affecting Ogoni and other parts of the Niger Delta is gas flaring. Although Nigeria has large gas reserves, it flares about 17 billion cubic meters of gas each year in conjunction with crude oil exploitation in the Niger Delta. This high level of gas flaring is equivalent to around one quarter of Africa's power consumption. In addition to the economic loss the nation suffers from gas flaring,[103] there are also environmental implications. A study examining the effects of gas flaring on the environment concluded that soils around areas where gas flaring occurs lose their fertility and capacity for sustainable agricultural activities due to soil acidification by different pollutants.[104] The same study also reported cases of 'acid rain' in communities where gas flaring occurs. For instance, corrugated roofs of houses in the region have witnessed rapid corrosion from the composition of rain that falls because of flared gas. Sulfur dioxide and nitrogen dioxide gases and their composite matter also contribute to poor visibility and cause public health issues in the affected communities.[105]

---

[102] *Ibid.*, 206.

[103] Effiong, S.A., and Etowa, U.E., "Oil spillage cost, gas flaring cost and life expectancy rate of the Niger Delta people of Nigeria," *Advances in Management & Applied Economics*, 2 (2012): 211-228.

[104] Friends of the Earth, "Gas Flaring in Nigeria, 2004". Accessed from: http://www.foe.co.uk [14 January 2017].

[105] Manby, B., *The Price of Oil: Corporate responsibility and human rights violations in Nigeria's oil producing communities* (New York: Human Rights Watch, 1999).

CHAPTER 3

THE MILLENNIUM DEVELOPMENT GOALS

This chapter presents and discusses the different Millennium Development Goals (MDGs). At the Millennium Summit in September 2000, the largest gathering of global leaders in history adopted the United Nations

Overview of the Millennium Development Goals

Goal	Targets
1. Eradicate extreme poverty and hunger	Target 1: To reduce the proportion of people whose income is less than US$1 per day by 50% by 2015. Target 2: To reduce the proportion of people who suffer hunger by 50% by 2015.
2. Achieve universal primary education	Target 3: To ensure that, by 2015, children everywhere, boys and girls alike, will be able to complete primary education.
3. Promote gender equality and empower women	Target 4: To eliminate the gender disparity in primary and secondary education, preferably by 2005 and in all levels of education not later than 2015.
4. Reduce child mortality	Target 5: To reduce the under-5 mortality rate by two-thirds between 1990 and 2015.
5. Improve maternal health.	Target 6: To reduce by three-quarters, between 1990 and 2015, the maternal mortality ratio.
6. Combat HIV/AIDS, malaria and other diseases	Target 7: To halt by 2015 and to start the reversal of the spread of HIV/AIDS. Target 8: To halt by 2015 and start the reversal of the incidence of malaria and other major diseases.
7. Ensure environmental sustainability	Target 9: To integrate the principles of sustainable development into the country's policies and development programs; and reverse the loss of environmental resources. Target 10: To cut by 50% the number of people, both in rural and urban areas, without sustainable access to safe drinking water. Target 11: To register significant improvement in the conditions of slum dwellers by 2020.
8. Develop a global partnership for development	Targets 12 to 18: These targets are concerned with the reduction and cancellation of bilateral debt among developing countries; the reduction of trade and financial policies that are discriminatory, especially to developing countries; investing in improving the productivity and wellbeing of youth in developing countries; making affordable drugs available to developing countries; and improving access to ICT for developing countries.

United Nations

Millennium Declaration, committing their respective countries to a new global alliance to decrease extreme poverty and identifying several targets with a 2015 deadline. These targets became what are now called the MDGs. Nigeria was one of the 189 countries that signed up to them.

In 2007, the MDG monitoring framework was revised to include four additional targets which were accepted by the UN member countries: full and productive employment and decent jobs for all, improved access to reproductive health, improved access to comprehensive treatment for people suffering from HIV/AIDS, and bio-diversity protection.[106] These new targets took effect from January 2008 and were integrated into the original MDG framework.

Eradicating Extreme Hunger and Poverty

This goal is concerned with addressing the problems of hunger and poverty in the world, especially in developing countries. The world continues to grapple with these problems and the related one of malnutrition, although some progress has been made by countries and by multilateral and bilateral development institutions such as the Food and Agriculture Organization (FAO), the World Bank, the European Union (EU), etc.

Sub-Saharan Africa and South Asia account for the most people living in extreme poverty. Poverty is both a cause and effect of hunger.[107] According to the FAO, an estimated 800 million people suffer face chronic hunger and an estimated 2 billion people globally face micronutrient deficiencies. Out of this 2 billion people, an estimated 160 million children aged under five suffer from severe acute malnutrition (SAM).[108] These observations highlight the scale of the problem of extreme hunger and poverty in the world, particularly in developing countries.

Poverty and food/nutrition security have been some of the most pressing global challenges of the 20th century. This has informed an increase in the scope of funding commitments and technical assistance by donor agencies and governments towards the food security and livelihoods (FSL) sector. Although these programs are partly responsible for the global decrease in the number of people living in extreme poverty, regional inequities remain when categorizing the scale and scope of these challenges. The overriding

---

[106] Asia Development Bank, “Introduction to the Millennium Development Goals. Key Indicators for Asia and the Pacific 2009.” Accessed from: https://www.adb.org/sites/default/files/publication/27727/mdg-introduction.pdf [15 February 2017].

[107] Kristof, N.D., “The Hidden Hunger,” *New York Times*, 23 May 2009. Accessed from: http://www.nytimes.com/2009/05/24/opin ion/24kristof.html [15 February 2017].

[108] Food and Agriculture Organization, *The State of Food Insecurity in the World* (Rome: United Nations, 2014).

goal of FSL interventions is usually, "food security must assure access by all individuals at all times to sufficient food for an active and healthy life".[109] The 1996 World Food Summit added nutrition aspects and defined food security as a situation in which all people, at all times, possess physical and economic access to enough, safe and nutritious food to satisfy their dietary needs and food preferences, thus supporting an active and healthy life.[110] Given this observation, food insecurity, on the other hand, can be referred to as a situation where there is limited access to sufficient, safe and nutritious food for a healthy and active life.

The creation and adoption of the FSL sector as an area of focus for humanitarian and development interventions is driven by the complex network of relationships among food security, hunger and poverty. Essentially, the unique situation of people living in extreme poverty predisposes them to hunger and malnutrition. For instance, poor people do not have sufficient financial resources to produce or purchase sufficient and nutritious food for themselves and their families and, in turn, tend to be weaker and can neither produce nor earn enough money to buy food in sufficient quantities. In view of this, a target was created at the 1996 World Food Summit to cut by 50% the number of people suffering SAM. This target was at the core of the Rome Declaration on World Food Security and laid the foundation for MDG1. At the time of this declaration, an estimated 700 million people were chronically malnourished and about 2 billion individuals suffered from various micronutrient deficiencies, including vitamin A, iodine and iron deficiencies.[111] Overall, what is clear here is that despite some progress in reducing the number of people living in extreme poverty and facing hunger, many countries are far from achieving the goal of decreasing the number of people in this category.

Poverty and Hunger in Nigeria

Over the last decade, living standards in Nigeria have continued to decline, thus affecting the quality of life of a majority of the Nigerian citizenry. Available statistics highlight the difficult living conditions that most Nigerians face. The National Bureau of Statistics notes that approximately

---

[109] World Bank, "From agriculture to nutrition: Pathways, synergies, and outcomes." Report No. 40196-GLB (2007).

[110] U.K. Department for International Development, *Eliminating hunger: Strategy for achieving the Millennium Development Goal on Hunger*. (London: DFID, 2003).

[111] Food & Agriculture Organization, *The World Food Summit Goal and the Millennium Development Goals* (Rome: United Nations, 2001).

50% of Nigerians live below the poverty line.[112] Considering that Nigeria has a population of more than 180 million, this statistic highlights the scale of the poverty problem in the country. Furthermore, the Vision 2010 Committee Report indicates that a majority of Nigerians consume less than one-third of the required minimum of protein and vitamins, and only an estimated 60% of the population have access to primary healthcare.[113]

The problem of poverty is closely associated with Nigeria's low human development indicators. For instance, Nigeria ranked 157th out of 189 countries on the UNDP's Human Development Index in 2016.[114] The standard of living and life expectancy of the average Nigerian has sharply declined over the last decade, and despite significant GDP growth until the recession in 2016 the number of people living below the poverty line continued to increase.[115] This situation has worsened with the recession as the inflation rate hit 20% in 2017 for the first time in twenty years.[116] This raises concerns about Nigeria's capacity to achieve MDG1 and the Sustainable Development Goals.

The lack of inclusive growth in Nigeria is partly responsible for the high poverty levels. For instance, between 2000 and 2011, Nigeria averaged an annual GDP growth rate of 7% while unemployment levels rose during the same period, hitting 19% in 2011.[117] This highlights structural problems within Nigeria's economy that make it difficult for an improvement in GDP to translate into improved standards of living for the Nigerian citizenry. Some of the other causes of the high levels of poverty in Nigeria are corruption, weak leadership, neglect of the agriculture sector (this sector is the highest employer of labour, with only 5% of the sector driven by mechanised farming),[118] weak infrastructure (*e.g.* inadequate power supplies and bad roads), a high debt burden and uncontrolled population growth.[119] Addressing these problems should improve the living standards of a significant number of Nigerians and reduce its poverty burden.

---

[112] National Bureau of Statistics, "Nigeria Poverty Profile" (2010). Accessed from: http://www.nigerianstat.gov.ng/pdfuploads/Nigeria%20Poverty%20Profile%202010.pdf [15 February 2017].

[113] *Ibid.*

[114] U.N. Development Programme, *Human Development Report 2016.*

[115] National Bureau of Statistics, "Nigeria Poverty Profile" (2010).

[116] *Ibid.*

[117] Institute of Chartered Accountants of Nigeria, "Growth without development in Nigeria: confronting the paradox." Paper presented at the 43rd Annual ICAN Conference, Abuja, 10 October 2013. Accessed from: http://www.icanig.org/speeches/inventory_images/26.pdf [4 March 2017].

[118] Federal Ministry of Agriculture, "Positioning the Agriculture Sector to support export-oriented growth," Policy Brief, 24 June 2014.

[119] Edoh, T., "Poverty and the survival of democracy in Nigeria," *Nigeria Journal of Political and Administrative Studies*, 1 (2003).

Achieving Universal Primary Education

Few global goals have been as consistently supported as the idea that every child deserves a chance at completing primary education. Education, and particularly primary education, is a goal in and of itself, but it is also a critical driver of progress toward the other MDGs. In particular, increased education for girls has a significant positive effect on the health of infants and children, immunization levels, family nutrition and level of school attainment.[120] Whilst examining the challenge of education in Africa, the World Bank notes that educating boys and girls may be the most effective preventive strategy against the spread of HIV/AIDS.[121] Furthermore, primary education also contributes to improved natural resource management, including conservation of forest reserves.[122] Education is one of the most potent weapons against hunger and poverty, especially as it equips people with the skills, confidence and independence to live meaningful lives.[123] When more of a country's population are educated, the country is likely to build sound public institutions, thus reducing the level of inequality. Increasingly, studies conducted on the positive externalities of education suggest that these benefits require a minimum threshold of five or six years of school attainment, hence the reason why added emphasis should be placed on completion rather than access to primary education.

When considered in parallel with sound macroeconomic policies, education is central to the construction of globally competitive economies and democratic societies. Education is critical to creating, applying and spreading new ideas and technologies which are required for sustainable economic growth; this, in turn, raises the productivity of a country's workforce.

Despite the intended and unintended benefits of educating a country's population, the world remains far from the core Education for All (EFA) target, *i.e.* universal primary school completion. The World Bank notes that the average rate of primary school completion in the developing world only improved in recent years from 72% to 77%, far short of the progress required to achieve MDG2.[124] When weighted by population, the global picture shows some improvement, supported by a strong increase in the high primary school completion rate in China, from 73% to 81%.[125] One of the reasons for regional disparities in access and completion rates for universal primary education is

---

[120] World Bank, *Achieving Universal Primary Education by 2015: A Chance for Every Child* (Washington DC: IBRD, 2003).

[121] *Ibid.*

[122] *Ibid.*

[123] Sen, A., *Development as Freedom* (Oxford: Oxford University Press).

[124] World Bank, *Achieving Universal Primary Education by 2015.*

[125] *Ibid.*

that the existing nomenclature for aid does not prioritize countries with the highest need.

According to the Overseas Development Institute (ODI), "the majority of developing countries register an average primary completion rate of only 57%, yet receive an estimated 10% of current official development assistance going to education.[126] Furthermore, the same study by the ODI suggests that poor funding for education in the most affected countries is also responsible for the poor primary school completion rate. Whatever basis is used to examine the issue of universal primary education, the global average conceals significant regional variations in both the distance from the MDG and the progress made over the last decade. Based on a study conducted by the World Bank, Sub-Saharan Africa registered the lowest completion rate by far, with barely half of all school-age children completing primary school; it is followed closely by South Asia, with an average completion rate of about 70%.[127] The Middle East and North Africa registered a disturbing trend of no growth in completion rates during the 1990s, with the average completion rate remaining around 74%. The same study notes that Europe and Central Asia are closest to fulfilling the target of universal basic education with a completion rate of 92%, followed by Latin America and the Caribbean (85%) and East Asia and the Pacific (83%)[128]. What is clear from this study is that many of the countries lagging behind in the realization of the goal of universal primary education are located in Sub-Saharan Africa.

Universal Primary Education in Nigeria

In response to MDG2 and the need to achieve Education for All, the Nigerian government launched the Universal Basic Education (UBE) scheme in 1999. The overriding objectives of the UBE are to eradicate illiteracy, poverty and ignorance, together with stimulating and supporting national development, increased political participation and national integration.[129] The UBE scheme is backed by legislation, *i.e.* the UBE Bill.[130] In becoming law, a government agency – the Universal Basic Education Commission – was established to oversee implementation of the scheme and support efforts to

---

[126] Overseas Development Institute, "Universal Primary Education: Uganda," Policy Brief, February 2006. Accessed from: https://www.odi.org/sites/odi.org.uk/files/odi-assets/publications-opinion-files/4072.pdf [24 February 2017].

[127] World Bank, *Achieving Universal Primary Education by 2015.*

[128] *Ibid.*

[129] Joyce Olunfunke Ogunsanmi, J.O., and Ibimiluyi, F.O., "From the Universal Primary Education (UPE) to Universal Education (UBE): Implications for counselling in primary and junior secondary schools in Nigeria," *International Journal of Psychology & Counselling*, 6 (2014): 89-93.

[130] The UBE Bill was signed into law in 2004.

achieve MDG2. The UBE scheme is in accordance with the National Policy on Education,[131] which states that a child should have access to basic or primary education so that he or she can obtain fundamental skills, thoughts and positive attitudes. According to the policy, "primary education is supposed to bring about the required and total development of the Nigerian child irrespective of the education system".[132]

The implementation of the UBE, in relation to intended outcomes, has been fraught with challenges that threaten the capacity of Nigeria to achieve MDG2. One is the low quality of teachers. Primary education is the foundation for other levels of education, so when this foundation is faulty it affects the secondary and tertiary levels. While the government has made some efforts to provide more quality teachers to government-run primary schools, this problem persists. UNESCO notes that in 1997, less than 70% of primary school teachers in Nigeria had Grade II Teacher's Certificates, the criterion then.[133] By 1999, Grade II had been replaced by a National College of Education (NCE) qualification, yet only 40% of primary school teachers had it at the time. UNESCO further notes that Nigeria has an average of 36.03 pupils per trained teacher, a high number that implies reduced access of pupils to trained teachers. Poor teachers produce poor pupils with limited capacity to perform well at higher levels of education. These observations show increased efforts are required to provide more quality education in primary schools.

Another challenge to effective implementation of the UBE scheme is inadequate funding.[134] To achieve universal basic education targets, sufficient funding is required to rehabilitate many primary schools across the federation which have suffered neglect from the federal and state governments. Funding is also required to attract the most qualified people to teaching. In Nigeria, there is a widespread impression that the teaching profession is one with particularly poorly paid jobs.[135] This discourages qualified and talented people from going into teaching. Consequently, some people enter the profession as a means to an end rather than with passion. In addition to rehabilitating infrastructure in primary schools, funding is required to motivate teachers and attract talented people to the profession.

Another problem with effective implementation of the UBE scheme concerns socio-cultural norms. In Nigeria, only 59% of the population aged

---

[131] Federal Republic of Nigeria, *National Policy on Education*, (Abuja: Federal Government Nigeria Publications, 2004).

[132] *Ibid.*

[133] UNESCO, "Education Web Master: World Conference on Higher Education Framework and Action" (2001). Accessed from: http://www.jyu.tilunesco2001/conference.html [23 February 2017].

[134] *Ibid.*

[135] *Universal Basic Education Programme, Annual Report 2006* (Abuja: UBEC, 2006).

15 and above can read and write.[136] Northern Nigeria accounts for the highest levels of illiteracy compared to the national average.[137] Culture has a significant role to play in poor education outcomes for Northern Nigeria.[138] The majority of people in Northern Nigeria are Muslims who prefer to enrol their children in informal education systems, such as Islamic schools. Again, Northern Nigeria accounts for the highest number of out-of-school children and a low enrolment of girls compared to the national average.[139] Consequently, improving access to basic education and improving completion rates will require significant investments in education in Northern Nigeria as that would influence Nigeria's performance with respect to MDG2.

Gender Equality and Women's Empowerment

MDG3, which focuses on gender equality and women's empowerment, is based on the premise that empowering women is an effective way of reducing poverty levels, lifting more people out of extreme hunger and disease, as well as supporting development that is truly sustainable. Furthermore, MDG3 was created to reduce gender disparities in education, particularly primary and secondary education. A critical element of achieving gender equality is via the empowerment of women, which can be achieved through increased political participation, improved access to sexual and reproductive health services, and improved access to economic opportunities. These channels align with the popular saying, "if you educate a girl, you educate the world". This saying reflects the important role that women play in keeping households together and in children's development.

Another critical way of reducing gender disparities is through the eradication of all forms of violence against women. Such violence, especially domestic violence and sexual violence, is a major public health concern and constitutes the violation of women's human rights. According to the World Health Organization, one in three women globally have gone through physical and/or sexual violence.[140] The majority of this intimate partner violence. Globally, about 30% of women who have been in relationships report that they have experienced some sort of physical and/or sexual violence by their close partners, *i.e.* a boyfriend or husband.[141] As much as 40% of murders of women

[136] U.S. Central Intelligence Agency, "World Factbook: Nigeria".

[137] World Bank, "Education for All: assessing the level of progress made by the Nigerian Government," Policy Brief, March 2014.

[138] Amos, E., *Education in Northern Nigeria* (London: George Allyn University Press: 1996).

[139] World Bank, "Education for All."

[140] World Health Organization, "Violence against women: Factsheet," November 2016. Accessed from: http://www.who.int/mediacentre/factsheets/fs239/en/ [5 March 2017].

[141] *Ibid.*

are committed by male partners.[142] Factors responsible for the rising perpetration of violence against females are low levels of education, negative cultural norms that subjugate women, child maltreatment, alcohol and substance abuse, etc.

A recent MDGs report highlighted some disturbing facts that show the difficulties that countries face when it comes to eliminating the barriers to achieving gender quality and improved women's empowerment in Nigeria:[143]

- Low school enrolment levels for girls.
- High levels of poverty, particularly in least developing and middle income countries.
- More men than women in paid employment and the formal economy.
- More women than men in the informal economy.
- Glass ceilings for women in the corporate world.
- Men are paid more than women, including when they carry out the same job.

Globally, women continue to face inequitable access to education, work and economic assets, and political participation. Violence in particular continues to undermine efforts aimed at fulfilling MDG3. Meaningful progress will largely depend on success in these interconnected challenges.

Gender Equality and Women's Empowerment in Nigeria

In accordance with global calls and treaties, Nigeria has taken some steps towards improving the conditions of women such as signing into law the National Policy on Women, which was influenced by the Convention on the Elimination of All Forms of Discrimination against Women (CEDAW). To achieve MDG3, Nigeria will need to adopt a pragmatic development approach that challenges structures which perpetrate gender disparities at all levels. Power relations between the male and female genders must be balanced to improve the conditions of Nigerian women.

One area where gender disparity in Nigeria is prevalent is the political space. There are barriers such as religious and cultural bias against the participation of women in politics at the federal, state, and local government levels. This has resulted in low membership levels for women in political parties and limited participation in the parties' decision-making structures. The aggressive and masculine nature of Nigerian politics also contributes to

---

142 *Ibid.*

143 United Nations, *The Millennium Development Goals Report, 2012* (New York: United Nations, 2012).

perpetrating the power imbalance. Although approximately 50% of Nigeria's population consists of women, they have continued to be sidelined with respect to elective and appointed political offices. [144] Low political participation of women also translates to low economic participation. To put this observation into proper perspective, it is essential to note that women have never held more than 15% of elective political positions.

There is also an economic dimension to the problem of gender inequality and low women's empowerment in Nigeria. One of the factors inhibiting women's empowerment is their limited access to economic assets. According to the United Nations, out of the three-quarters of all economic activities ascribed to men, women actually carry out 53% of the work, although most of this is in the informal economy.[145] In Nigeria, women are restricted from engaging in economic activities that would otherwise make them independent. Women lack equitable access to decent employment and are faced with occupational segregation when they have the same qualifications and academic credentials as their male counterparts.

The Gender in Nigeria Report,[146] funded by the U.K. Department for International Development (DFID) and prepared by the British Council, notes that Nigerian women earn less than men, even within the same sector. The report further highlights the inequitable access to land, credit, information and technology for women.[147] The reason for this is that entitlement structures are skewed by gender, thus influencing the allocation of economic assets. The report concludes that more equitable access to productive assets will reduce extreme poverty in Nigeria, especially in rural areas where a majority of the extreme poor are located.

Reducing Child Mortality

Child mortality is a critical indicator for assessing the health and well-being of children. The main target for MDG4 is to reduce the under-five mortality rate by two-thirds between 1990 and 2015. Although the UN notes that child deaths are declining, the decline has not met expectations. For instance, between 1990 and 2008, the death rate for children under five

---

[144] Ekpe, D., Eja, A.E., and John, E.I., "Women's gender equality in Nigeria: A critical analysis of socio-economic and political (gender issues)," *Journal of Research in Gender & Development*, 4 (2014): 15-20.

[145] U.N. Department for Economic and Social Affairs, *Achieving Equality, Women's Empowerment and Strengthening Development Cooperation*, (New York: United Nations, 2010). Accessed from: http://www.un.org/en/ecosoc/docs/pdfs/10-50143_(e)_(desa)dialogues_ecosoc_achieving_gender_equality_women_empowerment.pdf [23 February 2017].

[146] British Council, *Gender in Nigeria Report.*

[147] *Ibid.*

declined from 100 to 72 deaths for every 1,000 births.[148] The implication of this is that globally, there are 10,000 fewer deaths among under-fives per day.[149] Some countries have made significant progress towards reducing child mortality. UNICEF notes that almost one-third of the 49 least developed countries have reduced under-five mortality rates by 40% or more over the past two decades. Nevertheless, this falls significantly short of the MDG4 target of a two-thirds decrease by 2015.[150]

Since 1990, child mortality rates in North Africa, East Asia, West Asia, Latin America and the Caribbean have declined by about 50%.[151] On the other hand, the situation appears dire in SSA, where little progress has been made. Although SSA has recorded a 22% reduction in under-five mortality rates, high fertility rates and the slow pace of reducing deaths imply that the absolute number of children who have died has actually risen from about from 4 million in 1990 to 4.5 million in 2008.[152] SSA accounts for one-fifth of the world's under-five children and, as such, it accounted for 50% of their 8.8 million deaths in 2008.[153] What these statistics show is countries in SSA, including Nigeria, have underperformed when it comes to securing the health and well-being of children.

Child Mortality in Nigeria

Although under-five mortality has been reduced globally from 90 deaths per 1,000 live births in 1990 to 48 in 2012, Nigeria has not recorded a significant improvement in this measure. In fact, under-five mortality in Nigeria rose from 138 per 1,000 live births in 2007 to 158 per 1,000 live births in 2011, against the MDG4 target of 71 per 1,000 live births.[154] At present, Nigeria is one of the five countries that account for 50% of the world's under-five deaths.[155] It also accounts for 20% of the child deaths in SSA. UNICEF notes that an estimated 5 million children are born annually in Nigeria and

---

[148] United Nations, Goal 4: Reduce Child Mortality, Fact Sheet, September 2010. Accessed from: http://www.un.org/millenniumgoals/pdf/MDG_FS_4_EN.pdf [12 March 2017].
[149] *Ibid.*
[150] UNICEF, "Levels and trends in child mortality, 2015". Accessed from: https://www.unicef.org/publications/files/Child_Mortality_Report_2015_Web_9_Sept_15.pdf [22 March 2017].
[151] United Nations, Goal 4: Reduce Child Mortality, Fact Sheet.
[152] *Ibid.*
[153] *Ibid.*
[154] National Population Commission and ICF Macro, *Nigerian Demographic and Health Survey 2008* (Abuja: ICF Macro and Calverton, 2009).
[155] *Ibid.*

about 1 million of them die before they reach the age of five years.[156] There are regional disparities when it comes to under-five mortality rates in Nigeria, with Northern Nigeria accounting for the highest rate.

Regional Distribution of Under-Five Mortality in Nigeria

Region	*Mortality per 1,000 Live Births*
North East	269
North West	260
South West	176
South East	103

UNICEF

Several factors are responsible for poor child health and well-being in Nigeria. Among these are poor hygiene conditions, dirty feeding bottles and utensils, inadequate disposal of refuse, unsafe water and poor maternal education, especially in rural areas.[157] With respect to maternal education, a child born to a financially deprived and less-educated family is more likely to die within the first six months of life: the mother may be poorly nourished during pregnancy, lack access to proper antenatal care, and be likely to deliver in a poorly equipped facility. It is essential to note that rural areas account for the majority of the under-five deaths in Nigeria.

Maternal Health

According to the WHO, "one woman dies per minute in childbirth around the world and Sub-Saharan Africa accounts for 50% of these deaths".[158] Although some progress has been made towards improving maternal care globally, Africa continues to lag on maternal mortality indicators. The majority of women across the globe lack comprehensive

---

[156] UNICEF, "General Facts: Mother, Newborn and Child Health and Mortality in Nigeria," Fact Sheet, September 2012. Accessed from: https://www.unicef.org/nigeria/ng_publications_advocacybrochure.pdf [13 March 2017].

[157] Adetoro, G.W,, and Awoo, E.O., "A statistical analysis of child mortality: Evidence from Nigeria," *Journal of Demography and Social Statistics*, 1v(2014): 110-120. Accessed from: http://eprints.covenantuniversity.edu.ng/4262/1/A%20Statistical%20Analysis%20of%20Child%20Mortality%20-%20Gbemi%20%26%20Amoo.pdf [18 March 2017].

[158] Africa Progress Panel, "Maternal Health: Investing in a Lifeline of Healthy Societies and Economies," Policy Brief, September 2010. Accessed from: http://www.who.int/pmnch/topics/maternal/app_maternal_health_english.pdf.

access to care. Almost 75% of women who die in Africa would be alive if they had access to interventions that prevent pregnancy and reduce complications associated with childbirth. International organizations – multilateral and bilateral agencies – and national governments have realized the scale of the problem of maternal mortality and have made commitments towards reducing maternal deaths worldwide. MDG5 calls for national maternal mortality ratios to be decreased by three-quarters between 1990 and 2015. The maternal mortality ratio did decline by an average of 5% between 1990 and 2005,[159] an insuffient pace if efforts to address the problem are to have a significant effect on expected targets.

Countries face challenges when it comes to improving or increasing access to maternal care. Among these are limited funding, inadequate data resulting in poor primary healthcare planning, poor implementation of healthcare programs and the cost of healthcare services. Maternal deaths are preventable especially when they are caused by complications during pregnancy or during the postpartum period. The four main killers are severe bleeding, infections, hypertensive disorders in pregnancy and obstructed labour.[160]

Maternal Health in Nigeria

Nigeria accounted for 6 million births in 2007 – the third highest number in the world after India and China – and an aggregate fertility rate of 5.4. This highlights the level of population growth in Nigeria when viewed in absolute terms.[161] As a large number of Nigerians live in poverty, this impairs their capacity to afford healthcare. Poverty, demographic challenges and insufficient funding of public healthcare contribute to neonatal and maternal mortality. The United Nations estimates the lifetime risk of maternal death in Nigeria at 1 in 18. When benchmarked globally, the seriousness of maternal death in the country becomes evident: an estimated 1 of every 9 maternal deaths in the world occurs in Nigeria.[162]

The women who survive pregnancy and childbirth must also contend with compromised health as inadequate health facilities; the cost of services; the distance to healthcare facilities, particularly in rural areas; and cultural norms that discourage people – also especially in rural areas – from accessing

---

[159] *Ibid.*

[160] Harding, A. "The Private Health Sector: A key to reaching women with maternal health programmes," Women Deliver Conference 2010.

[161] UNICEF, "Maternal and newborn health in Nigeria: Developing strategies to accelerate progress," Policy Brief, June 2010. Accessed from: https://www.unicef.org/sowc09/docs/SOWC09-Panel-1.3-EN.pdf [11 March 2017].

[162] *Ibid.*

modern healthcare services highlight the unique challenges that pregnant and lactating women face.[163] This casts enormous doubt on Nigeria's ability to achieve MDG5. Focusing on the cultural dimension of the problem, attitudes and practices that discriminate against women and girls contribute to maternal mortality and morbidity. Child marriages and high levels of adolescent births are commonplace across Nigeria, especially in the North, which accounts for the highest level of maternal mortality.

HIV/AIDS, Malaria and Other Diseases

As at the end of 2010, approximately 34 million people were living with HIV around the world, including an estimated 3 million children under 15 years old.[164] In the same year, there were an estimated 2.7 million new cases of HIV infection, including 390,000 children under 15.[165] Internationally, the number of people infected with HIV continues to decline each year, although there are marked variations when considered regionally. In SSA, where most of the new HIV infections occur, about 1.9 million people became infected in 2010. Furthermore, the yearly number of AIDS-related deaths globally continues to witness a steady decline from a high of 2.2 million to about 1.8 million in 2010. The number of AIDS-related deaths in the Middle East and North Africa rose in the decade until 2010,[166] while the number of such deaths in SSA, South Asia, South East Asia and the Caribbean has steadily declined.[167]

While new incidences of HIV have declined slowly on a global basis, Eastern Europe and Central Asia have witnessed an acceleration since 2008. Introducing antiretroviral therapy has averted 2.5 million deaths in low- and middle-income countries worldwide since 1995. It is essential to note that SSA accounts for the majority of the averted deaths during this period: an estimated 1.8 million. Furthermore, offering antiretroviral prophylaxis to pregnant women living with HIV has prevented over 300,000 children from becoming infected with HIV since 1995.[168] Of these children who avoided infection, 85% reside in SSA, the region that has the greatest prevalence of HIV infection among women of reproductive age.

---

[163] *Ibid.*

[164] WHO, "Global HIV/AIDS Response: Epidemic Update and Health Sector Progress towards Universal Access," Progress Report 2012. Accessed from: http://www.who.int/hiv/pub/progress_report2011/hiv_full_report_2011.pdf [7 March 2017].

[165] *Ibid.*

[166] WHO, UNICEF, and UNAIDS, *A guide on indicators for the monitoring and reporting on health sector response to HIV/AIDS* (Geneva: World Health Organization, 2011).

[167] *Ibid.*

[168] World Health Organization, World Health Statistics 2011. Accessed from: http://www.who.int/whosis/whostat/EN_WHS2011_full.pdf [7 March 2017].

In addition to HIV/AIDS, malaria is another life-threatening disease that MDG6 seeks to address. Malaria is mostly found in the tropics. Essentially, there are more than 100 countries where there is a risk of malaria transmission, and these are visited by about 120 million international travellers annually.[169] Each year, many such travellers fall sick because of malaria they contracted in countries where the disease is endemic.

At the beginning of the millennium, the fight against malaria was being lost. In 2001, the roadmap towards the implementation of the United Nations Millennium Declaration noted that an estimated 1 million individuals die from malaria annually, and the number has been rising over the past 20 years. The deterioration of health systems (especially in low and middle-income countries), rising resistance to malaria drugs and insecticides, dirty environments and human migration are leading contributors to the spread of the disease. In 2000, children aged under five years accounted for 86% of malaria deaths globally.[170] Furthermore, children aged between 1 and 60 months accounted for 12% of all deaths globally and 22% in SSA, where malaria was the leading cause of death among children in this age bracket.[171]

Over the past decade, there has been some progress in reducing the malaria burden globally with incidence rates falling by about 60%. Some of the reasons for this include: more than two-thirds of children aged under five were sleeping under insecticide-treated nets; advocacy; and targeted messaging to highlight the benefits of keeping a clean environment, along with increased access and usage of artemisinin-based combination therapies (ACTs). It is essential to note that ACTs are increasingly preferred to antimalarial drugs for treating malaria in SSA. According to the WHO, "the number of febrile children treated with antimalarial drugs – the traditional approach – decreased from 45% in 2000 to 13% in 2015".[172]

Although there has been significant progress in fighting the scourge of malaria globally, the disease remains a serious health issue, especially in SSA. The WHO estimates that in 2016 there were 212 million cases of malaria and 429,000 malaria deaths.[173] It reported that 80% of the world's malaria cases and 92% of malaria deaths in 2015 were in Africa.[174] What is most worrying is that the majority of malaria cases and deaths happen in SSA: the Democratic Republic of Congo, Nigeria, Ethiopia and Uganda account for

---

169 WHO, Malaria Report, Working Paper, June 2012.

170 UNICEF and World Health Organization, "Achieving the Malaria MDG Target: Reversing the incidence of Malaria 2000-2015," Geneva: WHO (2015). Accessed from: http://apps.who.int/iris/bitstream/10665/184521/1/9789241509442_eng.pdf [18 March 2017].

171 *Ibid.*

172 United Nations General Assembly, "Roadmap towards the implementation of the United Nations Millennium Declaration," (2001). Accessed from: http://www.unmillenniumproject.org/documents/a56326.pdf [9 March 2017].

173 World Health Organization, World Malaria Report 2016: Summary (2017), 14.

174 *Ibid.*

Overview of Malaria-Specific Indicators

Indicator	*2000*	*2015*	*Change*
Incidence rate associated with malaria (per 1000 at risk)	146	91	-37%
Death rate associated with malaria (per 100,000 at risk)	47	19	-60%
Proportion of children under 5 sleeping under ITNs	2%	68%	>100%
Proportion of children under 5 with fever who are treated with appropriate antimalarial or ACTs	0%	13%	>100%

World Health Organization

50% of the global deaths attributed to malaria. Children under the age of five carry the largest burden, with more than two-thirds of all malaria-related deaths affecting this particular age group.

HIV/AIDS and Malaria in Nigeria

Malaria is a serious public health issue in Nigeria, where it accounts for more cases and deaths than in any other country. Fully 95% of Nigerians are at risk of malaria while the remaining 5% of the population resides in malaria-free highlands. There are about 100 million cases of malaria with over 300,000 malaria-related deaths annually. When compared with the number of HIV-related deaths, which is about 200,000 annually, it becomes clearer as to why malaria is a leading health concern for Nigeria. Furthermore, malaria accounts for about 12% of maternal mortality in Nigeria. The prevalence of malaria in children 6-59 months old is greatest in the South West, North Central, and North West regions, where it is about 50%, while the lowest is in the South East region, with 27.5%.[175]

Given the seriousness of malaria in Nigeria, significant amounts of funds have been committed by the Nigerian government and by multilateral and other foreign donor agencies to address this problem.

Despite the high funding levels, challenges and gaps remain in efforts to deal with the problem. Among the factors inhibiting progress is the widespread poverty in Nigeria, which poses serious challenges for malaria prevention and treatment. Moreover, vector control is highly reliant on a

[175] US Embassy in Nigeria, Nigeria Malaria Fact Sheet, December 2011. Accessed from: http://photos.state.gov/libraries/nigeria/231771/Public/December-MalariaFactSheet2.pdf [22 March 2017].

specific class of insecticides, *i.e.* pyrethroids, and resistance to these pesticides has been reported among people in 27 countries in SSA, including Nigeria.

Funding Commitments Towards Malaria in Nigeria

Donor and Project Description	*Amount*	*Period*
World Bank: Malaria Booster Program, which supports 7 Nigerian states and some national-level activities	US$280 million	2008-2009
UK DFID: SuNMAP (Support to Nigeria Malaria Program)	US$100 million	2008-2013
Global Fund: Grant towards fighting Malaria	US$500 million	2009-2014
US PMI: Initiative to scale up malaria prevention and treatment interventions	US$1.2 billion	2005-2015
US PMI: Malaria Action Program for States (MAPS), an integrated malaria project being implemented in 8 Nigerian states	US$500 million	2009-2015

Federal Ministry of Health Statistics Department

prevention and treatment. Moreover, vector control is highly reliant on a specific class of insecticides, *i.e.* pyrethroids, and resistance to these pesticides has been reported among people in 27 countries in SSA, including Nigeria.

Environmental Sustainability

The target of MDG7, which is concerned with ensuring environmental sustainability, is to integrate the principles of sustainable development into the policies and programs of countries. Climate change, a serious global concern, has a disproportionate effect on the fortunes of the world's poorest countries. For instance, Africa accounts for less than 3% of global emissions, yet its more than 800 million inhabitants are challenged with issues resulting from climate change in which these emissions have a key role, such as droughts.[176] What makes the situation worse for poorer countries is that they lack the knowledge, infrastructure, technology and financial resources to respond to the challenges of climate change.

---

[176] United Nations, "Goal 7: Environmental Sustainability," Fact Sheet, September 2008. Accessed from: http://www.un.org/millenniumgoals/2008highlevel/pdf/newsroom/Goal%207%20FINAL.pdf [19 February 2017].

There are enormous hurdles on the way to achieving MDG7. One of them is that an estimated 200,000 people per day lack access to latrines, toilets or other improved sanitation services.[177] Open defecation remains a problem, especially in SSA, where 70% of the population do not have access to clean, safe and hygienic sanitation facilities.[178] Another hurdle is that more than 800 million people inhabit slums in developing countries. Between 2000 and 2010, more than 200 million slum dwellers gained access to improved WASH services/facilities and less crowded housing, thus exceeding the MDG target of improving the living conditions of an estimated 100 million people who live in slums.[179] Between 2010 and 2012, there was a further significant improvement in the situation as 4 million people were no longer categorized as slum dwellers. Yet even if the target of significantly improving the living conditions of 100 million slum dwellers by 2020 is achieved, this figure represents only 10% of the estimated global slum population, which, at present expansion rates, is expected to triple to 3 billion by 2050.

Another hurdle to achieving environmental sustainability is in the area of conservation. Forests are disappearing at a rapid pace because of illegal or excessive logging and weak implementation of forest conservation laws in some countries. Limited access to cheap modern energy, especially in developing countries, is a further hurdle in efforts to achieve MDG7. In many developing countries, especially in SSA, women are the main users and providers of energy sources such as animal dung, wood and agricultural deposits; the result of excessive use of these primary energy sources is that women and children are affected by respiratory diseases associated with using solid fuels.

Environmental Sustainability in Nigeria

The inclusion of environmental sustainability as an MDG was informed by acknowledgement of the damage to the natural environment because of deliberate human activities. Environmental degradation is a serious problem in Nigeria. The UNDP notes that the country's natural resources, as national assets, are seriously threatened. Between 2000 and 2009, forested areas shrank from 14% to 10% of the total land.[180] Access to safe and clean sanitation and water remains another serious environmental problem in

---

[177] *Ibid.*

[178] *Ibid.*

[179] United Nations, *The Millennium Development Goals Report, 2013* (New York: United Nations, 2013).

[180] United Nations Development Programme, "Nigeria: The Human Development Index: Going Beyond Income," Human Development Report 2009. Accessed from: http://www.http://hdstats.undp.org/en/countries/country_fact_sheets/cty_fs_NGA.html [22 March 2017].

Nigeria. Limited progress has been made, bringing the proportion of the population accessing safe and clean water to 59% and the number of people accessing improved sanitation to 52%.[181] The main challenge here is to optimize public investments to further increase access to safe and clean water. In the area of sanitation, efforts have failed to meet expectations. The proportion of people with access to safe and hygienic facilities decreased from 54% in 2008 to 52% in 2009.[182]

Achieving MDG7 in Nigeria is also plagued by challenges such as the high population and high poverty incidence. Nigeria's population is growing at a higher rate than elsewhere and there seem to be no efforts towards addressing this problem. [183] There is a positive correlation between environmental resource use and population-driven pressure. Uncontrolled population growth will jeopardize the intended outcomes of government policies and programs that are designed to fulfil MDG7. As more people enter into poverty, environmental sustainability becomes an increasingly difficult challenge. As with high population growth, high levels of poverty place enormous strain on the natural environment as people feed off the environment to survive. For instance, there is excessive exploitation of groundwater in the Northern part of Nigeria and an influx of saline water in the South, so innovative solutions are needed across the country to deal with the strain on its natural resources.

MDG7 – Key Targets and Indicators

Target	*Indicators*
Integrate the principles of sustainable development into country policies and programs	- Proportion of land areas covered by forest - Proportion of gas flared - Energy use (kg oil equivalent) per US$1GDP - Carbon dioxide emissions (per capita)
Reduce by 50% the proportion of individuals who lack sustainable access to safe drinking water	- Proportion of aggregate population with access to safe drinking water (%) - Proportion of aggregate population with access to basic sanitation (%)
Achieve considerable improvement in the lives of at least 100 million slum dwellers	- Proportion of people with access to secure tenure (%) - Residential housing construction index

UN Millennium Development Goals

---

[181] *Ibid.*

[182] *Ibid.*

[183] The population growth rate was 2.5% in 2016, according to the CIA World Factbook.

Global Partnership for Development

MDG8 is mainly concerned with developing a global partnership for development. It involves giving developing countries fair and equitable access to foreign markets for trade, the global financial system, and access to information and communication technology (ICT) so that the living conditions of people in these countries can be improved. The levels of official development assistance (ODA) continue to increase despite challenges in the global economy, although aid to Africa remains below expectations. At present, ODA stands at 0.31% of the combined national income of developed countries, still below the UN target of 0.7%.[184] Despite this challenge, some level of progress has been made. For instance, the debt burdens of developing countries have declined considerably from historical levels. Out of the 40 countries that qualified for debt relief under the Heavily Indebted Poor Countries (HIPC) initiative, 35 of them have had future debt repayments decrease by US$57 billion, and 28 of them have obtained additional support of US$25 billion under the Multilateral Debt Relief Initiative.[185]

Another challenge in achieving this goal concerns access to ICT for developing and poorer countries. Limited access to ICT affects the standard of living of people. Improved access to ICT is also a key to achieving MDG7, which deals with environmental sustainability. In a similar vein, access to the internet is a key to advancing the interests of developing countries. Although internet access continues to grow, the majority of the world's population lacks it. By the end of 2008, 1.6 billion individuals, or 23% of the world's population, were using the internet.[186] In the developed world, the percentage is much higher than in developing countries, where only 16% of the people have access to it. In SSA, only 6% had access to the internet in 2010.[187]

---

[184] United Nations, "Goal 8: Develop a Global Partnership for Development," Fact Sheet, September 2010. Accessed from: http://www.un.org/millenniumgoals/pdf/MDG_FS_8_EN.pdf [21 March 2017].

[185] *Ibid.*

[186] *Ibid.*

[187] *Ibid.*

CHAPTER 4

KEY ACTORS OF THE DEVELOPMENT AGENDA

This chapter identifies and discusses the roles of the key actors of the development agenda in Nigeria. Discussing this is essential to understanding their commitments to addressing the various cross-sectoral development challenges. Nigeria's development sector consists of donors, international non-governmental organizations (INGOs), the private sector and the public sector (*i.e.* government ministries, departments and agencies). These entities collaborate at different levels and through different channels to respond to the country's development challenges. The chapter looks at their varying tasks – such as funding availability, coordination and implementation – and their perceived role in responding to Nigeria's development challenges.

Donor Agencies

Donor agencies are organizations – usually international development agencies – that provide wholesale funding to developing countries to help governments address cross-sectoral challenges. Their funding commitments also help governments to meet their national and international obligations as they relate to international development goals such as the MDGs. Often, developing countries do not have the financial resources or technical expertise to achieve development goals, which is why they are dependent on donor agencies' assistance. In addition to providing financial resources, the agencies can provide technical assistance to bridge perceived capacity gaps in implementing complex development projects.

Poverty, conflicts, pandemics, corruption, political instability and weak public institutions are among the factors that contribute to under-development in many countries. In addressing the human element of development challenges, the donor agencies also focus on addressing the underlying causes of these problems. In this regard, the assistance is designed to promote economic reforms or to improve production methods to have a significant impact on development outcomes.[188]

[188] Reci, A., "Advantages and disadvantages of foreign assistance in Albania," *Forum Scientiae Oeconomia*, 2 (2014): 124-132.

Although the funding and technical assistance provided by donor agencies can help in addressing some of these problems, it is also important to note that there is a downside to such foreign aid. One of the criticisms against foreign assistance is that multilateral and bilateral aid is often tied to the donors' strategic and political priorities rather than the development priorities of the recipient countries.[189] The conflict between the donors' objectives and the recipients' development priorities can lead to protracted aid dependence and also cause civil unrest where resources are channeled to less productive activities.

Despite the perceived disadvantages of foreign assistance, there are many cases where it has been beneficial, especially in terms of achieving development outcomes. For instance, foreign assistance played a key role in containing the recent ebola outbreak in West Africa. The US Center for Disease Control's (CDC) response to the 2016 ebola epidemic was the largest in the agency's history and happened in a region where the CDC had limited operational presence.[190] Over the course of the outbreak, the CDC deployed an estimated 2,000 personnel to provide technical support to health workers in Guinea, Nigeria, Sierra Leone and Liberia.[191] Furthermore, the early intervention of the World Health Organization and Medecins Sans Frontiers (MSF) proved pivotal in controlling the outbreak in these countries, especially in Nigeria. Foreign assistance also played a key role in reconstruction efforts in Europe after the Second World War.

Multilateral Agencies

Multilateral organizations play a critical role in addressing the cross-sectoral development challenges in Nigeria. Their support usually revolves around aid to the government at the national and state levels although it is more pronounced at the national level, where it tends to be channeled through state ministries, departments and agencies (MDAs). In addition to providing funds for development programs, their support also includes advocacy and technical assistance in specified areas. For instance, multilateral organizations such as the World Bank, the International Monetary Fund, the African Development Bank (AFDB), the UN system and the European Commission have provided funding and technical assistance in setting up the MDGs Office domiciled to the Presidency. This Office was responsible for coordinating

---

[189] *Ibid.*

[190] Dahl, B.A., Kinzer, M.H., Raghunathan, P.L., Christie, A., De Cock, K.M., Mahoney, F., Bennett, S.D., Hersey, S., and Morgan, O.W., "CDC's response to the 2014-2016 Ebola Epidemic: Guinea, Liberia, and Sierra Leone," *Morbidity & Mortality Weekly Report* (2016): 12-20.

[191] *Ibid.*

programs and projects across the different ministries that support the realization of the MDGs across Nigeria.

Some multilateral agencies also provide support through local implementing organizations such as international NGOs, local NGOs, civil society organizations (CSOs) and private sector organizations. This support relies on the experience and specific expertise of these organizations to complement government interventions across key sectors such as health, agriculture, water and sanitation, education, social enterprise development, nutrition, etc. Although this support is often aligned to the federal government's development priorities, there is nonetheless a tendency of these agencies to tailor their support to the foreign policy objectives of their funding sources.[192] The following overview of several multilateral donor agencies provides a sense of their involvement.

- World Bank

The World Bank is part of the UN system, however, it operates as a stand-alone entity given the financial nature of its interventions. In Nigeria, the International Bank for Reconstruction & Development (IBRD), one of the World Bank's institutions, is more prominent than its parent entity given its development ethos. Consequently, IBRD offers a useful lens for considering the World Bank's development interventions in Nigeria. It is essential to note here that although the World Bank is a development-oriented institution, most of its support to the government is in the form of loans with low interest rates. In addition, it also provides technical assistance where necessary to ensure that loans for development projects are implemented in a way that contributes to the realization of the project development objective (PDO) with an emphasis on improving the living standards of the citizenry. The World Bank Group is the largest donor in Nigeria, contributing in excess of 42% of aggregate donor commitments or development assistance to the country.

To understand the strategic thrusts of the IBRD's interventions in Nigeria, the Country Partnership Strategy (CPS) FY2014-2017 is a useful resource.[193] It builds on the previous CPS (FY 2010-2013) in accordance with the need to transition from the MDGs to the SDGs, although some of its strategic priorities replicate the previous CPS in terms of fulfilling the MDGs. This document highlights poverty reduction and reducing inequalities as the overriding goals governing the IBRD's relationship with the Nigerian government. To fulfil them and support the realization of the development

---

[192] Reci, A., "Advantages and disadvantages of foreign assistance in Albania."

[193] World Bank, "Country Partnership Strategy for the Federal Republic of Nigeria: FY2014-2017," Report No. 82501-NG. Accessed from: http://documents.worldbank.org/curated/en/214371468098983763/pdf/825010CAS0P133040Box385166B00OUO090.pdf.

goals more generally, it provides funding in sectors such as education, water and sanitation, health, governance and energy with a view to reducing regional disparities as reflected in the lives of the populace. For instance, in the health sector, a key thrust of its support is addressing malnutrition (which contributes to addressing MDG4) and improving access to sexual and reproductive health services (which contributes to addressing MDG5). The latest CPS builds on the previous CPS by focusing on three pillars:[194]

> *1. Achieving sustainable and inclusive growth:* to be achieved through funding support and technical assistance in specified areas such as agriculture, energy, public sector reforms and private sector development.
>
> *2. Sustainable human development:* to be achieved through funding support and technical assistance in community development, improved healthcare delivery (*i.e.* primary healthcare), basic and post-basic education outcomes, etc.
>
> *3. Governance for results:* under this pillar the IBRD is committed to strengthening public financial management, improving the allocation and monitoring of government expenditures, strengthening personnel control mechanisms in the civil service, etc.

Upon close observation, it is clear that the second pillar is more aligned to the MDGs given its emphasis on human development. This is underpinned by the IBRD's commitment to reducing poverty and hunger in Nigeria. For instance, the IBRD provided technical assistance and funding to the federal government in establishing a social safety net to take care of the needs of the most vulnerable, especially in rural areas. In addition to technical support, it also committed US$500 million to fund this program,[195] whose effective implementation should contribute to realizing MDG1.

- African Development Bank

Africa's capacity to achieve the MDGs and the SDGs remains questionable given high levels of corruption, low levels of human capacity and limited funding. The AFDB's strategy for achieving the MDGs and SDGs

---

[194] *Ibid.*

[195] Momoh, M., "World Bank commits US$500mn to Nigeria's social protection programme," *Africa Review*, 30 March 2016. Accessed from: http://www.africareview.com/business-finance/World-Bank-supports-Nigeria-social-protection-programme/979184-3139066-g2fwnkz/index.html.

in Nigeria hinges on addressing its food insecurity problem. For the AFDB, food insecurity predates the MDGs, hence its focus is on agriculture and climate change issues.[196] In this way, it addresses MDG1, MDG4, and MDG7.

The AFDB's focus on food security hinges on the dynamic relationship between food insecurity and poor education, bad health and poverty, which can last generations. For example, hungry children have weak immune systems and die prematurely from communicable diseases that are ordinarily preventable and treatable, *i.e.* dysentery, malaria, etc. In accordance with this, the AFDB has continually contributed to the Comprehensive Africa Agricultural Development Programme (CAADP), an initiative co-financed by national governments to boost agricultural productivity. The CAADP is a multi-donor-funded US$50 million program that is based on four pillars:[197]

1. Extending the area under sustainable land management and reliable water control systems
2. Improving rural infrastructure and trade-related capacities for market access
3. Increasing food supply, reducing hunger and improving responses to food emergencies
4. Improving agricultural research as well as dissemination and adoption of technology

Bilateral Agencies

Bilateral donor agencies also play a significant part in funding and supporting development programs in Nigeria. The bilateral and multilateral agencies are similar by way of their high-level engagement with federal and state governments. One difference is that bilateral agencies are more involved at the state and local government levels by engaging with civil society organizations. While bilateral agencies are similar in their approach to project design and implementation, they tend to differ in terms of their development priorities and program strategies. For the purposes of this section, we will focus on three bilateral agencies: the US Agency for International Development (USAID); the UK Department for International Development (DFID) and the European Commission.

---

[196] UNECA, AU, AFDB and UNDP, "Food Security in Africa: Issues, challenges, and lessons." MDG Report (2013). Accessed from:https://www.afdb.org/fileadmin/uploads/afdb/Documents/Publications/Millennium_Development_Goals__MDGs__Report_2013.pdf.

[197] *Ibid.*

• US Agency for International Development

USAID's support to the Nigerian government encompasses strategies and approaches to address the country's governance challenges, economic issues and human development challenges. Its assistance to Nigeria is aligned with the development priorities of the government as outlined in documents such as the National Health Strategy Plan, Vision 20:2020, Transformation Agenda, etc.[198]

USAID's commitment to Nigeria is based on four strategic thrusts: democratic governance, improved access to healthcare and education, strengthening economic growth and stimulating trade, and peace and security.[199] In line with its global commitment on promoting gender equality, USAID invests in addressing issues affecting women and adolescent girls, such as improved access to sexual and reproductive healthcare, girls' education, etc. The US$225-million USAID-funded project Strengthening Integrated Delivery of HIV/AIDS Services (SIDHAS) has women and adolescent girls as its main beneficiaries.[200] Another project targeting adolescent girls is the US$45-million Northern Education Initiative (NEI),[201] designed to address the marked disparities in education outcomes between Northern and Southern Nigeria.[202] Given that educational outcomes in Northern Nigeria are lower than the national average – especially in relation to girls – the NEI seeks to bridge this gap as poor outcomes in the North can hamper Nigeria's progress and performance on MDG2 & MDG3.

Among the bilateral agencies, USAID is the leading donor, given the size of its funding commitments to Nigeria annually. On average, USAID commits between US$500 million and US$600 million annually to fund a range of cross-sectoral projects in Nigeria.[203]

• UK Department for International Development

DFID is another bilateral agency that plays a critical role in shaping the development landscape in Nigeria. DFID's vision for Nigeria is one of a peaceful and prosperous country. This vision encompasses the MDGs and the SDGs. To achieve it, DFID funds many organizations that are working to end extreme poverty. Its funding commitments support wealth creation, especially

[198] usaid.gov/Nigeria
[199] USAID, "Nigeria Strategy 2010-2013."
[200] USAID, "Nigeria: Strengthening Integrated Delivery of HIV/AIDS Services (SIDHAS)" (2015). Accessed from: http://pdf.usaid.gov/pdf_docs/PA00KNBT.pdf.
[201] usaid.gov/Nigeria
[202] National Population Commission, "National Demographic Health Survey," 2013.
[203] http://beta.foreignassistance.gov/?OUID=175&FY=2013&AgencyID=0.

women's empowerment in rural areas; health; education; water and sanitation; governance; and poverty and vulnerability. With regards to the MDGs in Nigeria, DFID is committed to realizing the targets on malaria, child mortality and maternal mortality.

Considering the scale of Nigeria's development challenges, DFID has increased its funding allocation to the country. This allocation emanates from the United Kingdom's spending pledge for international development: 0.7% of its national income.[204] Funding commitments for Nigeria in 2016-17 were GBP266 million,[205] up from GBP20 million in 2001-02, making it DFID's second largest program in Africa and third largest in the world.[206] Most of these funds are used to channel development interventions that support the realization of the MDGs and SDGs in Nigeria.

- European Commission

The European Commission, acting through the EU Delegation to Nigeria, is one of the leading donors to the country. The current allocation to Nigeria from the European Development Fund (EDF) is around EUR512 million over the period 2014 to 2020.[207] Additional funding to Nigeria is provided through other instruments such as humanitarian aid and support for civil society and counter-terrorism.[208] The EU's commitment hinges on three priority areas:

> *1. In the social sector*, improving access to quality primary healthcare, addressing the problem of malnutrition, and measures to improve resilience and social protection for the most vulnerable members of society.
>
> *2. In the economic sector*, ensuring sustainable electricity, improving conditions for economic growth, developing the private sector, promoting trade and investment (especially between Nigeria and the EU), improving public financial management systems at both the federal and state levels, and promoting renewable energy.

---

[204] Provost, C., "Everything you need to know about UK aid and the 0.7% spending pledge," *Guardian*, 13 June 2016.

[205] The significant size of DFID's commitment to Nigeria for 2016-17 is largely informed by the humanitarian emergency stemming from the Boko Haram conflict in North East Nigeria.

[206] House of Commons International Development Committee, "DFID's Programme in Nigeria: Second Report of Session 2016-17."

[207] EU Delegation Commitment to Nigeria: https://eeas.europa.eu/delegations/nigeria/1622/eu-projects-nigeria_en.

[208] *Ibid.*

3. In the governance sector, strengthening Nigeria's democracy, reducing corruption and human trafficking, and managing the country's borders.

The EU Delegation's work in the social sector is closely linked to MDG4 and MDG5. The EU Delegation also coordinates with government MDAs to develop and coordinate programs that support the realization of the MDGs and SDGs.

Foundations

As with multilateral and bilateral agencies, foundations play a critical role in shaping the development agenda in Nigeria. Their significant funding commitments address some of Nigeria's cross-sectoral development challenges. Most of these foundations can trace their origins to private-sector initiatives aimed at giving back to society. In certain cases, private-sector organizations have been known to create foundations as an extension of their corporate social responsibility (CSR). Foundations are largely philanthropic, contributing to the improvement of well-being in society with a focus on improving the conditions of the most vulnerable people.

Increasingly, foundations play a crucial role in international development. According to the Index of Global Philanthropy and Remittances, official development assistance from OECD members amounted to US$120 billion in 2009, private capital investment in developing countries amounted to another US$258 billion, international remittances – transfers of money by workers in foreign countries to their home countries – reached US$174 billion,[209] and philanthropic funding was US$53 billion – a smaller but nonetheless considerable portion of aggregate funding commitments to international development.[210] Some of these foundations have assets in excess of US$1 billion,[211] such as the Rockefeller Foundation, with assets of more than US$4 billion.

In Nigeria, foundations contribute a significant amount of financial resources to addressing development challenges. A number of foundations operate in Nigeria, and we will focus here on two – the Bill & Melinda Gates Foundation and the Ford Foundation.

---

[209] Hudson Institute, Index of Global Philanthropy and Remittances 2011. Accessed from: https://s3.amazonaws.com/media.hudson.org/files/publications/201703IndexofGlobalPhilanthropyandRemittances2011.pdf.

[210] *Ibid.*

[211] "Foundations play an increasing role in international development," *Philanthropy News Digest*, 10 November 2011.

• Bill & Melinda Gates Foundation

The Bill & Melinda Gates Foundation (BMGF) is a significant player in development in Nigeria. It works with the government, the private sector and civil society organizations to support efforts to lift people out of poverty. The BMGF focuses on the following goals in Nigeria:[212]

> *1. Polio eradication:* BMGF works at the global level with the WHO and UNICEF, as well as at the country level with the National Primary Healthcare Development Agency (NPHCDA)[213] and state governments, to ensure regular and proper vaccinations and immunizations.
>
> *2. Improving family health:* BMGF focuses on reducing preventable deaths with added emphasis on maternal and child health, investing in programs that offer prenatal through postnatal care, as well as childhood immunization programs. BMGF also addresses common healthcare issues such as pneumonia, diarrhea and the "neglected tropical diseases" (NTDs), and works to improve access to safe water and promote hygiene.
>
> *3. Healthcare systems strengthening*: BMGF supports efforts, through funding and technical assistance, to improve primary healthcare and explore ways of integrating healthcare services to ensure a strong healthcare delivery system for Nigerian citizens.
>
> *4. Nutrition*: BMGF partners with the Dangote Foundation and INGOs to address severe malnutrition and improve nutrition among under-five children.

BMGF is the largest donor foundation in terms of its funding. In 2014-2016, it committed about US$1 billion to the health sector in Nigeria, of which an estimated US$400 million went toward efforts to eradicate malaria.

• The Ford Foundation

The Ford Foundation is the oldest foundation in Nigeria. Its first office in Lagos State was opened in 1960. It has three other offices in Africa,

---

212 Bill & Melinda Gates Foundation, "Supporting Nigeria's Progress." Accessed from: http://www.gatesfoundation.org/Where-We-Work/Africa-Office/Focus-Countries/Nigeria.

213 BMGF channels funds through the primary healthcare agencies to address maternal, nutrition, and child health issues in Nigeria, given that these agencies can reach people in rural areas.

in Johannesburg, Nairobi, and Cairo. Lagos is its West Africa operational hub. Nigeria is the largest beneficiary of the foundation's funding for development projects in Africa, accounting for 75% of it yearly. The Ford Foundation's strategic priorities are:

1. Promoting governance that is transparent, accountable and effective
2. Improving access to quality sexual and reproductive health
3. Improving the capacity of media organizations to support good governance
4. Promoting heritage and legacy

Across these areas of focus, the foundation supports individuals, organizations and initiatives aimed at improving the accountability of government – at all levels – to the citizenry. The foundation also funds initiatives aimed at strengthening government institutions and civil society organizations to achieve the MDGs.

Implementing Agencies

Implementing agencies play a critical role in shaping the development agenda in Nigeria. Their role is more operational, as most donors lack the capacity to deploy their development programs across the six geopolitical regions of Nigeria. The implementing organizations usually demonstrate strong knowledge of development challenges in different sectors, and some have sector-specific expertise and project management expertise that donors leverage to implement their development programs. Some of these implementing agencies are private-sector organizations (*i.e.* subcontractors) and not-for-profit organizations such as INGOs, local NGOs and CSOs. Donor agencies usually rely on the expertise and experience of these entities in implementing large and complex projects. Private-sector implementing partners include ABT Associates, Crown Agents, Deloitte, etc.[214] Not-for-profit implementing partners include Christian Aid, Oxfam, Catholic Relief Services, Save the Children, Plan International, Mercy Corps, etc.

Gradually, donors have realized that public-private collaboration in the field of advocacy and public policy can be beneficial for both sides. The

---

[214] Private sector organizations increasingly play a key role in addressing development challenges. Donors have realized that they can leverage the technical expertise and economic power of the private sector to deliver on their programme and project objectives. In certain cases, private sector organizations have demonstrated more value for money in implementing development projects than their not-for-profit counterparts. They also can have the economic power to implement projects on a large scale to reach more people.

private sector carries considerable political weight and is able to address development challenges and market constraints that can hamper the capacity of development projects to fulfil their obligations to target beneficiaries.[215]

Most of the time, the implementing organizations access funds allocated for development programmes through a bidding process. Successful bidders implement projects that align to the program goals and strategic priorities of the donors, adhering to conditions stipulated in the grant agreements as they relate to financial management, procurement, reporting, results-based management, etc. Besides fulfilling operational requirements for implementing development projects, the agencies are expected to achieve the projects' objectives. The activities of these implementing agencies are thus vital to achieving donors' program development goals.

Government

The government is primarily responsible for addressing Nigeria's development challenges. Political governance in Nigeria is at three levels: federal, state; and local. We will focus here on the federal and state governments since local governments are stifled by the dominance of state governance structures, especially from the funding perspective. Political interference and excessive dependence on the state governments are partly responsible for the ineffectiveness of the local governments in delivering on grassroots or rural development.[216] Constitutional reform is required to address this problem, especially with regards to making local governments more autonomous. Many of Nigeria's development challenges are in rural areas, and if the local governments remain ineffective, progress is less likely to be made toward the MDGs and SDGs.[217]

Although the state governments enjoy some level of independence, they still depend on the federal government for revenues under the Allocation Formula.[218] This formula exemplifies the unbalanced nature of federalism in Nigeria, and has contributed to national cohesion remaining an illusion given the intensity and frequency of ethno-religious conflicts in the country.[219] Nigeria's federal system is highly centralized, which hinders its efficiency.[220]

---

[215] UNDP, *Partners in Development: How Donors Can Better Engage the Private Sector for Development in LDCs*, (New York: UN Global Impact, 2011)

[216] Agbodike, F.C., Igbokwe-Ibeto, C.J., and Nkah, B.C., "Local government administration and the challenges of sustainable development in Nigeria," *Review of Public Administration & Management*, 3 (2014): 95-105.

[217] *Ibid.*

[218] The Federal government uses 51% of the national revenue while the remaining 49% is shared by the 36 states of the federation.

[219] Agbodike, F.C., Igbokwe-Ibeto, C.J., and Nkah, B.C., "Local government administration."

[220] Peil, M, *Nigerian Politics: The People's View* (London: Cassel, 1976).

Since the majority of donor development assistance in the country is coordinated at the federal level through the MDAs, this section considers the role of two ministries that are key for Nigeria's development.

Federal Ministry of Health

The Federal Ministry of Health (FMoH) is charged with providing quality stewardship and services for the health of every Nigerian. It is also responsible for developing health policies that cascade down to the states and local government given the revenue allocation formula. Here, the federal government offers policy guidance and strategic support to states, local government administrations and the private sector in their efforts at creating health systems that are primary healthcare-oriented and accessible to all Nigerians, especially those in rural areas. The policies developed by the ministry are meant to strengthen the national health system such that it will be able to offer effective, efficient, quality and affordable health services that will improve the health status of Nigerians through the achievement of the MDGs and SDGs. The health policy has targeted the same objectives as those outlined in the MDGs, namely:[221]

- A two-thirds reduction in the under-five mortality rate between 1990 and 2015.
- A three-quarters reduction in the maternal mortality rate between 1990 and 2015.
- A 50% reduction in the spread of HIV/AIDS.
- Stemming the incidence of malaria and other major diseases by 2015.

The ministry is also responsible for developing and implementing health programs that respond to emerging challenges in the sector. Donor agencies and implementing partners also provide support in developing and monitoring the implementation of projects under such programs, some of which – such as the Comprehensive Integrated Essential Health Services[222] – are geared towards realization of the health-related MDGs.

Federal Ministry of Education

The Federal Ministry of Education (FMoE), through its agencies and parastatal entities, is responsible for developing, implementing and monitoring initiatives that are aimed at ensuring equal and adequate

[221] Federal Ministry of Health, *National Health Management: Revised Policy Programme and Strategic Plan of Action* (Abuja: Department of Health Planning & Research, 2006).
[222] *Ibid.*

educational opportunities for all. This includes reducing the marked disparities between Northern and Southern Nigeria as it relates to education outcomes. The ministry also has the responsibility for developing coherent national policies and for ensuring that the states' policies operate within the parameters of national policies as adapted for local needs. Responsibility for educational institutions at the primary, secondary and tertiary levels is shared between the federal, state and local governments, communities, and private organizations.

Governments at all three levels, NGOs and local communities offer funding for education at the primary school level. Government funding levels are considered inadequate as allocations from the federal government have remained unchanged as the annual cost of educating pupils has risen.[223]

The FMoE has over the years benefitted from financial and technical assistance from donor agencies. For instance, the World Bank has played a prominent role in addressing the challenges associated with universal primary education. This includes providing assistance in the form of a credit to support the Primary Education Project, which was implemented in two phases. The main objective of this project was aimed at upgrading and monitoring quality in primary education, improving planning and research capacities, and contributing to the improvement of resource allocations.[224] This project, alongside other health policies of the government, is designed to support the realization of MDG2, *i.e.* achieve universal primary education.

---

[223] Teboho Moja, T., "Nigeria Education Sector Analysis: An Analytical Synthesis of Performance and Main Issues." Report Produced for the World Bank, January 2000.
[224] *Ibid.*

SECTION 2

NIGERIA'S PERFORMANCE ON THE MDGS

CHAPTER 5

POVERTY ERADICATION

This chapter explores Nigeria's performance as it relates to the first MDG, which concerns extreme hunger and poverty. In examining its progress, a comparative analysis is conducted with other countries in Sub-Saharan Africa – South Africa, Kenya and Angola. These countries were selected based on their positions in the top ten countries by GDP. Only three countries were chosen to narrow the scope of this review. This MDG will be analyzed according to the following framework:

1. Background of the problem
2. Challenges of poverty eradication in Nigeria
3. Evaluation of goal-specific performance – the poverty prevalence rate (*i.e.* the proportion of the population living below US$1 per day, and prevalence of underweight children under five years of age).
4. Recommendations for addressing challenges

In subsequent chapters, this framework will be adapted to analyzing Nigeria's performance on the other MDGs to provide consistency in the analyses while identifying gaps that require attention as they relate to the SDGs.

Background: Poverty and Hunger

Poverty remains one of the most significant challenges to development in Nigeria as people lack access to the most basic necessities of life. There are different effects and problems connected with this. Evidence of the intensity of poverty in Nigeria is found in the country's poor health outcomes and related consequences of low income, such as a high infant mortality rate, declining standards of living and a low life expectancy. For instance, there was a sharp decline in the per capita income of Nigerians from a high of US$1,280 in 1980 to US$263 at the time of the MDGs.[225] Given the abundance of natural resources in Nigeria, it remains a paradox as to how the country's per capita income falls well short when compared to some less resource-rich countries. For instance, Nigeria's per capita income of US$240 in 1990 was significantly lower than the average of about US$500 for Sub-Saharan Africa.[226] The Vision 2010 Committee Report indicates that an estimated 50% of Nigerians live below the poverty line. With a population of more than 180 million, the implication of this statistic becomes clearer given the potential for social unrest and instability.

The prevalence of poverty is all-encompassing and this is largely responsible for Nigeria's low performance indicators. Several factors account for the growing poverty rate in the country. These include corruption and embezzlement, poor leadership, ineffective poverty reduction and eradication programs, and inadequate infrastructure.[227] The persistence of these problems frustrates the effectiveness of initiatives aimed at reducing poverty in the country, and casts significant doubt on Nigeria's ability to halve poverty levels as targeted by the MDGs.

Challenges to Poverty Eradication in Nigeria

Identifying and understanding some of the contributing factors to poverty is critical to determining what is needed to address this problem. We focus here on three causes of poverty in Nigeria: unemployment, corruption and non-diversification of the economy.

Unemployment

Unemployment contributes to poverty because when individuals do not have jobs, their livelihoods are affected and they are unable to satisfy their basic needs. Studies show that there is a positive correlation between poverty and unemployment.[228] The high rate of unemployment in Nigeria stems from the combination of relatively slow growth in demand for labour and a rapidly growing labour supply, considering the high population growth rate and increased levels of rural-urban migration.

---

[225] Igbuzor, O., "The Millennium Development Goals: Can Nigeria meet the goals in 2015?" Paper presented at the Symposium on Millennium Development Goals and Nigeria, Institute of Chartered Accountants of Nigeria, Abuja District, 27 July 2006.

[226] OXFAM, *Measuring Poverty in Nigeria*, (Abuja: Oxfam, 2003).

[227] UNDP, Human Development Report, 2007, Country Fact Sheet: Nigeria, Accessed from: http://hdrstatsundp .org/countries/countryfactsheets/ctyfsMGA.html.

[228] Nwagwu, E.J., "Unemployment and poverty in Nigeria: a link to national insecurity," *Global Journal of Politics and Law Research*, 2 (2014): 19-35.

Unemployment Rate in Nigeria, 1999-2006 and 2010-2012 (%)

Description	*1999*	*2000*	*2001*	*2002*	*2003*	*2004*	*2005*	*2006*	*2010*	*2011*	*2012*
National	19.9	18.1	13.7	12.2	14.8	11.8	11.9	5.30	21.10	23.90	24.30
Composite	n/a	14.2	10.3	9.5	17.1	11.0	n/a	n/a	n/a	n/a	n/a
- Urban	n/a	19.8	15.1	13.3	13.8	12.2	n/a	n/a	n/a	n/a	n/a
- Rural	n/a	n/a	n/a	n/a	n/a	n/a	n/a	n/a	n/a	n/a	n/a

National Bureau of Statistics, Labour Market Assessment Report, 2012

In Nigeria, like many other African countries, unemployment is greater among people who have attained higher levels of education. Many graduates in Nigeria lack jobs and, consequently, they find themselves engaged in activities that detract from their academic and professional qualifications. High levels of graduate unemployment leave many highly-qualified people in poverty and contribute to substantial under-utilization of capacity in Nigeria. This situation represents an institutional failure on the part of the government.

Corruption

Corruption is a leading contributor to the high incidence of poverty in Nigeria. It is linked to massive looting by public officials of public resources that would otherwise have been invested in wealth creation and improved public service delivery, thus decreasing poverty levels.[229] The looting and mismanagement of public funds occurs at all levels of government.

A study conducted by Action Aid Nigeria highlighted the strong correlation between corruption and poverty.[230] Essentially, as Nigeria's ranking on the CPI index worsens, the proportion of those living in poverty increases as resources meant to improve the welfare of citizens is diverted for private purposes.

Relationship between Corruption and Poverty in Nigeria

Indicators	*2009*	*2010*	*2011*
Corruption Perception Index (CPI) ranking	130th	134th	143rd
Proportion of people living on less than US$1.25 per day	53.5%	56%	59.6%

Transparency International, National Bureau of Statistics

---

[229] Olu Aina, O., "How corruption contributes to poverty." Paper presented at the International Conference on Development of Social Enterprise and Social Business for Eradication of Extreme Poverty and Street Begging, Chittagong, Bangladesh, 19-20 December 2014.

[230] Action Aid Nigeria, *Corruption and Poverty in Nigeria: A Report*, (Abuja: Action Aid, 2015).

Furthermore, corruption increases poverty by having a negative effect on economic performance, employment opportunities and access to quality public services. The poor – especially those at the bottom end of the income spectrum – are most affected by corruption since it diverts resources from being used for improving public services such as schools and healthcare facilities. Statistics indicate that the proportion of people categorised as extremely poor has risen over the last thirty years: 6% (1980), 12% (1985), 13.9% (1992), 29.3% (1996); 22% (2004) and 39% (2010).[231]

Geopolitical Disaggregation of Poverty in Nigeria (2010)

Region	*Proportion of Population Categorised as 'Food Poor'*
North Central	38.1%
North East	51.5%
North West	51.8%
South East	41.0%
South Central	35.5%
South West	25.4%

National Bureau of Statistics, The Nigerian Poverty Profile 2010 Report (2012)

Poverty in Nigeria varies by geopolitical region, sector and gender.[232] The table above shows there is a marked North-South divide when it comes to the incidence of poverty, with the North accounting for the majority of the extreme poor. In addition to corruption, several factors account for this, including low levels of literacy, poor human capacity development and a weak enabling environment for capacity development.[233] Over the years, several programs – such as the Poverty Alleviation Program – have been launched by the federal government to address the problem of poverty in Nigeria. However, the majority of these programs have failed to deliver improved human development outcomes. The failure of these programs can be traced to the erroneous belief that paying stipends is the best means of lifting people out of poverty without emphasising the need to empower them to be self-reliant. The stipend approach tends to be exploited by public administrators who fill available places with their own relatives and cronies to the detriment of target beneficiaries.

---

[231] *Ibid.*

[232] National Bureau of Statistics, *The Nigerian Poverty Profile 2010 Report* (Abuja: 2012).

[233] World Bank, *Voices for the Poor* (Washington DC: World Bank, 2003).

Non-Diversification of the Economy

Nigeria's mono-economic status is another factor responsible for the growing levels of poverty. The Nigerian economy is largely dependent on the oil and gas sector, which accounts for 90% of revenues. Before 1970, the economy was largely driven by the agricultural sector. By 2008, oil and gas had grown to account for 95% of export revenues, 80% of government revenues and 18% of the gross domestic product.[234]

The growth in the oil sector has been at the expense of others, especially agriculture, whose output has suffered as a result of the government's focus on hydrocarbons.[235] Consequently, many jobs have been lost due to limited domestic and foreign direct investment inflows.[236] The oil sector – which has been marred by high levels of corruption and mismanagement – cannot provide sufficient employment in its current form for the teeming youth population in Nigeria. Despite earning about US$2 billion in excess crude oil money, the downstream sector remains moribund, coupled with declining levels of public service delivery. A bribery scandal involving the U.S.-based company Halliburton and highly placed Nigerian government officials highlights the high level of corruption and resource wastage in the sector.[237] Evidenced by revenue leakages, corruption contributes significantly to the high levels of inequality in Nigeria as resources meant for collective benefit are diverted by a few.

MDG1: Goal-Specific Performance

As can be seen in the data on the next page, Nigeria has made significant progress in MDG1, especially as it relates to poverty prevalence, which declined from 65% in 1990 to 40% in 2014 – short of the target by about 8% - even as the actual number of people living in poverty has risen. When compared to other countries, Nigeria and South Africa made significant progress although both of them failed to halve the proportion of those living below US$1 by 50%. Angola and Kenya failed to make any progress on this particular indicator as the number of those living in poverty increased significantly in both countries. The growing inequality in Nigeria is partly responsible for its inability to meet the set target. On the issue of the proportion of children under five who are underweight, Nigeria recorded a

---

[234] Ministry of Finance, "Fiscal Policy Review," *Quarterly Report*, August 2008.

[235] Joshua, S.T., Happy, D.G., and Dankumo, A.M., "Growth of non-oil sectors: A key to diversification and economic performance in Nigeria," *Public Policy and Administration Research*, 6 (2016): 64-75.

[236] *Ibid.*

[237] This involved payment of bribes estimated at US$180 million to secure contracts with an estimated value of US$6 billion to build liquefied natural gas facilities in Nigeria.

reduction from 35.7% in 1990 to 25.5% in 2015, short of the target. The other countries also recorded declines in the prevalence of underweight children.

Targets & Indicators for MDG1

MDG1: Eradicate Extreme Poverty & Hunger	
Target 1: Halve, between 1990 and 2015, the proportion of people living on less than US$1 per day	Proportion of population below US$1 (PPP) per day
Target 2: Halve, between 1990 and 2015, the proportion of people who suffer from hunger	Prevalence of underweight children under five

	Nigeria		***South Africa***		***Kenya***		***Angola***	
Indicator	***1990***	***2015***	***1990***	***2015***	***1990***	***2015***	***1990***	***2015***
Population below US$1 (PPP) per day (%).	65	40	29.3	17.6	23.1	34	29	34
Underweight children under five (%)	35.7	25.5	22	14	19	11	36	22

World Bank, UNDP, UNICEF

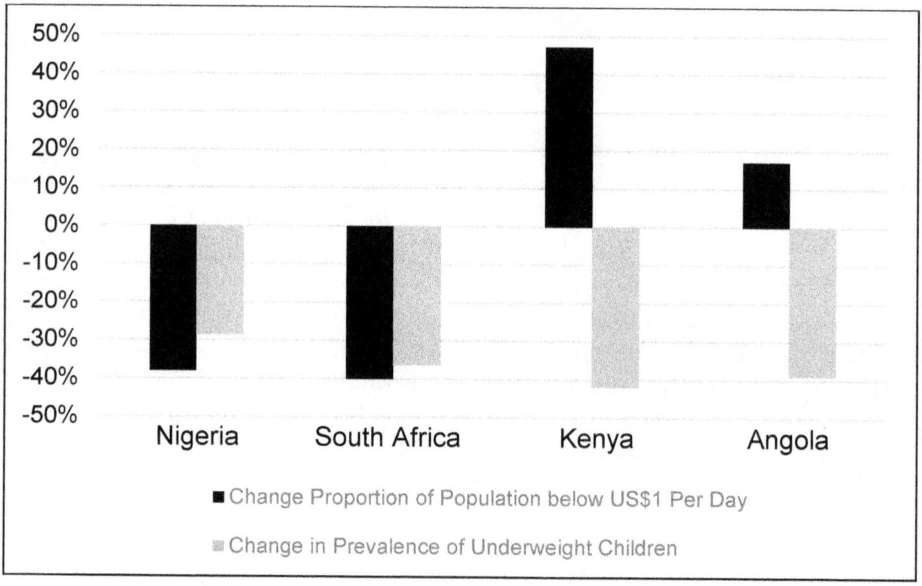

A number of factors account for the high poverty prevalence in Nigeria. For one, poverty is extreme in rural areas, where 80% of the population lives on less than US$1.25 per day. This is compounded by poor infrastructure and inadequate public service delivery in these areas, where large numbers of people reside. Another problem is that productivity in the agricultural sector is low despite 60% of the workers being rural farmers.[238] Corruption by public officials is largely responsible for Nigeria's inability to meet basic development expectations as it has a negative effect on economic performance, employment opportunities, poverty levels and access to quality public services. The poor – especially those at the bottom end of the income spectrum – are most affected when resources meant for improving public services, such as schools and healthcare facilities, are diverted by government officials or public administrators.[239]

Under the administration of President Muhammadu Buhari, the public space has been awash with revelations of billions of dollars found by anti-graft agencies – the Economic and Financial Crimes Commission (EFCC) and the Independent Corrupt Practices Commission (ICPC) – in the homes and bank accounts of government officials. In fact, EFCC reports that it has recovered over a billion dollars of stolen funds from its investigation of public officials.[240] These are funds that would have been used to implement social protection programs for the most vulnerable in society. What makes corruption seem like an insurmountable challenge for every administration is the collective reluctance to allow justice to run its course. Consequently, appropriate punitive measures are not applied to offenders; most of the time, corrupt officials are given a "slap on the wrist" as punishment for large-scale embezzlement. This situation encourages other government officials to engage in corrupt practices, given the potential to bribe judicial officials and influence their judgment in corruption cases.[241]

Despite sustaining a growth rate of 6 to 7% over the last decade, the number of those living in poverty has continued to increase. This is partly due to the current economic recession in the country, stemming from the decline in commodity prices, especially crude oil, which hit US$38 per barrel in December 2015 and has remained below US$70 after reaching around US$100 between 2011 and 2013.[242] The worsening economic situation has scaled back the progress achieved in poverty alleviation. The Nigeria Bureau of Statistics reported that Nigeria's unemployment rate rose from 14.2% in 2016 to 18.8% in December 2017.[243]

---

[238] U.S. Central Intelligence Agency, "World Factbook: Nigeria".

[239] Action Aid Nigeria, *Corruption and Poverty in Nigeria.*

[240] Okakwu, E., "Despite challenges, EFCC making progress in anti-corruption war," *Premium Times*, 30 August 2017.

[241] *Ibid.*

[242] "Brent Crude falls under US$100, lowest in 14 months," Financial Post, 8 September 2014.

[243] "Nigeria Bureau of Statistics: Unemployment in Nigeria." *The Vanguard*, 23 December 2017. Accessed from: https://www.vanguardngr.com/2017/12/nigerias-unemployment-rate-rises-14-2-18-8/ [27 December 2017].

In addition to its failure in achieving poverty alleviation targets, Nigeria has also failed to meet child nutrition targets, as measured by the proportion of under-five children who are underweight. In addition to growing social inequality, the conflict in the North East region of the country has eroded any progress achieved in this area. Overall, Nigeria fell short of the target by 10%, but this gap has broadened between 2015 and 2017 as more children face severe acute malnutrition in North East Nigeria. To put things into proper perspective, UNICEF estimated that 400,000 children – the majority of whom are under the age of five – face acute malnutrition in the North East.[244] This is understandable, considering that an estimated 2 million people have been displaced by the Boko Haram insurgency in the region. Consequently, improved security and political stability would have a significant effect on child health in Nigeria. Counter-insurgency operations by the armed forces in the region have helped some communities in Borno state – the most affected area – shift from the "emergency phase" to the "early recovery phase". However, challenges still remain with continued guerrilla-like attacks on rural communities. Currently, the North East has the worst human development indicators of any of Nigeria's regions.

Overall, although Nigeria failed to meet the targets for MDG1, it made some progress that must be sustained under the SDGs. Some key institutional and policy drivers contributed to this, such as the setting up of the Office of the Senior Special Assistant to the President on the MDGs (OSSAP-MDGs) and the establishment of the Small and Medium Scale Enterprises Development Agency of Nigeria (SMEDAN).

---

[244] UNICEF, "400,000 children in North East Nigeria at riskof severe acute malnutrition". Accessed from: https://www.unicef.org/nutrition/nigeria_94178.html.

CHAPTER 6

ACHIEVING UNIVERSAL PRIMARY EDUCATION

Introduction

The second MDG (MDG2) focuses on achieving universal primary education by the end of 2015. More specifically, the target for this goal is "to ensure that all boys and girls complete a full course of primary schooling". This chapter will examine the background to the problem in Nigeria and the degree to which Nigeria has achieved this goal, and will compare its progress with those of the selected countries – South Africa, Kenya and Angola. First, it is essential to outline some global statistics related to this issue. According to the United Nations:[245]

- Enrolment in primary education in developing countries reached 90% in 2015, an increase from 83% in 2000.
- The number of out-of-school children of primary school age reached 57 million in 2015.
- Among people aged between 15 and 24, the global literacy rate has improved from 80% in 1990 to 91% in 2015. Furthermore, the literacy gap between males and females has narrowed.
- In conflict-affected countries, the proportion of out-of-school children rose from 30% in 1996 to 35% in 2012. This statistic is noteworthy as the Boko Haram insurgency in North East Nigeria has increased the number of out-of-school children in Nigeria.

Background of the Problem

The level of literacy in any country usually influences its level of economic development because development is largely the result of the

[245] United Nations, Goal 2: Achieving Universal Primary Education. Accessed from: http://www.un.org/millenniumgoals/education.shtml [23 May 2017].

contributions of its citizens. In a study examining the importance of literacy on India's economic growth, Veman Desai discovered that low levels of literacy facilitate income disparity and increased economic inequality.[246] The literacy level is also a key indicator of a country's economic situation, as an increased literacy rate supports the enhancement of its human capital. Another study, funded by UNESCO, indicated that there is a positive correlation between literacy rate and GDP per capita.[247] Essentially, countries with high levels of literacy usually have higher GDP and GDP per capita compared to countries with low literacy rates.

In Nigeria, the literacy rate was 59.6% in 2015, *i.e.* 59.6% of the population aged 15 and over could read and write. Broken down by gender, the rate was 69% for males and 49% for females.[248]

Literacy Rate for Nigeria, 1995-2015

1995	*2003*	*2007*	*2010*	*2015*
56%	67%	64%	61%	59.6%

CIA World Fact Book

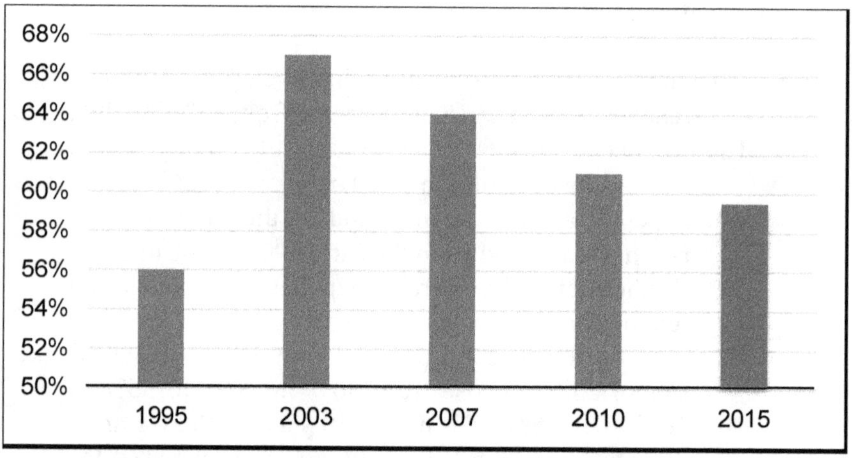

UNESCO

The literacy rate in Nigeria has been on the decline since a peak of 67% in 2003. This contributes to its low GDP per capita.

---

[246] Desai, V.S., "Importance of literacy in India's Economic Growth," *International Journal of Economic Research*, 32 (2012): 112-124.

[247] Cameron, J., "The Economic Benefits of Increased Literacy." Paper prepared for the Education for All Global Monitoring Report "Literacy for Life," 2006.

[248] U.S. Central Intelligence Agency, "World Factbook: Nigeria".

In accordance with the need to fulfil MDG2, the Nigerian government introduced Universal Primary Education (UPE) in 1999 as a program to address the low levels of literacy. The expected impact of this program was to stimulate and fast-track national development. UPE was later replaced by the Universal Basic Education scheme. UBE involves six years of tuition-free primary education and three years of free junior secondary education, translating into nine years of free uninterrupted education geared towards addressing the problem of illiteracy.

While UBE has improved the net enrolment of primary school children, there are still concerns as to whether it has improved qualitative education. The mass education planned by the program will not produce the desired results if the issues of quality, efficiency and relevance are not dealt with. On the issue of relevance, for instance, there are concerns about the usefulness of the curriculum, *i.e.* whether it is oriented toward the skills required to produce economic growth in a rapidly evolving global economy. There also are concerns about the quality of teachers being recruited to teach in primary and secondary schools. Some lack the teaching skills and qualifications required to properly inculcate the appropriate skills in the students, and some are there because they lack other jobs.

Despite the efforts made with the UPE and UBE programs, the Nigerian education sector is still plagued with a number of challenges that have affected access to education for many boys and girls. Data from the 2006 census conducted by the National Bureau of Statistics showed a net enrolment figure of 22,422,918, consisting of 13,302,269 males (54%) and 11,120,649 females (45.5%), highlighting how girls are disadvantaged when it comes to education outcomes in Nigeria.

Challenges to Universal Primary Education in Nigeria

Universal primary education in Nigeria is bedeviled by several challenges that inhibit unfettered access for boys and girls. For instance, one of the factors that has affected net enrolment rates in primary schools is poor planning. Weak management structures within the education system have propagated the negative trends in education outcomes such as literacy levels and net enrolment rates.[249] Poor management of the education budget – in addition to its insufficient level – has also affected the capacity to meet expectations for universal basic education in Nigeria.

Another issue affecting improved access to primary education concerns quality. The public perception in Nigeria is that the quality of education offered at all levels is far below expectations and that standards

---

[249] Maduagwu, S., *Development of education in Nigeria: Past, present and future* (Port Harcourt: Japan Foundation, 1999).

have diminished sharply.[250] These perceptions stem from the lack of adherence to best practices in education management. The poor quality of education is highlighted by the following: teachers with inadequate qualifications and experience; overcrowded classrooms, *i.e.* high teacher-pupil ratios; poor learning environments,[251] *i.e.* dilapidated classrooms; and the absence of basic facilities, teaching and learning resources in most primary schools – especially government-run schools. These factors have contributed to low primary school completion rates.[252]

A further problem is the lack of qualified teachers. As noted earlier, many primary school teachers have not held the National College of Education (NCE) qualification. Teachers have a responsibility for the realization of educational objectives together with ensuring the survival of the educational system. The quality of teachers affects literacy levels and aggregate human capacity in Nigeria. This then affects the quality of output from students.

In addition to low enrolment and completion rates in primary schools, gender and regional disparities also present a challenge to improving access to primary education. The gender disparity at the primary school level was 82% in 2006.[253] A World Bank survey indicated that the average dropout rate at the primary school level between 1999 and 2005 was 44%, and girls accounted for the majority of this. There also are disparities in participation across the six geopolitical regions. Primary school enrolment was as high as 80% in Southern Nigeria and as low as 20% in Northern Nigeria.

MDG2: Goal-Specific Performance

The goal of MDG2 was to "ensure that by 2015, children everywhere, boys and girls alike, will be able to complete a full course of primary schooling". The analysis in this section takes into account the indicators identified for this goal:

- The net enrolment ratio in primary education
- The proportion of pupils starting grade 1 who reach the last grade of primary education, *i.e.* the primary school completion rate
- The literacy rate of 15-24-year-olds, women and men

[250] Igbuzor, O., "Review of Nigeria Millennium Development Goals: 2005." Paper presented at the MDG/CAP Nigeria planning meeting, Abuja, 2006.
[251] The average teacher-pupil ratio in Nigeria was 1:76 as at 2007, according to the Education Data Bank of the Federal Ministry of Education.
[252] The primary school completion rate in Nigeria was 61.02% and the Northern region had the lowest percentage at 46% (National Bureau of Statistics, 2006).
[253] National Bureau of Statistics, National School Census (2006).

Net Enrolment Ratio

The net primary school enrolment ratio assesses the number of children enrolled in a level (*i.e.* primary or secondary), regardless of age, divided by the population of the age group that officially corresponds to the same level.[254] For the purposes of this review, we focus on enrolment at the primary education level.

Net Enrolment Ratio, 1990 and 2015

Country	*1990*	*2015*	*Change*
Nigeria	58%	68.7%	+18.4%
South Africa	73%	83.2%	+14.0%
Kenya	64%	82%	+28.1%
Angola	69.3%	88%	+27.0%

UNICEF, World Bank

Increase in Net Enrolment Ratio, 1990-2015 (%)

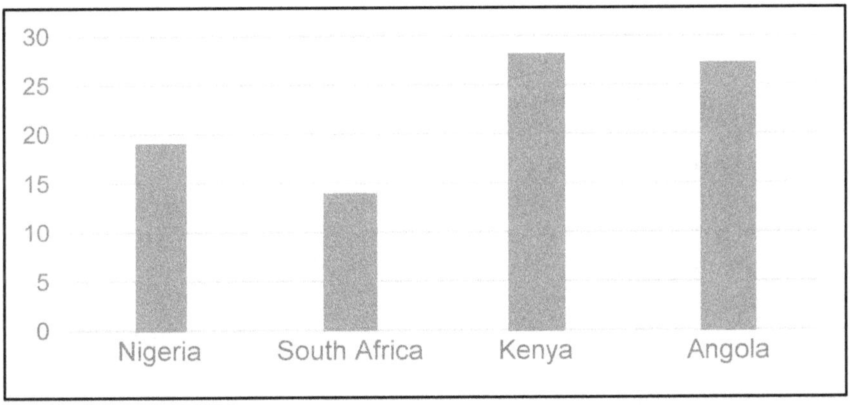

UNICEF, World Bank

In 2015, the net primary school enrolment ratio for Nigeria was 68.7%, lower than the other countries in the comparative analysis presented here. This shows that more needs to be done by the government to improve access to basic or primary education for boys and girls.

Over the 25 years shown in the tables, Nigeria's net enrolment ratio improved by 18.4%, outperforming only South Africa, which recorded a 14.0% increase. The highest performer was Kenya, which recorded an

---

[254] United Nations, "Statistics: MDG Indicators." Accessed from: https://mdgs.un.org/unsd/mdg/Host.aspx?Content=Indicators/OfficialList.htm [19 May 2017].

increase of 28.1%. Nigeria's improvement over this period is seen as insufficient to address the challenges in the education sector. This observation is important because results for this indicator carry far-reaching implications for literacy levels in a country.

In noting this, it is still essential to acknowledge the progress achieved. A number of factors are responsible for this improvement: a slight increase in the education budget, although still insufficient; improved investment in improving infrastructure in government schools, especially through the Universal Basic Education Commission and, at the state level, the State Universal Basic Education Board; and increased fulfilment of counterpart obligations for donor-funded education projects. The Universal Basic Education Act of 2004 provides for basic education comprising of ECCE, primary and junior secondary education. The funding of basic education is supposed to be the responsibility of state and local governments; however, the federal government has decided to intervene in the provision of basic education with 2% of its Consolidated Revenue Fund.[255]

At the same time, many communities, especially in rural areas, still lack classrooms with some students learning in appalling conditions. This situation has contributed to the North-South divide in education attainment outcomes in Nigeria.[256] Furthermore, cultural stereotypes also contribute to the poor education outcomes, such as the reluctance of parents to send girls to school, preferring to give them out as child brides.[257] These factors are likely to impede continuous improvement in this indicator.

Primary School Completion Rate

The primary school completion rate is the aggregate number of students attending the last grade of primary school, irrespective of age, expressed as a percentage of the official last grade of the primary school-age population.[258] Essentially, it is the number of those who graduate or complete their primary school education.

The information on the next page makes it clear that Nigeria has underperformed on this indicator, weakening any progress achieved in the net enrolment ratio. Increased enrolment rates have been accompanied by certain challenges, and chief among them is that quality education has been negatively impacted as resources are spread more thinly across an increased

---

[255] Universal Basic Education Commission (UBEC), Universal Basic Education Act of 2004. Accessed from: https://ubeconline.com/ [23 October 2017].

[256] Asodike, J.D., and Ikpitibo, C.L., "Basic Issues in Primary Education Delivery in Nigeria," *European Scientific Journal*, 8 (2010):150-164.

[257] British Council, "Girls' Education in Nigeria: Issues, Influencers, and Actions" (2014). Accessed from: https://www.britishcouncil.org/sites/default/files/british-council-girls-education-nigeria-report.pdf [24 September 2017].

[258] United Nations Statistics: Millennium Development Goals Indicators.

number of students. While encouraging enrolment in primary education is key to laying the foundation for higher literacy rates, driving completion rates is key to improving education attainment outcomes.

Primary School Completion Rate, 1990 and 2015

Country	*1990*	*2015*	*Change*
Nigeria	82%	71%	-13.4%
South Africa	56%	68%	+21.4%
Kenya	66%	74%	+12.1%
Angola	51%	70%	+37.3%

UNICEF, World Bank, Federal Ministry of Education, South Africa Department of Education

Change in Primary School Completion Rate, 1990-2015 (%)

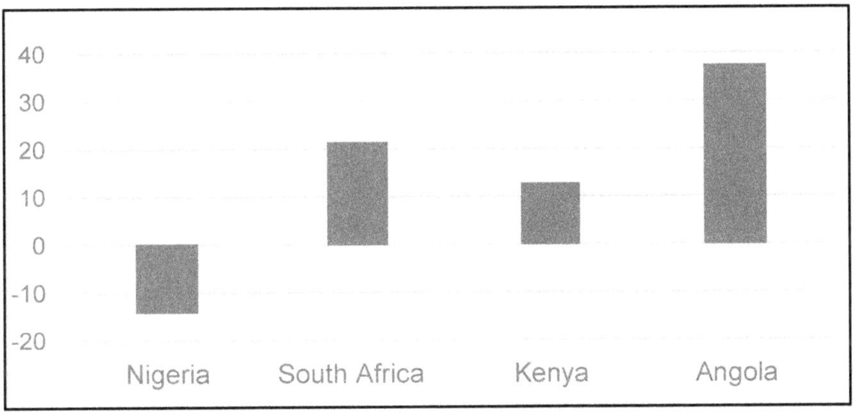

UNICEF, World Bank

Some of the reasons for Nigeria's dismal primary school completion rate include culture, poverty and the low emphasis on girls' education. With respect to culture, Northern Nigeria has the lowest female primary school enrolment and completion rates. The extremely conservative culture in the region renders women as second-class citizens where they are seen as mainly fit for domestic duties as opposed to going to school. The problem of early marriage in the North is also responsible for inherent gender disparities in education outcomes. For instance, the primary school completion rate for females was 56% compared to 69% for males.[259] This result carries far-

[259] Federal Republic of Nigeria, *National Policy on Education*, (Abuja: Federal Government Nigeria Publications, 2004).

reaching implications for Nigeria's performance on MDG3, which deals with gender equality and women's empowerment.

Nigeria can learn from Angola, which recorded a sharp improvement in its primary school completion rate. One of the ways that the Angolan government achieved this result was by collaborating with international development partners, particularly UNICEF, to improve water, sanitation and hygiene (WASH) conditions in primary schools. This includes building proper gender-disaggregated toilets in target schools. Investment in WASH infrastructure, together with increased funding for the education sector from the national budget, contributed to Angola's performance in this indicator.[260] In its review of girls' education in Nigeria, the British Council noted that poor WASH conditions in primary and secondary schools – especially the absence of hygienic gender-disaggregated toilets – contributes to poor enrolment and completion rates for girls. The World Health Organization notes that 11% more girls attend school when sanitation is available.[261] Furthermore, the school absenteeism of many children in both developed and developing countries is attributable to diseases contracted within the school environment.[262]

Given these observations, some state governors are taking steps to address this problem in collaboration with international development partners and the broader civil society. In fact, the construction of gender-disaggregated toilets is central to ongoing reconstruction efforts in North Eastern Nigeria. In its policy recommendations for improving girls' education outcomes in the region, Connected Development, an NGO, suggests integrating strategies for promoting and improving girls' education at the primary and secondary levels, while making schools gender-friendly and creating safe spaces for girls.[263]

Literacy Rate

The literacy rate among 15-24 year olds, *i.e.* youth literacy, measures the number of people in this age bracket who can read and write. As of 2015, Nigeria had a youth literacy rate of 71%, lower than its peers in this study,

---

260UNICEF, "WaSH in Schools in Angola." Accessed from: https://issuu.com/unicefangola/docs/wash_schools_angola_2016.

261 World Health Organization, "The World Health Report: Reducing Risks, Promoting Healthy Life" (2002). Accessed from: http://www.who.int/whr/2002/en/whr02_en.pdf [16 September 2017].

262 Koopman, J.S., "Diarrhea and school toilet hygiene in Cali, Colombia," *American Journal of Epidemiology*, 107 (1978): 412-420.

263 "Connected Development (CODE), An examination of girls' education policies in Nigeria with a focus on the North East," *Policy Brief*, February 2017. Accessed from: http://connecteddevelopment.org/wp-content/uploads/2017/02/Girl-Child-Education-Policies-in-Nigeria-and-Its-North-Eastern-Part...pdf [12 September 2017].

which indicates that Nigeria still needs to invest in education if it is to have the necessary human capacity to compete in a global economy.

Literacy Rate Among 15-24-Year-Olds, 1990 and 2015

Country	*1990*	*2015*	*Change*
Nigeria	65.4%	71%	+8.6%
South Africa	79%	92%	+16.5%
Kenya	81%	86%	+6.2%
Angola	78%	73%	-6.4%

UNICEF, World Bank

Change in Literacy Rate Among 15-24-Year-Olds, 1990-2015 (%)

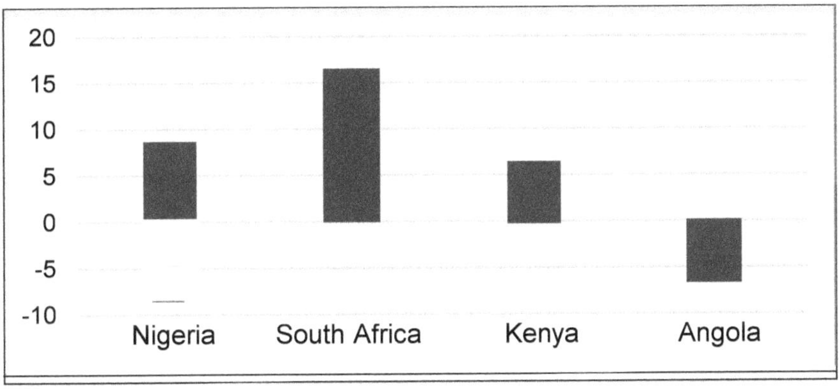

UNICEF, World Bank

The highest performer on this indicator was South Africa, whose literary rate increased from 79% to 92%. With a youth literacy rate of 71% in 2015, Nigeria needs to invest in education if it is to have the necessary human capacity to compete in a global economy. Several factors account for Nigeria's modest improvement in literacy levels. These include declining allocations for education in the national budget; the poor quality of education, especially in rural areas; and low primary school completion rates.[264] These factors must be addressed if youth and adult literacy rates in Nigeria are to improve significantly.

[264] "Review of Nigeria Millennium Development Goals: 2005."

CHAPTER 7

GENDER EQUALITY AND WOMEN'S EMPOWERMENT

Introduction

This chapter focuses on analysing Nigeria's performance on MDG3: "gender equality and women's empowerment". Around the globe, an estimated 90 million girls are not in school. Furthermore, 1 in 3 girls will face gender-based violence in their lifetime.[265] The situation is more dire in developing countries, such as Nigeria, where 1 in 7 girls is married before they reach 15 years of age, with some child brides as young as age nine.[266] Furthermore, women make up more than 40% of the workforce in the agriculture sector but only 3% of them own or have access to land for farming. In Africa, only 10% of all businesses are owned by women.[267]

These statistics indicate that the world, especially Africa, is not harnessing the opportunities inherent in empowering women. Investing in gender equality and women's empowerment can unlock human potential on a transformational scale, considering that women make up one-half of the potential human capital in any country. A recent inequality report produced by the World Bank suggests that countries with higher levels of gender equality are more competitive and prosperous than countries with lower levels of gender equality.[268] For instance, Tanzania achieved marked improvement in the living conditions of the bottom quintiles of the population as a result of a significant decrease in income inequality. The same report indicates that high levels of gender equality contribute towards inclusive growth and shared prosperity.[269]

---

[265] USAID, "State of Gender Equality and Women Empowerment in the World." Accessed from: https://www.usaid.gov/what-we-do/gender-equality-and-womens-empowerment
[266] *Ibid.*
[267] UNICEF, *Promoting Gender Equality: An Equity-Focused Approach to Programming* (New York: UNICEF, 2011).
[268] World Bank, *Poverty and Shared Prosperity: Talking on Inequality* (Washington DC: World Bank, 2016).
[269] *Ibid.*

One of the ways of improving gender equality is to increase access to education for girls. A study conducted by the US Agency for International Development suggests that an extra year of secondary school for girls has the potential to significantly increase their future earnings.[270] The same study also suggests that girls with secondary schooling are up to six times less likely to marry as children than those with little or no education. Furthermore, countries that invest in educating girls are more likely to record lower levels of infant and maternal mortality rates than countries with poor levels of girls' education.

The main target for MDG3 is to eliminate gender disparity in primary and secondary education, preferably by 2005, and in all levels of education no later than 2015. This chapter analyses Nigeria's performance on MDG3 from the perspective of two indicators: (1) the ratio of girls to boys in primary, secondary and tertiary education, and (2) the proportion of seats held by women in the national parliament.

Background of the Problem

Although some progress has been achieved, especially with the establishment of gender policy, gender equality and women's empowerment remain a serious problem in Nigeria. Enrolment levels, literacy levels and primary school completion rates for females have not improved despite investments in education.[271] Available statistics also highlight the persistently widening gap between employment and other income-generating opportunities for males and females.[272] In 2004, for instance, male participation in the industrial sector was substantially higher than female participation.[273] Negative perceptions of women have contributed to Nigeria's inability to properly harness the productive capacity in women.

Gender-based discrimination is a pervasive global issue that is largely responsible for low levels of gender equality in many countries, including Nigeria. This is evident in low health and socio-economic development outcomes for women in Nigeria, as buttressed by some of the statistics already highlighted. Negative perceptions of women in Nigeria contribute to feminized poverty and limit the country's economic potential. A number of factors account for the reduced involvement of women in employment and

---

[270] USAID, "Gender Equality and Female Empowerment Policy: Fact Sheet." Accessed from: https://www.usaid.gov/sites/default/files/documents/1870/Gender_Equality_Female_Empowerment_Policy_Factsheet.pdf.

[271] Igbuzor, O., "The Millennium Development Goals: Can Nigeria meet the goals in 2015?."

[272] *Ibid.*

[273] Federal Ministry of Finance, *National Capacity Assessment Report of Nigeria* (Abuja: Federal Ministry of Finance, 2012).

other income-generating opportunities. For one, Nigeria's failure to locally embrace Article 1 of the Convention on the Elimination of All Forms of Discrimination against Women (CEDAW) has limited efforts to emancipate women, who constitute about 49% of Nigeria's population.[274] This situation has affected effective implementation of the National Gender Policy,[275] which is supposed to improve conditions for Nigerian women, especially as they relate to participation in political governance, education and private enterprise.

The structure of Nigeria's society and culture is another factor that has stifled women's empowerment, especially from a political and economic standpoint. Nigeria operates a patriarchal society which is highlighted by its high masculine and power distance scores based on Geert Hofstede's Cultural Dimensions.[276] The implication of a high power-distance score is that less powerful and vulnerable members of society, such as women, accept that power is distributed unequally.[277] The culture in Nigeria sees women as inferior to men and this is why more preference is placed on boys. Nigerian culture restricts women to the stereotyped roles of performing domestic chores, child bearing, child rearing, etc.[278] This prevents women from reaching their full potential as most parents prefer to invest more in their male children. Local customs (*e.g.* child/forced marriage), traditional practices (*e.g.* non-involvement of women in decision-making at the community level) and customary law also serve to subjugate women in Nigeria. Both urban and rural women still face significant levels of discrimination and violence. On a broader scale, these conditions diminish their socio-economic status. For instance, politics in Nigeria is seen as a male-dominated area, thus limiting female participation in political governance.

Several programs and projects have been initiated by development agencies to address the inherent limitations that Nigerian women face. One such project is the DFID-funded "Voice to the People (V2P) Project"[279] which is being implemented by Christian Aid, a British NGO. A key outcome of this good governance project is to get youths and women involved in decision-

---

[274] CIA World Factbook, "Nigeria: People & Society." Accessed from: https://www.cia.gov/library/publications/resources/the-world-factbook/geos/ni.html.

[275] Geert Hofstede, "Nigeria: Cultural dimensions". Accessed from: https://geert-hofstede.com/nigeria.html.

[276] Nigeria scored 60 on the masculinity dimension and 80 on the 'power distance' dimension. See *ibid.*

[277] With respect to patriarchy, the higher power-distance in Nigeria also carries far-reaching implications for the hierarchical relations between men and women.

[278] Ifemeje, S., and Ikpeze, O., "Global trend towards gender equality: Nigeria's experience in focus," *Kuwait Chapter of Arabian Journal of Business & Management Review*, 2 (2012): 51-63.

[279] Voice to the People (V2P) Project. Accessed from: http://voicetothepeople.org/.

making at the rural level. The project is currently being implemented in the South-Eastern region of Nigeria. A similar project is the DFID-funded "Voices for Change Project"[280] which is being implemented by Palladium. This project adopts a bottom-up approach to getting women involved in decision-making at the community level by leveraging traditional structures such as traditional leaders and religious leaders. The buy-in of these traditional leaders has generated positive results, such as the involvement of women in traditional cabinet meetings and being accorded the right to vote during them.

Another contributing factor to low gender equality in Nigeria is the structure of the legal system. The laws have, in certain respects, been instruments of gender inequality. The language of the Nigerian constitution is masculine as highlighted by references to "He" throughout the document. Section 6 of the Nigerian Criminal Code appears to have legalized marital or spousal rape by way of its wording: "unlawful carnal knowledge means carnal connection which occurs otherwise than between husband and wife". With the rising amount of spousal rape in Nigeria, there is no law at present to deal with it, leaving women who suffer it with no legitimate avenue to seek justice. Another part of the criminal code which is discriminatory towards women is Section 360, which provides for 2 years' imprisonment when the victim of an assault is female and 3 years' imprisonment when the victim is male.

MDG3: Goal-Specific Performance

Ratio of Girls to Boys in Education

The ratio of girls to boys enrolled in public and private schools offers insights into the level of gender parity. Since we have already examined the net enrolment ratio and completion rate at the primary school level whilst discussing MDG2, we focus here on the secondary level.

Compared to the other countries, Nigeria recorded the highest level of improvement when it comes to increasing the number of girls to boys in secondary school. However, like Angola, the ratio of girls to boys is low when compared to South Africa, where there were more girls than boys in secondary schools as at 2015. The fact that there are still more boys than girls enrolled in Nigeria's secondary schools is a situation that must change if gender parity in the country is to be improved. Some of the inherent challenges to gender equality earlier discussed are responsible for this result.

Challenges still remain when it comes to improving girls' education outcomes in Nigeria. The problem is more pronounced in Northern Nigeria, where girls are less likely to enrol in primary/secondary schools; and even when they enrol, they are less likely to complete primary and secondary education compared to their Southern counterparts. A number of factors

---

[280] Voices for Change (V4C) Project. Accessed from: http://www.v4c-nigeria.com/about/.

Ratio of Girls to Boys at the Secondary Level

Country	*1990*	*2015*	*Change*
Nigeria	0.74	0.89	+20.3%
South Africa	0.98	1.07	+9.2%
Kenya	0.90	0.96	+6.7%
Angola	0.78	0.76	-2.6%

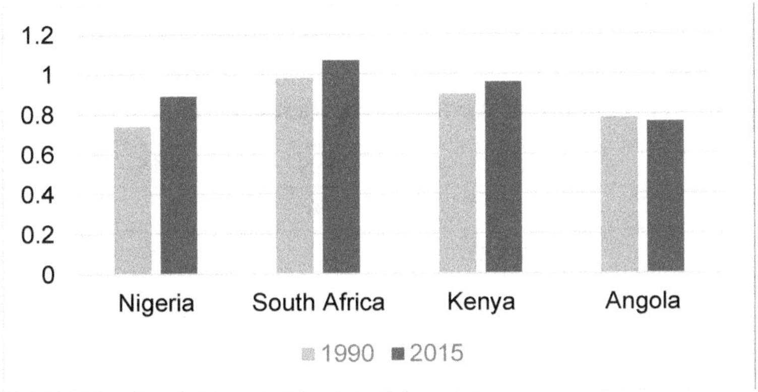

UNICEF, World Bank

account for the poor outcomes of girls' education in Nigeria. The distance to schools coupled with the poor security situation in the North discourages many girls from attending school.[281] Again, there is the cultural perception in the North that the girl is created to attend to domestic chores. Parents are more likely to send their boys to school and leave the girls at home deliberately.[282] This problem is more prevalent among poorer households, where marrying off girls is seen as a means of survival both for them and their parents. Very few child brides in Nigeria's rural areas can continue school in view of the challenging burden of combining all the responsibilities associated with being a wife. These cultural factors contribute to low attendance rates for girls compared to their male counterparts.[283]

---

[281] British Council, "Girls' Education in Nigeria: Issues, Influencers, and Actions".

[282] Africa Check, "Education for the Girl Child in Northern Nigeria: Girl Education in Nigeria," August 2007. Accessed from: https://africacheck.org/wp-content/uploads/2017/03/July-info-graphic.pdf [21 December 2017].

[283] *Ibid.*

Proportion of Seats Held by Women in National Parliament

This indicator measures the number of women voted as permanent or temporary members of the parliament.[284] It is a useful way of measuring gender equality as it offers insights into the level of women's participation in decision-making, *i.e.* involvement in political governance. Since Nigeria returned to uninterrupted democratic rule following nearly two decades of military rule, the time period for the analysis is 1999-2015. Furthermore, since Nigeria operates a bicameral legislature, the number of women in the Senate and House of Representatives is treated holistically.

Proportion of Women in the National Parliament

Country	1999	2015
Nigeria	3%	6%
South Africa	3%	42%
Kenya	1%	20%
Angola	15%	37%

UNICEF, World Bank

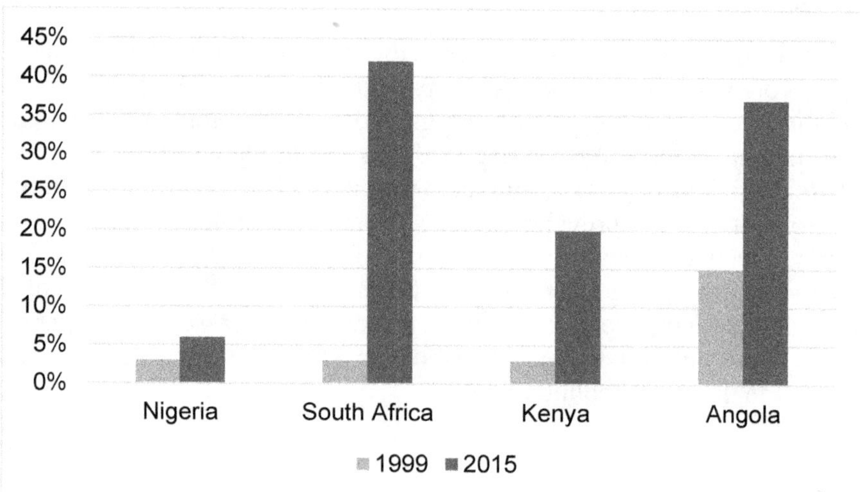

UNICEF, World Bank

[284] United Nations, "Millennium Development Goals Indicators." Accessed from: https://mdgs.un.org/unsd/mdg/Host.aspx?Content=Indicators/OfficialList.htm.

The preceding tables show that Nigeria has underperformed on the proportion of women in the national parliament, reflecting the country's low gender parity and high levels of gender inequality.[285] Earlier, we identified steps being taken by DFID to address the problem of women's representation through participatory projects designed to get women involved in decision-making. Some of the factors responsible for the low proportion of women in the national parliament are the patriarchal and highly masculine nature of Nigeria's society; negative perceptions of the role of women; low enrolment ratios for females at all levels of education; and the structure of Nigeria's constitution and customary laws, sections of which are discriminatory against women.

Going by comparative statistics of women contestants in the 2007 and 2011 general elections in Nigeria, there was an impressive rise in the number of women seeking elected positions – a 70% increase in their participation.[286] Increased awareness from the Gender Awareness Desk of the Independent National Electoral Commission (INEC) and the work of development partners contributed to this improvement. In noting this, it is essential to add that the progress in this regards appears to have diminished considerably, based on the statistics related to the 2015 general elections.

Viewed through the measures discussed here, it can be said that Nigeria underperformed on MDG3 with respect to its targets.

---

[285] Nigeria scored 0.52 on the Gender Inequality Index for 2015, an indicator under the UNDP's Human Development Index, as opposed to South Africa, which had a score of 0.66.

[286] Olurode, L. "State and Political Participation: Women in Nigeria's 2011 Elections." Discussion Paper, April 2013. Accessed from: http://library.fes.de/pdf-files/bueros/nigeria/10192.pdf [25 September 2017].

CHAPTER 8

CHILD MORTALITY

Introduction

This chapter examines Nigeria's performance on MDG4, which deals with reducing child mortality. One of the ways of studying the level of well-being is through examining the state of child health. Given this observation, the target for MDG4 is "to reduce the rate of under-five mortality by two-thirds". Over the years since the launch of the MDGs in 1990, the governments of different countries have made and renewed commitments towards improving child health. However, challenges remain, especially in developing countries. In June 2012, governments, notably in the developed world, launched the "A Promise Renewed" campaign to address the issues of child health, especially as it relates to preventable deaths both during and after the termination of the MDGs in 2015. Therefore, child health is also reflected in the Sustainable Development Goals (SDGs).

Under MDG4, countries are expected to devote considerable resources and efforts towards ending preventable child deaths. An evidence-based assessment of child mortality is the foundation for staking stock of what has been achieved so far under MDG4. The goal-specific performance assessment of Nigeria, in addition to the peer analysis, provides a useful approach to determining how much progress has been achieved and what gaps exist so that they can be addressed during the coverage period for the SDGs.

There has been significant progress towards addressing MDG4 globally. On a positive note, this progress has been accelerating in recent times as signified by a global decline in child mortality. The under-five mortality rate worldwide declined from 91 deaths per 1,000 live births in 1990 to 43 in 2015.[287] During the same time, the yearly number of under-five deaths was reduced from 12 million to 5.6 million. On a regional level, progress has also been made with a reduction in under-five deaths, *i.e.* 180 deaths per 1,000 live births in 1990 compared to 83 deaths per 1,000 live births in 2015.[288] This is short of the target of 60 deaths per 1,000 live births set for SSA. Some of the

[287] UNICEF, "Levels and trends in child mortality, 2015".

[288] *Ibid.*

reasons for the inability of African countries, especially Nigeria, to achieve the target for child mortality are discussed in the next section. Here, the challenges to improved child health in Nigeria are identified and discussed with a view to understanding the reasons for underlying gaps in its performance under this goal.

Challenges of Child Mortality in Nigeria

Child mortality is a useful way of ascertaining a country's level of socio-economic development together with the quality of life of its citizens, especially pregnant and lactating women (PLAW). Under-five mortality is an indicator that measures the likelihood of a child who survives to age one dying between age one and age five.[289] Africa accounts for 45% of all child mortality in the globe, and it occurs mainly in SSA.[290] Although significant progress has been achieved with regards to under-five mortality, Nigeria's progress has not been steady, as evidenced by a rise in under-five mortality from 138 per 1,000 live births in 2007 to 158 per 1,000 live births in 2011.[291]

Several factors account for this. One is low education attainment, with poor education outcomes – especially for girls. Some studies have demonstrated that there is a positive correlation between education attainment and low mortality rates.[292] Educated or literate mothers are more likely than non-educated mothers to ensure a healthy environment for their infants and children, feed them with nutritious and healthy food, access reproductive health services in healthcare centres, and have improved understanding of the importance of reproductive health.

Another reason for high child mortality in Nigeria is poor water, sanitation, & hygiene (WASH) conditions. A lack of access to safe water is one of the largest contributors to this problem. A significant number of child deaths from unsafe water have been reported in the North East as a result of the severe humanitarian crisis stemming from the Boko Haram insurgency in the region. This conflict has affected public services and displaced about 2 million people. Children, including infants and under-fives, and PLAW have been worst-hit by the crisis as access to safe water and healthy sanitation facilities are at a premium. As a result, the humanitarian response has prioritized the WASH sector in a bid to manage the dangers to children and

---

[289] In some definitions, under-five mortality refers to deaths of all infants and children under five years old.

[290] UNICEF, "Levels and trends in child mortality, 2015".

[291] National Population Commission and ICF Macro, *Nigerian Demographic and Health Survey 2008*.

[292] Antai, D., "Regional inequalities in under-5 mortality in Nigeria: A population-based analysis of individual and community-level determinants". *Population Health Metrics*, 9 (2011).

mothers.[293] The humanitarian crisis in the North East is a negative factor in Nigeria's performance on MDG4 and the SDGs. Furthermore, a critical aspect of WASH interventions in North Eastern Nigeria is hygiene promotion programs that encourage mothers and broader communities to practice safe hygiene practices such as safe disposal of infant faeces, washing of hands after using the toilet, washing of hands before preparing food for infants and children, and reduction in open defecation.

Another factor responsible for high child mortality in Nigeria concerns limited access to quality reproductive health services, both pre- and post-natal, especially in rural areas where poverty is severe. Primary healthcare in Nigeria has suffered from insufficient funding, poor management and weak implementation of the budget allocation for the health sector. Even when where primary healthcare centres exist, the distance and cost of transportation has discouraged many women from visiting such facilities.[294] Related to this problem is the lack of qualified healthcare workers in some of them; as a result, many women still rely on traditional means of childbirth by midwives without the knowledge and expertise to deal with complications which may occur. The majority of child deaths occur in rural areas and understandably so, considering the high levels of poverty and illiteracy and the lack of healthcare facilities.

MDG4: Goal-Specific Performance

Two indicators are used to assess Nigeria's performance on MDG4 in relation to the three other African countries. The target for MDG4 is: "to reduce the rate of under-five mortality by two-thirds". This put the target for Nigeria at 70 deaths per 1,000 live births. The two indicators used to conduct this analysis are (1) the under-five mortality rate, and (2) the infant mortality rate.

Under-Five Mortality Rate

As already highlighted, the under-five mortality rate is a useful indicator for measuring a country's level of well-being because it considers the quality of child health, which is fundamental to socio-economic development. The under-five mortality rate measures the likelihood of a child

---

[293] United Nations Office of the Coordinator Humanitarian Affairs (UNOCHA), Nigeria, "Humanitarian Response Plan for North East Nigeria, 2017." Accessed from: http://reliefweb.int/sites/reliefweb.int/files/resources/ocha_nga_hrp_2017_summary_16122016.pdf.

[294] Okoye, I., "Access to primary healthcare services and child mortality in Orumba North Local Government Area, Anambra State." Thesis submitted to the Department of Sociology/Anthropology, Faculty of Social Sciences, University of Nigeria, Nsukka, 2009.

who survives to age one dying between age one and age five, *i.e.* the number of infants and children under the age of five that die per 1,000 live births.

Under-Five Mortality Rate (Deaths per 1,000 Live Births)

Country	***1990***	***2015***	***Change***
Nigeria	212	109	-49%
South Africa	60	41	-32%
Kenya	102	49	-52%
Angola	226	157	-31%

UNICEF, NDHS, World Bank

Under-Five Mortality Rate (% Decrease)

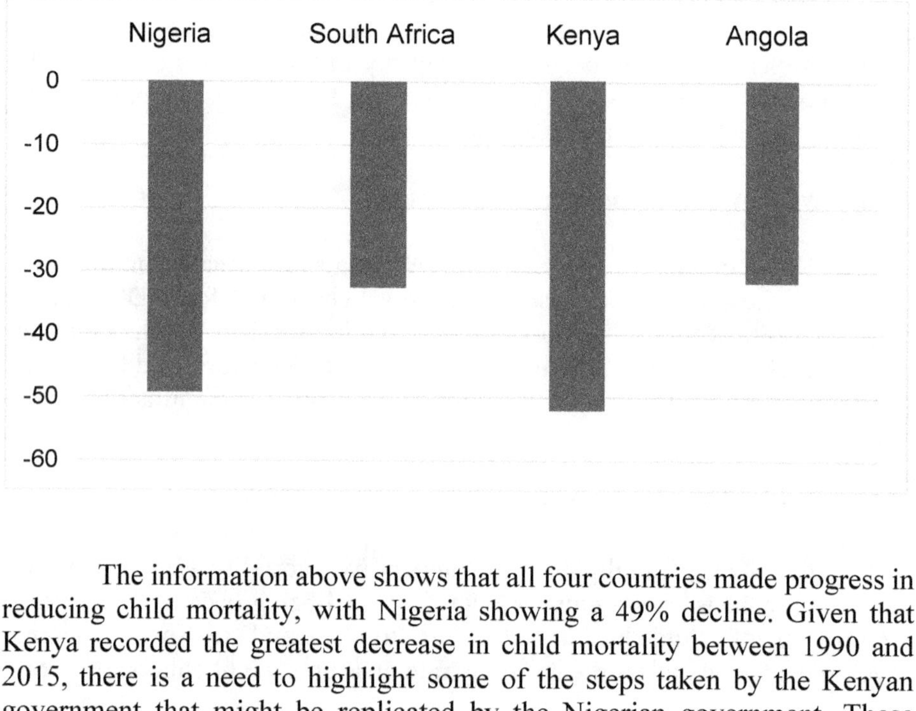

The information above shows that all four countries made progress in reducing child mortality, with Nigeria showing a 49% decline. Given that Kenya recorded the greatest decrease in child mortality between 1990 and 2015, there is a need to highlight some of the steps taken by the Kenyan government that might be replicated by the Nigerian government. These include better breastfeeding practices (*i.e.* exclusive feeding), increased adoption of family planning practices and uptake of reproductive health services (*e.g.* pay-for-performance to healthcare providers and conditional cash transfers to households),[295] increased immunization (especially against preventable diseases such as measles), improved control of the spread of HIV, and a reduction in malaria-related deaths as a result of increased provision of mosquito nets. These approaches indicate that a spectrum of factors must be considered by the Nigerian government when addressing child mortality, which is closely related to maternal mortality.

Infant Mortality Rate

The infant mortality rate measures deaths of infants under the age of one per 1,000 live births. It is another useful indicator for measuring the level of a country's socio-economic development, notably its health status.[296]

Infant Mortality Rate (Deaths per 1,000 Live Births)

Country	*1990*	*2015*	*Change*
Nigeria	126	69	-45%
South Africa	47	34	-28%
Kenya	66	36	-45%
Angola	134	96	-28%

World Bank

Infant Mortality Rate (% Decrease)

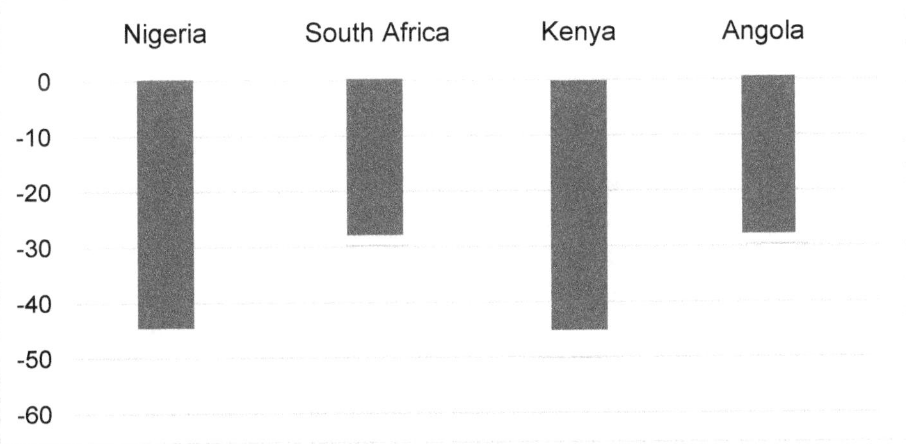

[295] Norman, C., "Utilizing incentives for global family planning and reproductive health services uptake: Altruistic or a euphemism for population control?" Master's thesis, Graduate School of Arts and Sciences, Brandeis University, 2013.
[296] United Nations, "Millennium Development Goals Indicators."

On the infant mortality rate indicator, Nigeria recorded a 45% decrease from 126 deaths per 1,000 live births in 1990 to 69 deaths per 1,000 live births in 2015. While this represents significant progress, it was still short of the targeted reduction of 50%. South Africa and Kenya have the lowest infant deaths per 1,000 live births at 34 and 36 respectively. Both countries have exceeded the target of 45 infant deaths per 1,000 live births set for SSA. Significant effort – especially on the part of the government, private sector and development partners – is required to ensure that Nigeria meets expectations for this target under the post-2015 development agenda.

On average, 70% of child deaths in Africa are attributed to a few mainly preventable causes such as malaria, diarrhoea, measles, acute respiratory infections and malnutrition. Malaria alone is responsible for 24% of child deaths annually in Nigeria. The majority of these deaths can be eliminated through targeted maternal neonatal and child health (MNCH) interventions. UNICEF outlined certain child survival interventions which are needed to address the most common causes of child deaths. MNCH interventions by international development partners are largely responsible for the progress recorded by Nigeria under the infant mortality indicator. However, added investments are required to meet the target. Most importantly, the government – especially at the federal and state levels – must meet its counterpart obligations for MNCH programs.

CHAPTER 9

MATERNAL HEALTH

Introduction

This chapter complements discussions in the previous chapter by examining the issue of maternal mortality, which is MDG5. An assessment of maternal health is another way of measuring well-being or the level of socio-economic development. Maternal health is correlated with child health, as countries with improved maternal health are likely to have improved child health.

Maternal mortality is a critical global concern. It can be viewed as a situation whereby the death of a woman occurs while pregnant or within 42 days of termination of pregnancy, regardless of the duration and place of the pregnancy.[297] According to the World Health Organization (WHO), an estimated 800 women die from pregnancy or childbirth-related complications daily.[298] In fact, in 2015 alone, an estimated 300,000 women died during and following pregnancy and childbirth.[299] Developing countries such as Nigeria accounted for the majority of these deaths, most of which are preventable. Some countries have recorded significant progress in reducing maternal-related deaths in Sub-Saharan Africa; however, challenges remain and other countries have lagged behind.

As this is a serious issue, maternal mortality is also reflected in the SDGs, *i.e.* SDG3. Countries that have poor maternal mortality ratios are usually characterised by underlying inequities in access to quality healthcare services, especially reproductive health services. This is why MDG5 has two targets, one of which is "to increase universal access to reproductive health services by 2015". In some cases, traditional practices and customs in developing countries also contribute to the low utilization of available reproductive health services, thus leading to complications that can be fatal for PLAW. To put this into proper perspective, the maternal mortality ratio in

---

[297] Shay, I.H., and Say, L., "Maternal mortality and maternity care from 1990-2005: Uneven but important gains". *Reproductive Health Matters* 15 (2005): 17-27.

[298] World Health Organization, "Maternal Mortality: Fact Sheet" (2016).

[299] WHO and UNICEF, *Trends in Maternal Mortality: 1990 to 2015* (Abuja: WHO, 2015).

developing countries was 236 deaths per 100,000 live births as opposed to 12 deaths per 1,000 live births in developed countries, according to the WHO.[300] Furthermore, the risk of maternal mortality is higher for adolescent girls under the age of 15, and pregnant/childbirth-related complications is one of the leading causes of death among these girls. This problem is likely to persist in countries where outdated norms and customs prevent or restrict sex education in secondary schools.

Maternal mortality is also a serious problem in Nigeria, where underlying socio-cultural and socio-economic inequities in access to quality healthcare services lead to significant fatalities from pregnancy and childbirth-related complications. The primary healthcare model being implemented in Nigeria has improved service delivery to pregnant women and under-five children; however, the maternal mortality ratio has yet to meet the expectations of relevant stakeholders. Weak organization and insufficient access to maternal health services have always been serious problems. The following table outlines reproductive health indicators that show the scale of the problem in Nigeria.

Reproductive Health Indicators in Nigeria, 2007

Average number of children per woman	6
Maternal deaths per 100,000 deliveries	1,100
Antenatal Coverage	47%
Institutional Delivery	33%
Infant deaths per 1,000 births	97
Birth registration	33%

UNICEF

A number of factors account for Nigeria's poor maternal health indicators. These include poor maintenance of health infrastructure at the primary, secondary and tertiary levels;[301] chronic shortages of essential medicines; the limited number of health workers; unskilled health workers,

---

[300] WHO and UNICEF, *Trends in Maternal Mortality: 1990 to 2015.*

[301] The healthcare model in Nigeria can be categorized into three categories namely: primary; secondary; and tertiary. At the primary level, healthcare centres are located in local government areas. Here, pregnant women receive ante-natal care, delivery and post-natal care in the centres closest to them. Essentially, the primary healthcare centers are supposed to address healthcare needs in rural areas. At the secondary level, healthcare centers are managed by the state government. At the tertiary level, healthcare is managed by the federal government.

especially birth attendants; and poor services delivered by caregivers. These factors are discussed in more detail in the next section.

Challenges of Maternal Health in Nigeria

In 2000, the WHO ranked the performance of Nigeria's healthcare system 187th out of 191 countries sampled. A study revealed that only 4% of public facilities in Nigeria satisfied globally accepted standards for basic obstetric care.[302] Perhaps this is one of the reasons why two-thirds of all women in Nigeria deliver outside designated health centres and without medically skilled attendants around.[303] The poor performance of Nigeria's healthcare system can best be appreciated by considering the country's protracted problem of poor governance, especially as it relates to transparency and accountability in the use of collective resources. Coupled with the low annual budget allocation to the health sector, corruption in public service has meant that meagre resources allocated to the health sector are diverted by public officials. This has placed the health of citizens in peril. The situation is even worse in rural areas where primary healthcare centres have failed to meet the basic obstetric and paediatric needs of the rural populace.

A factsheet published by the WHO indicates that internationally, the majority of maternal deaths are attributable to four main causes: (1) severe bleeding, (2) infections, (3) hypertensive problems associated with pregnancy and child birth, *i.e.* eclampsia, and (4) obstructed labour.[304] Complications post-abortion are responsible for another 12% of maternal mortality.[305] There are also indirect causes of maternal deaths, such as malaria, anaemia, hepatitis, anaesthetic death, meningitis, HIV/AIDS, sickle cell anaemia and renal failure. Furthermore, maternal mortality can be the result of poor health at conception and a lack of sufficient care for the healthy outcome of the pregnancy for women and their babies.

In Nigeria, over 75% of maternal deaths are attributable to haemorrhage, infection, hypertensive disorders and obstructed labour.[306] Inadequate access to and utilization of health services also contribute to the high mortality rate in the country.[307] In examining the problem of maternal

---

[302] Harrison, K.A., "The struggle to reduce high maternal mortality in Nigeria," African Journal of Reproductive Health, 13 (2009).

[303] *Ibid.*

[304] World Health Organization, "Factsheet: Maternal Mortality" (2011).

[305] *Ibid.*

[306] Omoruyi, G., "Causes of maternal mortality in Nigeria," *Sunday Observer*, 24 May 2008.

[307] *Ibid.*

mortality in Nigeria, certain studies[308] have categorized the factors responsible into five main types: medical factors, health factors, reproductive factors, unwanted pregnancy and socio-economic factors. Furthermore, direct obstetric or maternal deaths occur as a result of pregnancy complications, delivery or management. On the other hand, indirect obstetric or maternal deaths occur as a result of the worsening of existing medical conditions in the patient, such as hepatitis or HIV/AIDS.[309] In describing the problem of maternal deaths in Nigeria, health factors must be considered. Among those responsible for the high maternal mortality rate are weak medical treatment; limited availability of skilled manpower; poor compensation/remuneration for skilled health workers, leading to low staff morale; a lack of essential supplies such as medicines; limited access to maternity services;[310] and poor pre- and post-natal care.[311] Together, these factors have characterised the poor performance of Nigeria's healthcare delivery system.

Having identified and discussed the challenges plaguing the health sector in Nigeria, it is equally essential to note that certain steps have been taken by the government – especially at the federal and state levels – to address them. The problem is that these efforts have failed to produce the desired results, especially in relation to reducing the burden of preventable maternal deaths. Some states have seized the initiative by implementing schemes such as free medical care for pregnant women. Other states have included a budget line for free maternal health services. While these initiatives are well-intentioned, they have not confronted the problem of maternal mortality. This is largely the result of weak implementation, poor funding and inadequate monitoring. As these initiatives may not be properly planned, they can fail to outlive the administration that initiated them. This gives credence to the suggestion that a high level of political commitment is required to improve maternal health outcomes and contribute to the realization of MDG5.

MDG5: Goal-Specific Performance

The target for MDG5 is to "reduce by three-quarters between 1990 and 2015 the maternal mortality ratio". The indicators used to assess Nigeria's performance are as follows:

---

[308] Mojekwu, J.N., "Maternal mortality: Natural risk to women." *Ghana Journal of Development Studies*, 2 (2005): 129-141

[309] *Ibid.*

[310] Ogunjimi, L.O., Ibe, R. and Ikorok, M.M., *"Curbing maternal and child mortality: The Nigerian experience," International Journal of Nursing & Midwifery*, 4 (2012): 33-39.

[311] Omoruyi, G., "Causes of maternal mortality in Nigeria"; World Health Organization, "Proportion of Births Attended by a Skilled Health Worker: Factsheet" (2008).

- The maternal mortality ratio (MMR): this measures the yearly deaths per 100,000 live births from any cause or complications associated with pregnancy or its management. This is a useful indicator for assessing obstetric risk in any country.
- The proportion of births attended by skilled health personnel: this measures the percentage or number of births attended by a skilled health worker. Skilled health personnel include doctors, nurses and midwives. Like the maternal mortality ratio, this indicator is a useful way of measuring the quality of maternal health, especially considering that where more child deliveries are attended by skilled health personnel, the probability of deaths resulting from pregnancy complications would decline. Consequently, there is a positive correlation between maternal mortality and the number of births attended by skilled health personnel.[312]

Maternal Mortality Ratio

This peer analysis for the maternal mortality ratio looks at the situation in 1990 and 2015, outlining Nigeria's performance relative to South Africa, Kenya and Angola.

Angola recorded the greatest reduction in maternal deaths with a 59% decrease, followed by Nigeria with a 40% reduction. Although South Africa had a 28% increase in the MMR, it is essential to note the country has the best maternal health compared to the others, *i.e.* 138 deaths per 100,000 live births in 2015. One of the factors responsible for the reduction in the MMR in

Maternal Mortality Ratio, 1990 and 2015

Maternal deaths per 100,000 births	*1990*	*2015*	*Change*
Nigeria	1,350	814	-40%
South Africa	108	138	+28%
Kenya	687	510	-26%
Angola	1,160	477	-59%

World Bank

[312] World Health Organization, "Proportion of Births Attended by a Skilled Health Worker: Factsheet" (2008).

Change in Maternal Mortality Ratio, 1990-2015 (%)

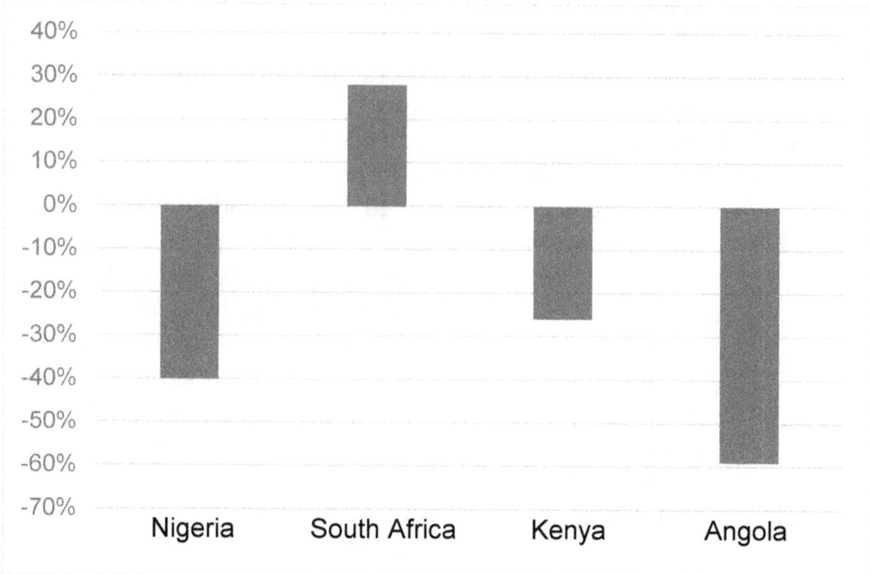

World Bank

Angola was a political commitment to addressing the problem, exemplified by a number of policies, such as the Joint Gender Policy, designed to enhance equal access to healthcare, especially sexual and reproductive health. Furthermore, increased investment by the Angolan government in the health sector is partly responsible for this improvement; its budget allocation to the health sector increased from 8% in 2007 to 12% in 2014.

Although Nigeria failed to meet the target for MDG5, the 40% reduction in its MMR is still worthy of note. Some initiatives and policies implemented by the government at the state and federal levels are responsible for this. At the federal level, a 15% increase in the budget allocation to the health sector between 2012 and 2014 played a role, as did the establishment of the Primary Healthcare Development Agency (PHCDA) with technical support from donors such as the World Bank and the WHO. The PHCDA has helped to improve access to pre-natal and post-natal care in rural areas, where there have been disparities with urban areas, by acting as a channel for ensuring that the federal government's development priorities for the health sector reach rural areas. At the state level, certain state governments, such as that in Lagos State, have built and equipped primary and secondary health centres with facilities and medical equipment with the objective of improving the quality of care provided to PLAWs.

Although the 15% improvement in funding for the health sector between 2012 and 2014 contributed to the progress achieved in reducing maternal deaths, the budget for the health sector is still below accepted standards and levels required to achieve meaningful and broad-based improvement in healthcare delivery in Nigeria.

The dwindling status of public healthcare delivery in Nigeria is likely to persist given the brain drain in Nigeria's health sector. The exodus of healthcare professionals is clearly reversing progress in the sector. Poor remuneration of health workers is at the heart of this exodus. According to a report by the *Sun* newspaper, less than one-third of the registered Nigerian doctors practice in the country while in the rest are migrating abroad, solely to earn improved salaries and access better working conditions. A number of factors account for this besides poor wages;[313] they include difficult work conditions, limited opportunities for professional and career development,[314] under-funding of the sector (*i.e.* insufficiently resourced and neglected healthcare systems), and mismanagement of financial resources by civil servants and appointed public officials.[315]

Besides the problem of brain drain is the geographical distribution of health workers in Nigeria. The majority of them are concentrated in urban areas, leaving rural dwellers with limited access to skilled healthcare personnel. Doctors and nurses are often reluctant to practice in rural areas, citing poor work conditions and limited opportunities for career growth. If this trend continues, progress achieved in the maternal mortality indicator may be scaled back, given that the majority of maternal deaths in Nigeria occur in rural areas. The urban-rural maternity mortality ratio in Nigeria was 1:2 in 2011, according to the Federal Ministry of Health. Women in rural areas – especially in the Northern part of the country – are less likely to use skilled providers and formal health facilities at delivery. Although culture has its role to play, there is also the problem of poorly staffed and poorly equipped primary healthcare centres (PHCs).

Proportion of Births Attended by Skilled Health Personnel

This indicator looks at the number of births attended by a skilled health worker – a doctor, nurse or midwife.

Angola's sharp increase in this particular indicator is in line with its improved funding for the healthcare sector and policies such as the Joint Gender Policy with its focus on sexual and reproductive health. It

---

[313] Iredale, R., "Luring overeas trained doctors to Australia: Issues of training, regulating and trading," *International Migration Journal*, 47 (2009): 31-65.

[314] World Health Organization, "Surgical workforce in Nigeria: Stock and flow of medical and dental practioners in Nigeria, with special focus on health workforce training in Cross River State: Case Study, 2015". Accessed from: http://www.who.int/workforcealliance/031616NigeriaCaseStudyweb.pdf [22 September 2017].

[315] *Ibid.*

Proportion of Births Attended by Skilled Health Personnel

Country	*1990*	*2015*	*Change*
Nigeria	30.8%	37.4%	+21.4%
South Africa	79%	96%	+21.5%
Kenya	50.2%	61.8%	+23.1%
Angola	20.5%	52.1%	+154.1%

World Bank

Change in the Proportion of Births Attended by Skilled Health Personnel, 1990-2015 (%)

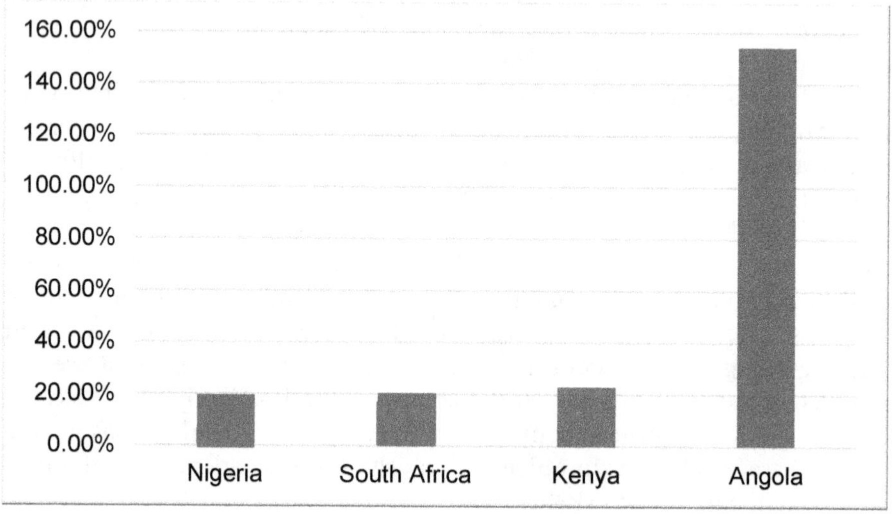

demonstrates the results of the country's political commitment to improving healthcare. By contrast, Nigeria recorded a much more modest improvement that was similar to those of South Africa and Kenya.

As the Angolan government's increased investment in the social sector contributed to that country's remarkable results, they should provide pointers for actions to be taken by the Nigerian government to improve performance. Following a protracted civil war, Angola has been rebuilding its society, including the health system. Investments in its heath sector, together with technical support provided by development partners, have contributed to increased availability of skilled health workers, even in rural provinces. The Community Health Workers (CHW) scheme has also played a significant role in improving the availability of skilled health workers to attend to childbirths and provide post-natal care.[316] This scheme includes training midwives to provide standard care during deliveries in remote or hard-to-reach areas.

A scheme like the CHW can improve the availability of skilled health workers in Nigeria, especially in rural and deprived areas. Under-investment and poor planning has left Nigeria's healthcare system in a fragile state. Government-owned hospitals, especially at the primary and tertiary levels, which were supposed to increase universal access to basic healthcare on the basis of affordability, are in a bad state. Poor remuneration of health workers, a lack of obstetric equipment and drugs, poor working conditions and other factors have contributed to limit the availability of skilled health personnel to attend to births.[317] The situation is worse in rural areas, where primary healthcare centres remain largely underutilized and understaffed. Poor remuneration of health workers is discouraging a significant number of people from entering the medical profession. As a result, some medical doctors are left with establishing their own practice or abandoning medical practice altogether for lucrative consulting or full-time engagements with donor-funded health programs. This has led to a shortage of skilled health workers, especially obstetricians and paediatricians.

---

[316] Giugliani, C., Duncan, B.B., Harzheim, E., Lavor, A.C., Lavor, M.C., Machado, M.M.T., Barbosa, M.I., Bornstein, V.J., Pontes, A.L., and Knauth, D.R., "Community Health Workers Programme in Luanda, Angola: An Evaluation of the Implementation Process". *Human Resources for Health* (2014): 26-58.

[317] Idowu, A.E., Osinaike, M.O., and Ajayi, M.P., "Maternal health challenges and prospects for national development: A case study of Badagry local government, Lagos State". *African Journals*, 9 (2011).

CHAPTER 10

COMBAT HIV/AIDS, MALARIA AND OTHER DISEASES

Introduction

This chapter discusses MDG6, which is concerned with combating HIV/AIDS, malaria and other diseases such as tuberculosis (TB). This goal bears seminal relevance for developing countries, including Nigeria.

The spread of HIV/AIDS, malaria and TB across the world poses a serious global health challenge. Most countries have increasingly acknowledged the humanitarian burden of these diseases and their threat to global integration, economic development and global security. Developing countries are impacted the most by the effects of such diseases. Their vulnerability largely stems from a raft of micro and macro factors. At the micro level, poor health-seeking behaviours and archaic cultural values and norms are responsible for the spread of these diseases. At the macro-level, high levels of illiteracy, fragile health systems and limited human/financial resources are equally responsible for their spread.

Overall, a complex myriad of material, socio-cultural and behavioural variables inform the nature, process and outcome of the epidemics in developing countries, especially in Africa. Developing countries account for the highest number of those infected with HIV, for instance. In 2002, the WHO reported that 42 million people had HIV/AIDS, and Sub-Saharan Africa accounted for 70% of this number.[318] Furthermore, the WHO indicated that an estimated 5 million new HIV infections occurred that year, and Sub-Saharan Africa accounted for 70% of them.[319] The estimated number of children orphaned by the disease in Africa is 10 million. Considering the significant investments by both governments and international development partners in combating HIV/AIDS and malaria, life expectancy in Africa has improved.[320] The United Nations notes that access to HIV treatment in low-and-middle-income countries increased ten-fold over a span of just five years.

---

[318] World Health Organization, "World Health Report 2003". Accessed from: http://www.who.int/whr/2003/en/Chapter3-en.pdf.

[319] *Ibid.*

[320] In 2015, the WHO indicated that life expectancy in Africa was 60.

Malaria is another global health burden that is of concern to the international community. In fact, 50% of the world's population is at risk of malaria. In 2008, the United Nations reported that there were an estimated 240 million cases of malaria, leading to over 800,000 deaths, and Sub-Saharan Africa accounted for 80% of these deaths.[321] The disease is also responsible for causing anaemia in infants, under-five children and pregnant mothers. Governments and international development partners have contributed significant resources to controlling the spread of malaria. External funding for malaria control increased from US$400 million in 2002 to US$1.5 billion in 2009. This figure was still below the minimum threshold of US$6 billion required in 2010 alone to satisfy the targets for MDG6.[322]

Like malaria, the Zika virus is a disease transmitted primarily by certain mosquitoes. Among its consequences, it adversely affects pregnant women and newborns in the form of microcephaly,[323] and it has also become an international health problem.

Tuberculosis is another disease that MDG6 seeks to address as it, too, poses a global health concern. It is more of a problem in Africa, where the disease is more prevalent.

HIV/AIDS, Malaria and Tuberculosis in Nigeria

This section discusses the problem of HIV/AIDS, malaria and tuberculosis in Nigeria. Each disease is treated separately so that the problem can be properly appreciated, as each presents peculiar challenges.

HIV/AIDS in Nigeria

AIDS is the leading infectious cause of deaths among adults globally. When untreated, HIV carries a fatality rate that nears 100%. This disease has torn families apart and created a significant number of orphaned children in Africa. One of the reasons why HIV is the leading infectious disease is that it fuels other epidemics, particularly TB. The first two cases of HIV and AIDS in Nigeria were identified in 1985 and reported at the International AIDS Conference in 1986. The Global AIDS Response Progress Report indicated that an estimated 2% of the population in Nigeria is infected with HIV. The same report indicated that HIV prevalence had previously increased from 4%

---

[321] United Nations, "Goal 6: Combat HIV/AIDS, Malaria and Other Diseases. Factsheet" (2010).

[322] *Ibid.*

[323] The Zika virus can be transmitted by pregnant women to infants. It is a congenital condition associated with incomplete brain development and an abnormal smallness of the head.

in 1983 to 5.5% in 1999.[324] Following a high of 6% in 2001, it declined gradually to 4% in 2010[325] before arriving at its current level.

The Nigerian government has taken steps to address the burden of the disease in coordination with financial and technical support from international partners. To create a focused and coordinated approach to tackling the epidemic, the National Action Committee on AIDS (NACA) was created to efficiently and effectively direct financial resources toward the problem across the 36 states of Nigeria. In 2010, NACA launched its comprehensive National Strategic Framework to cover the period 2010-2015. This framework complements initiatives to fulfil MDG6. It outlines modalities for improving results on the performance indicators for the different goals, including those relating to HIV/AIDS, malaria and tuberculosis.

The creation and work of NACA has helped to reduce HIV infection and prevalence rates, however some states show slow progress. In Nigeria, by 1999, 55% of people aged 15 to 49 were infected with the virus.[326] The broad variance in HIV prevalence rates illustrates the significance of constant surveillance at different layers in a country with the land mass, diversity, and population size as Nigeria. In 2003, the states with the highest HIV prevalence rates were Cross River (13%), Benue (9%), Adamawa (8%) and Akwa Ibom (7.3%), while the Federal Capital Territory had a rate of 8.5%. On the other hand, the states with the lowest prevalence rates were Osun (1.3%), Ogun (1.4%), Ekiti (2%), Jigawa (2%), Ondo (2.3%) and Kebbi (3%).[327]

In Nigeria, the main modes of transmission are through heterosexual and homosexual intercourse as well as blood-borne and mother-to-child transmission; these have accounted for 80% of all transmissions.[328] Significant progress has been achieved in reducing mother-to-child transmission in Nigeria through Prevention of Mother-to-Child Transmission (PMTCT) initiatives, which have been effective because of the high uptake of voluntary counselling and testing by women.[329] ARV prophylaxis has also been effective in reducing infection rates and deaths from the disease.

---

[324] WHO, "Global Aids Response Progress Reporting, 2016". Accessed from: https://aidsreportingtool.unaids.org/static/docs/GARPR_Guidelines_2016_EN.pdf.

[325] Federal Ministry of Health, National HIV Sero-Prevalence Sentinel Survey 2008 (Abuja: Federal Ministry of Health, 2012).

[326] USAID, HIV/AIDS in Nigeria, (Abuja: USAID, 2005).

[327] *Ibid.*

[328] Nasidi, A., and Harry, T.O., "The Epidemiology of HIV/AIDS in Nigeria". Accessed from: http://www.apin.harvard.edu/Chapter2.pdf.

[329] *Ibid.*

Malaria in Nigeria

Malaria kills more people than HIV/AIDS or any other killer disease and it is endemic throughout Nigeria, accounting for 25% of infant deaths and 30% of childhood mortality.[330] The economic impact of malaria costs Africa an estimated US$12 billion annually,[331] a figure that includes the cost of healthcare (*i.e.* treatment/drugs), working days and school days lost as a result of illness, reduced productivity due to brain damage from cerebral malaria, loss of investment as a result of funds committed to treatment, and diversion of material and non-material resources.[332] The economic effects of malaria in Nigeria are significantly pronounced. The Federal Ministry of Health[333] has estimated that the effects of malaria lower gross national income per capita by US$260.

Opting for vector control seems more feasible in preventing the disease in that it protects individuals from mosquito bites. In 1998, the WHO, in collaboration with UNICEF, UNDP and the World Bank, launched the Roll Back Malaria (RBM) Global Partnership to coordinate efforts in tackling malaria. Insecticide-treated nets (ITNs) were introduced as one of the strategies under this program in Nigeria. Malaria is a risk for 97% of Nigeria's population. [334] The remaining 3% reside in malaria-free highlands. Furthermore, an estimated 100 million malaria cases with over 350,000 deaths occur annually in Nigeria.[335] This compares with 200,000 deaths annually in Nigeria from HIV/AIDS. Malaria accounts for 60% of outpatient visits and 30% of hospitalizations among children under the age of five years. In children aged from 6 to 59 months, malaria has the most significant prevalence – an estimated 50% – in the South West, North Central, and North West regions. It has the least prevalence – 27.6% - in the South East region. Over the years, huge funds have been committed by governments and development agencies to fighting malaria. In Nigeria, the World Bank committed US$180 million for the Malaria Booster Program,[336] which assists seven states and some national-level activities coordinated by the federal and state ministries of health.

Another such program is the "Support to Nigeria Malaria Program," (SuNMaP), a US$100-million DFID-funded 5-year program that started in 2009 and ended in 2014. The UK government's funding commitments were

[330] Federal Ministry of Health, 2005.

[331] World Health Organization.

[332] Greenwood, B.M., Bojang, K., Whitty, C.J.M., and Targett, G.A.T., "Malaria". *Lancet*, 265 (9469): 1474-1480.

[333] Federal Ministry of Health, National Malaria Control Programme (2014).

[334] U.S. Embassy, Abuja, Malaria Fact Sheet (2012).

[335] Arowolo, T., "Ending Malaria in Nigeria: The WHO Agenda" (Abuja: NHIM, 2016).

[336] U.S. Embassy, Abuja, Malaria Fact Sheet (2011).

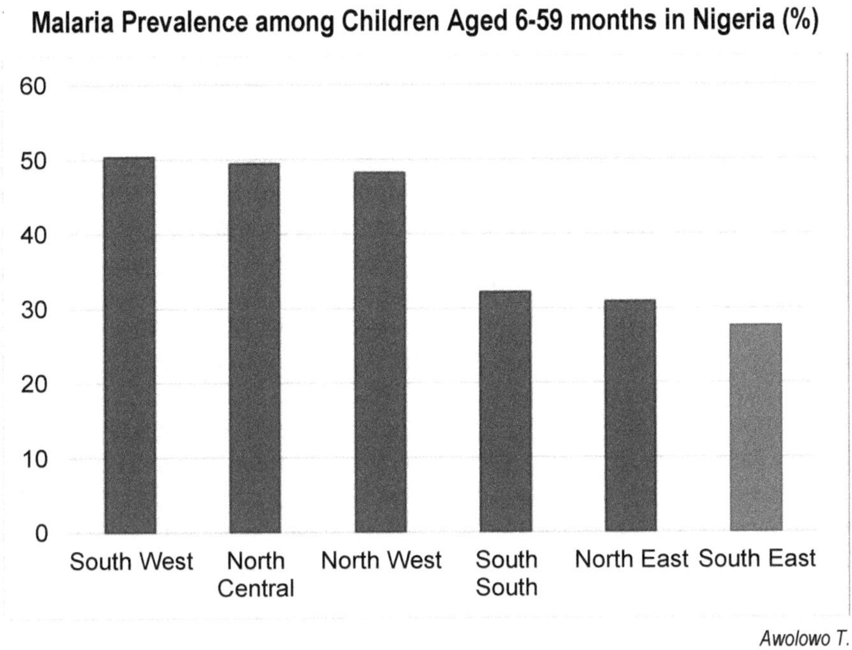

supplemented by the Global Fund, which awarded a US$500-million 5-year grant for the period 2009 to 2014. The US government has also committed huge funds to tackling malaria in Nigeria. The US Presidential Malaria Initiative (PMI), through USAID, launched a 5-year program estimated at US$1.2 billion to address the malaria burden in Nigeria.[337] This funding, meant to scale-up prevention and treatment interventions, ended in 2015.

Tuberculosis in Nigeria

The World Health Organization proclaimed tuberculosis a global emergency in 1993, and it remains one of the world's major causes of death. TB is an airborne disease that affects the lungs and is caused by bacteria. It is both preventable and curable. The WHO notes that one third of the globe's population (an estimated 2 billion people) are infected by TB,[338] and over 9 million infected people become sick each year with active TB that can be spread to other people. At the same time, it is essential to note that latent TB cannot be spread.

---

[337] *Ibid.*

[338] Federal Ministry of Health, "National Tuberculosis and Leprosy Control Programme (NTBLCP)" (2010).

TB disproportionately affects people in resource-poor environments, especially in Africa and Asia. It poses considerable challenges to developing countries as it mainly affects people during their most productive years. Thus, developing countries account for the majority of TB cases and TB-related deaths.[339] In Nigeria, the WHO estimates that 210,000 new cases of all types of TB occurred in the country in 2010, equivalent to 133 per 100,000 of the population. There were about 300,000 prevalent TB cases in 2010, equivalent to 200 per 100,000 of the population. Nonetheless, 83% of TB cases identified in 2009 were successfully treated.[340]

These statistics highlight the weight of the TB burden in Nigeria. What makes it even more pronounced is the high prevalence of HIV in the country. The prevalence of HIV among TB patients rose from 2% in 1991 to 12% in 2001 and 25% in 2010.[341] The percentage of TB patients tested for HIV was 78% in 2010, with a 25% TB-HIV co-infection rate. Furthermore, the proportion of HIV cases that developed TB was 5% in 2010 and 4% in 2011.[342] What this data shows is that TB in Nigeria is largely HIV-driven. Thus, controlling the TB burden in Nigeria is largely dependent on controlling the HIV prevalence rate.

MDG6: Goal-Specific Performance

This section analyses Nigeria's performance on MDG6 by examining the following indicators:

- HIV prevalence among pregnant women 15-24 years old
- Contraceptive prevalence rate
- Malaria prevalence rate
- Tuberculosis incidence rate

HIV Prevalence Rate

The HIV prevalence rate among pregnant women aged between 15 and 24 measures the number of such women affected by the disease at a particular time.

Of the four countries in the peer group, only Kenya recorded a decline in the HIV prevalence rate among pregnant women between 1990 and 2015. This implies that Nigeria failed to meet its target for MDG6 as it relates to controlling HIV/AIDS. South Africa performed very poorly, registering an

---

[339] U.S. Embassy, Abuja, Tuberculosis Fact Sheet (2012).

[340] *Ibid.*

[341] Federal Ministry of Health, "Strategic Plan for Tuberculosis Control: Towards Universal Access to Prevention, Diagnosis, and Treatment 2015-2020" (2015).

[342] *Ibid.*

HIV Prevalence Rate among Pregnant Women Aged 15-24

Country	*1990*	*2015*	*Change*
Nigeria	0.9%	1.3%	+44%
South Africa	1.3%	11.6%	+792%
Kenya	7.9%	4.0%	-49%
Angola	0.3%	0.9%	+200%

World Bank

Change in HIV Prevalence Rate among Pregnant Women Aged 15-24, 1990-2015 (%)

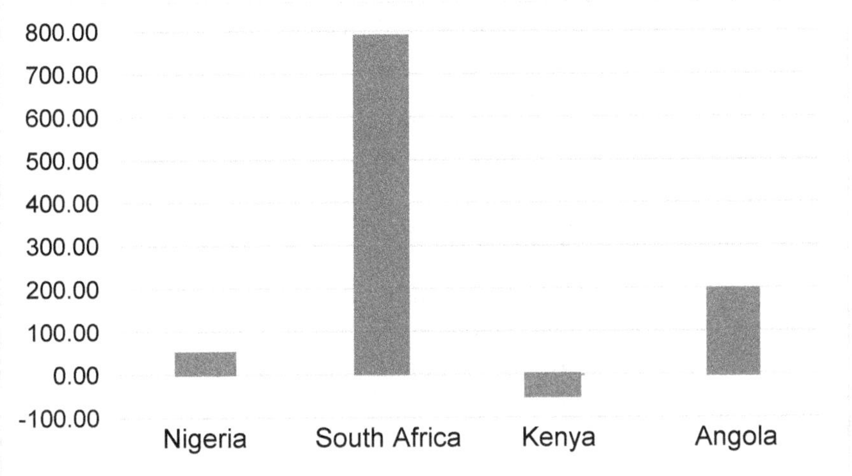

increase of nearly 800% in its female HIV prevalence rate. Before understanding the reasons for the contrasting results between Kenya and South Africa, there is the need to understand some of the reasons for Nigeria's inability to cut its HIV prevalence rate. Although some progress has been achieved in managing HIV/AIDS in Nigeria, the problem is now more situated in rural areas where contraceptive usage rates are low and health-seeking behaviours are poor. Essentially, the rural areas accounted for the majority of the increase in Nigeria's HIV/AIDS prevalence rate. The only consolation that can be taken from this is that Nigeria's female HIV/AIDS prevalence increased at a decreasing rate.

Kenya, which has a high HIV prevalence among women relative to men, has achieved progress in controlling the spread of HIV by increased usage of antiretroviral therapy among adults.[343] Furthermore, intense sex education and family planning programs (sponsored by donor agencies and the government) in both rural and urban areas has helped in controlling the spread of the disease. South Africa, on the other hand, has the largest and most high-profile HIV epidemic in the world, with an estimated 7 million people living with HIV in 2015.[344] In the same year, there were 380,000 new infections while 180,000 South Africans died of AIDS-related complications.[345] Among the reasons for South Africa's precarious position is low condom use, outdated cultural practices that discourage contraceptive use and low male circumcision rates.

Contraceptive Prevalence Rates

The contraceptive prevalence rate is another useful indicator for tracking progress in efforts aimed at controlling the spread of HIV/AIDS. Contraceptive prevalence is the proportion of women who are currently using, or whose sexual partner is currently using, at least one method of contraception, irrespective of the method utilized.[346] The belief is that contraceptive prevalence is positively correlated with HIV prevalence. Consequently, Nigeria's performance on this indicator would be discussed in respect with HIV prevalence.

All four countries under study achieved improvements in the contraceptive prevalence rate. Kenya recorded the highest increase, a result that is significant as it confirms that there is a positive correlation between HIV prevalence and contraceptive prevalence. However, this observation must be taken with caution, considering that South Africa has the highest

Contraceptive Prevalence Rate

Country	*1990*	*2015*	*Change*
Nigeria	6%	15.1%	+151.6%
South Africa	57%	59%	+3.5%
Kenya	17%	58%	+241.2%
Angola	5.2%	17.4%	+234.6%

World Bank

343 AVERT, "HIV Situation in Kenya". Accessed from: http://blog.opendata.go.ke/hiv-situation-in-kenya/.

344 AVERT, "HIV and AIDS in South Africa". Accessed from: https://www.avert.org/professionals/hiv-around-world/sub-saharan-africa/south-africa.

345 *Ibid.*

346 WHO, "Sexual and Reproductive Health: Contraceptive Prevalence". Accessed from: http://who.int/reproductivehealth/topics/family_planning/contraceptive_prevalence/en/.

Change in Contraceptive Prevalence Rate, 1990-2015 (%)

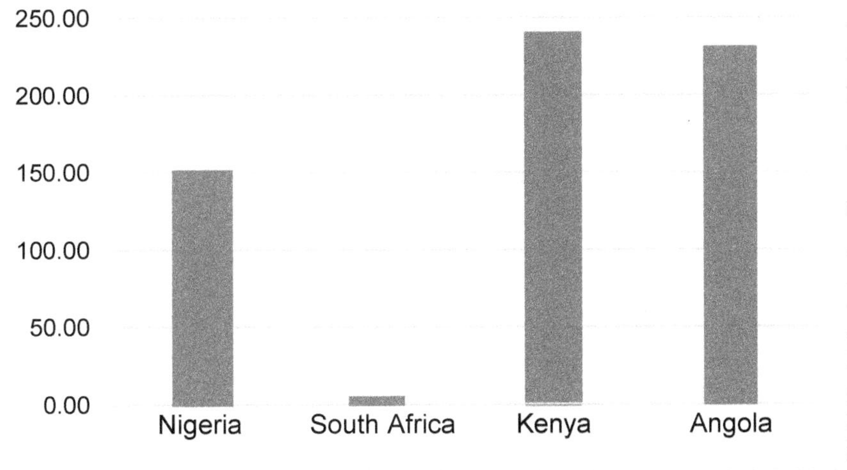

World Bank

contraceptive prevalence rate yet it also has the highest HIV prevalence. Nonetheless, it is essential to note that contraceptive prevalence in South Africa increased only slightly between 1990 and 2015. Perhaps this explains why the disease has reached epidemic proportions in the country.

Nigeria, on the other hand, achieved an increase of more than 150% in contraceptive prevalence.[347] This explains why its HIV prevalence increased at a slower rate. Consequently, a further significant increase in contraceptive prevalence is required to reduce its HIV prevalence. Contraceptive prevalence rates have also been associated with maternal mortality, and it has been shown that countries that have low contraceptive prevalence rates – such as Nigeria – tend to have high maternal mortality rates. Indeed, Nigeria has one of the highest maternal mortality rates in Sub-Saharan Africa and ranks as the country with the second highest number of maternal deaths in the world, with unsafe abortion contributing to an estimated 30% of the 60,000 annual maternal deaths.[348]

---

[347] World Health Organization, "Global Aids Response Progress Reporting, 2016". Accessed from: https://aidsreportingtool.unaids.org/static/docs/GARPR_Guidelines_2016_EN.pdf.
[348] World Health Organization, "Maternal mortality ratio in 2005: Estimates by UNICEF, WHO, UNFPA, WorldBank". Accessed from: http://www.who.int/reproductivehealth/publications/ maternal_mortality_2005/index.html [17 March 2010].

Malaria Incidence Rate

The Malaria incidence indicator looks at the number of new cases of malaria per population at risk at a given time, *i.e.* the incidence of malaria per 1,000 people at risk.

Malaria Incidence Rate (Cases per 1,000 People at Risk)

Country	*1990*	*2015*	*Change*
Nigeria	498	381	-23.5%
South Africa	12	3	-75.0%
Kenya	274	176	-35.8%
Angola	315	124	-60.6%

World Bank

Change in Malaria Incidence Rate, 1990-2015 (%)

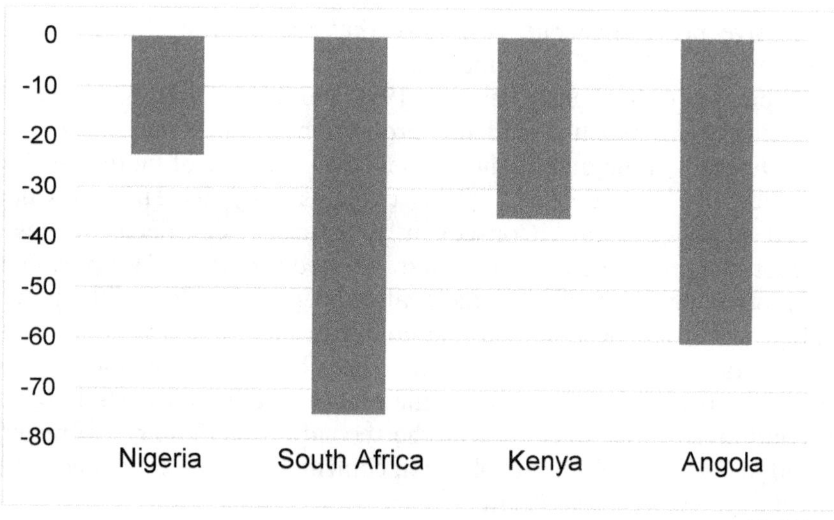

World Bank

As can be seen from the data above, all four countries achieved declines in the malaria incidence rate. South Africa recorded the largest percentage decrease, but it is important to note that this was from a very small number of cases among the population at risk. Nigeria also recorded a significant decrease in the incidence of malaria, but in percentage terms it was the smallest among the countries where malaria is considerably more prevalent. This shows that the funds committed by development partners and the government towards eradicating or controlling malaria have proved effective to some degree; however, more efforts are required to bring the disease's burden to a manageable level.

A number of factors are responsible for the decline in malaria prevalence achieved by Nigeria between 1990 and 2015. These included increased funding of malaria programs by the government and international development partners, [349] improved knowledge about the disease and preventive measures among local communities, increased availability of Artemisinin-based combination therapy (ACT), and increased use of insecticide-treated nets (ITNs) by households.[350] The success of programs to fight malaria is largely attributed to an integrated approach to tackling the problem. Essentially, donor-funded malaria programs involve the implementation of preventive and treatment-related activities. The preventive component involves advocacy and community mobilization, plus the sensitization of communities on the importance of maintaining clean environments, together with added health education regarding the importance of using ITNs to prevent the disease and save lives. Even with the reduced prevalence of malaria, however, the disease is one of the largest contributors to child mortality in Nigeria.

The distribution of ITNs, including in remote locations, has helped to reduce morbidity across all six geopolitical regions of Nigeria. In fact, the decrease in the malaria prevalence rate achieved by Nigeria is largely informed by the increase in the ownership of ITNs, especially in rural areas. According to a recent study, ownership of ITNs increased from 41% in 2010 to 68% in 2013.[351] Funding through malaria interventions has helped in reducing the price of ITNs and ACT.

Tuberculosis Incidence Rate

This section discusses Nigeria's performance on controlling the spread of TB. The indicator selected for this purpose is the TB incidence rate, which measures the number of new cases per 100,000 people within the population at risk.

Only Kenya achieved a decrease in the tuberculosis incidence rate, while South Africa and Angola registered increases. These results are significant as they confirm the correlation between the HIV/AIDS burden and the TB burden. South Africa's results can be explained by its HIV/AIDS

---

[349] For instance, the Bill & Melinda Gates Foundation has committed in excess of US$100 million to fighting malaria in Nigeria.

[350] Dawaki, S., Al-Mekhlafi, H., Ithoi, I., Ibrahim, J., Atroosh, W., Abdusalam, A., Sady, H., Elyana, F., Adamu, A., Yelwa, S., Al-Areeqi, M., Subramaniam, L., Nasr, N., and Lau, Y., "Is Nigeria winning the battle against malaria? Prevalence, risk factors and KAP assessment among Hausa communities in Kano state," *Malaria Journal*, 15 (2016): 351-355.

[351] *Ibid.*

Tuberculosis Incidence Rate (per 100,000 people)

Country	*1990*	*2015*	*Change*
Nigeria	325	322	0%
South Africa	585	834	+42%
Kenya	286	233	-18%
Angola	297	370	+25%

World Bank

Change in Tuberculosis Incidence Rate, 1990-2015 (%)

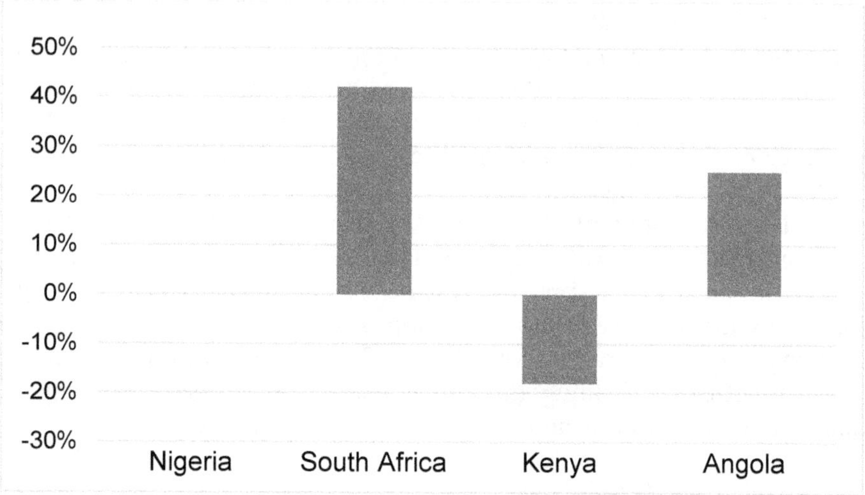

World Bank

prevalence rate. The TB burden in any country is largely HIV-driven.[352] The implication of this is that controlling HIV/AIDS will have a significant effect on controlling TB.

Nigeria recorded essentially no change in the TB incidence rate. This shows that no progress has been achieved in reducing TB, which is understandable as less than significant progress was achieved in reducing Nigeria's HIV prevalence rate.

[352] Federal Ministry of Health, "Strategic Plan for Tuberculosis Control: Towards Universal Access to Prevention, Diagnosis, and Treatment 2015-2020" (2015).

CHAPTER 11

ENVIRONMENTAL SUSTAINABILITY

Introduction

This chapter discusses MDG7, which deals with 'environmental sustainability'. Environmental sustainability seeks to sustain indefinitely the global systems that support human existence.[353] Essentially, these systems provide human beings with food, water, air, energy, etc. Some of these resources are finite, hence the need to put in place measures to manage their utilization and make them available for subsequent generations. Excessive or uncontrolled exploitation of them – such as deforestation, excessive fishing, etc. – affects the capacity of the natural environment to provide for human beings and protect them from ultraviolet (UV) radiation. Put simply, environmental sustainability deals with the 'preservation of natural capital'.[354]

Protecting human existence is at the core of environmental sustainability efforts. MDG7 is informed by the ongoing debate about climate change. Global disasters such as storm surges, floods, droughts, famine and extreme weather conditions have informed the need to implement measures aimed at managing natural resources and preventing these disasters. Although every geographical location is susceptible to the effects of climate change, it appears that developing countries, especially countries in Africa, are the most vulnerable given their significant exposure to climate change impacts coupled with their limited capacity to cope with these effects when they materialize.[355]

Water resource management is one the issues addressed by the environmental sustainability mantra. For one, water use has grown astronomically as a consequence of global population growth. Although there is no global shortage of water, the UN estimates that 40% of the world's

---

[353] United Nations, "Goal 7: Environmental Sustainability". Accessed from: http://www.un.org/millenniumgoals/2008highlevel/pdf/newsroom/Goal%207%20FINAL.pdf.
[354] Goodland, G., "The Concept of Environmental Sustainability," *Annual Review of Ecology and Systematics*, 26 (1995): 1-24.
[355] United Nations, "Ensure Environmental Sustainability: Fact Sheet". Accessed from: http://www.un.org/millenniumgoals/pdf/Goal_7_fs.pdf.

population face water shortages.[356] In fact, an estimated 1 billion people face conditions of physical water scarcity, which happens when more than 70% of river flows are diminished.[357] Women are the most affected by water shortages given their domestic role, particularly in developing countries. The issue of water availability also includes the quality of water, *i.e.* safe drinking water and sanitation facilities. The UN notes that the percentage of people utilizing improved sources of drinking water is about 60% in Sub-Saharan Africa; however, it is much higher in other regions such as East Asia (89%), Western Asia (90%), and Northern Africa (90%).[358] Concerning the issue of safe sanitation facilities, much of the world's population lacks access to healthy and hygienic sanitation facilities with open defecation still common in many countries, especially developing countries.

Environmental sustainability can also be perceived from the perspective of the 'distribution of slums' globally. These slums are a concern, considering the health risks faced by those who reside in them. UN-Habitat notes that about 800 million people live in slums in developing countries.[359] A number of factors account for this high number, but chief among them is the rise in inequality globally, *i.e.* fewer and fewer individuals controlling the world's economic resources. Some progress has been achieved in dealing with the spread of slums around the world. For instance, UN-Habitat notes that between 2000 and 2010, over 200 million slum dwellers gained access to improved water, sanitation and less-crowded housing spaces. Furthermore, between 2010 and 2012, conditions improved to the point where a further 40 million individuals were categorised as no longer living in slum dwellings. The United Nations notes that although the MDG slum target has been achieved from a global standpoint, the number of slum dwellers continues to grow. Globalization is largely responsible for this situation.

Challenges of Environmental Sustainability in Nigeria

Sustainable environmental management has remained consistently poor over the years, and this is partly the result of inadequate attention across all levels. Poor management of the environment is partly responsible for the high rate of poverty in Nigeria. Population growth in the country over the past decade has been accompanied by insufficient investment in infrastructure, natural resource management and development. The implication of this is far-reaching and includes increased waste generation coupled with poor waste management; limited access to decent water, sanitation, and hygiene facilities

[356] United Nations, "Goal 7: Environmental Sustainability".
[357] *Ibid.*
[358] *Ibid.*
[359] UN-Habitat, "Chapter 1: Development Context and the Millennium Agenda – The Challenge of Slums". Accessed from: https://unhabitat.org/wp-content/uploads/2003/07/GRHS_2003_Chapter_01_Revised_2010.pdf.

(WASH); an insufficient supply of water; poor land use; the limited availability of decent and affordable housing, leading to increased slum dwellings; poor land use; and high rural-urban migration.

The lack of environmental sustainability in Nigeria is evidenced by the low quality of life of the majority of citizens. One of the reasons for poor environmental sustainability in Nigeria is poor funding. This is the case with most developing countries, where government alone carries the responsibility for managing the environment – a situation that is no longer sustainable as the private sector has to be brought in to finance the demands of sustainable environmental management. In Nigeria, environmental management is done by the government through some MDAs such as the Federal Ministry of Environment (FME), the Federal Environment Protection Agency (FEPA), the Niger Delta Development Commission (NDDC), the Department of Agriculture and Forestry, etc.

Improved environmental sustainability in Nigeria can be achieved by attention to mass housing; adequate safe drinking water; safe and hygienic sanitation facilities; municipal solid waste management, etc.

MDG7: Goal-Specific Performance

This section analyses Nigeria's performance on MDG7. The targets and indicators that are used to analyse Nigeria's performance are as follows:

Selected Targets & Indicators for MDG7

Target	Indicators
Integrating the principles of sustainable development into country policies and programs.	Carbon dioxide emissions per capita.
Reduce by half the proportion of people without sustainable access to safe drinking water.	1. Proportion of population with access to safe drinking water (%) 2. Proportion of population with access to basic sanitation (%)

United Nations

Carbon Dioxide Per Capita

The carbon dioxide per capita indicator looks at CO2 emissions per individual. It is a useful way of gauging environmental sustainability as it offers useful insights into a country's resource management and its standard of living. It tells how much a country is contributing to global warming since it considers the carbon footprint at the per capita level.

Carbon Dioxide Emissions per Capita (tonnes)

Country	*1990*	*2015*	*Change*
Nigeria	0.1	0.6	+500%
South Africa	5.6	8.8	+57%
Kenya	0.3	0.3	0%
Angola	0.1	1.2	+1,100%

World Bank

Carbon Dioxide Emissions Per Capita, 2015 (tonnes)

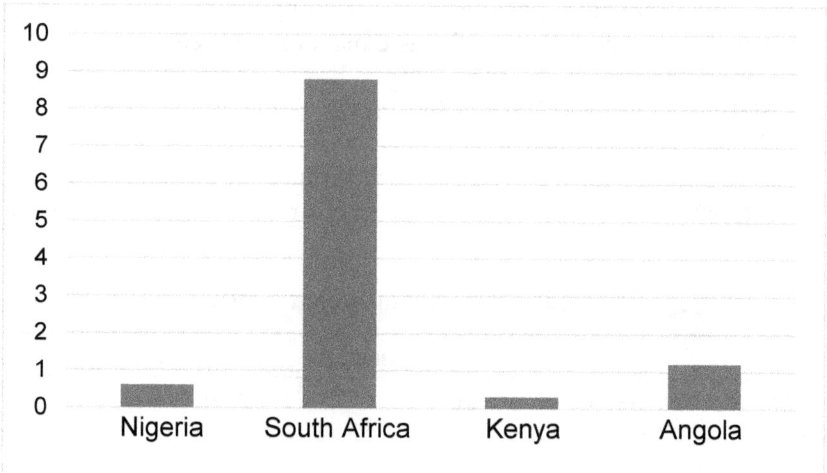

South Africa has the highest carbon dioxide emissions per capita, while Kenya has the lowest. Kenya's surge in the use of wind power and its forest conservation program are among the reasons for its low carbon footprint per capita. Nigeria, on the other hand, registered a 500% increase in CO2 emissions per capita between 1990 and 2015. This is the result of the use of energy for cooking, meeting the demands of small business, etc.

Developing countries are likely to have low carbon footprints per capita compared to developed countries. One of the reasons for this is that developing countries have yet to harness the benefits of industrialization. Despite this, there have been increases in all four countries examined.

Adverse weather conditions stemming from global warming have been a challenge for Nigeria in recent times. Excessive flooding and desertification are currently affecting parts of Nigeria and the government appears to have been late in waking up to the challenges of global warming. Major floods in 2012 captured the severity of the threat to life and property. Based on the post-disaster needs assessment (PDNA), the impact of the disaster was very high in terms of human, material, and economic losses with 363 people killed, 5,851 injured, 3,891,314 affected and 3,871,350 displaced. In fact, the PDNA report estimated that the collective damage caused by the flood at US$100 million.[360]

When it comes to dealing with the challenge of adverse weather conditions, the policy direction of the federal government is opaque. The 2012 floods provide a hint of the economic hits that Nigeria can sustain from future adverse weather conditions. This is not the problem of developing countries alone. Developed countries must be willing to provide support – by way of funding and meaningful technical assistance – to developing countries to help them build their climate change adaptability. This adaptability is critical for developing countries like Nigeria, who suffer the most from warming of the atmosphere by the industrial activities of developed nations.[361] Without extensive support, the capacity of developing countries to meet development targets is compromised. At the moment, international development partners such as USAID, the World Bank and the African Development Bank have been providing technical assistance to the Federal Ministry of Environment in developing a strategy and policy framework for building climate change resilience in Nigeria. One of the documents that has emanated from this engagement is the Climate Change Policy and Response Strategy.[362] At present, this is the overarching policy document outlining the climate change priorities and direction of the government. The document identifies some of the activities that should be implemented by the government over a 10-year period. They include stemming the widespread erosion in Southern Nigeria, afforestation and the clean-up of the polluted environment in the Niger Delta region.[363]

---

[360] Federal Republic of Nigeria, World Bank, EU, UN, and other partners, "Nigeria: Post-Disaster Needs Assessment of the 2012 Floods, PDNA Report 2013". Accessed from: https://www.gfdrr.org/sites/gfdrr/files/NIGERIA_PDNA_PRINT_05_29_2013_WEB.pdf [27 October 2017].

[361] Ijeoma, S., "Nigeria & Climate Change Adaptation," *ISSP Insight*, May 2012. Accessed from: https://www.sustainabilityprofessionals.org/system/files/May%202012-Nigeria%20and%20Climate%20Change%20Adaptation.pdf.

[362] International Centre for Energy, Environment & Development (ICEED), "Nigeria adopts climate change policy document". Accessed from: http://iceednigeria.org/ic/nigeria-adopts-climate-change-policy-document/ [12 September 2017].

[363] Building Nigeria's Response to Climate Change (BNRCC) Project, "National Adaptation Strategy & Plan of Action on Climate Change for Nigeria," Technical Report, November 2011. Accessed from: http://csdevnet.org/wp-content/uploads/NATIONAL-ADAPTATION-STRATEGY-AND-PLAN-OF-ACTION.pdf [12 October 2017].

Access to Safe Drinking Water

This indicator examines the percentage of people with access to safe drinking water from improved sources. These include household connections (*i.e.* drilling of boreholes), public stand pipes, protected wells and springs, etc. Although billions of people have gained access to safe drinking water between 1990 and 2015, significant inequalities still remain, especially in developing countries, where women are the most affected. In addition to gauging the level of environmental sustainability, this indicator is useful in measuring the quality of life of a country's citizenry.

Proportion of Population with Access to Safe Drinking Water

Country	*1990*	*2015*	*Change*
Nigeria	40	69	+72.5%
South Africa	83	93	+12.0%
Kenya	43	63	+46.5%
Angola	46	49	+6.5%

UNICEF

Change in Proportion of Population with Access to Safe Drinking Water, 1990-2015 (%)

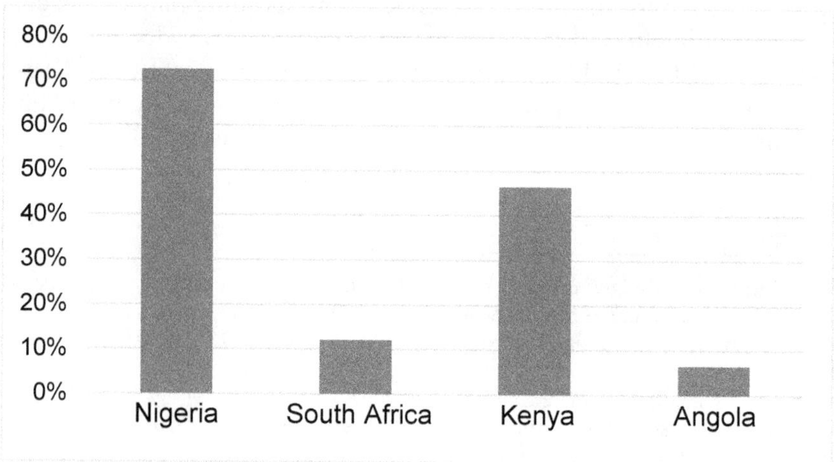

In measuring access to safe drinking water, Nigeria recorded the best result among the countries examined. Some of the factors responsible for this were increased budget allocations to the Federal Ministry of Water Resources and increased commitment to WASH interventions by development partners such as DFID, USAID, the World Bank, etc. Despite this positive result, it is essential to note that Nigeria is well short of the target of 75% coverage for access to safe drinking water. Furthermore, the significant disparity between water coverage in urban and rural areas needs to be addressed if Nigeria is to improve on this indicator under the SDGs.

Water supply coverage is more limited in rural areas than in urban areas. According to the Water & Sanitation Monitoring Platform (WSMP), a working group consisting of donor agencies and civil society, "a rural dweller has a less than 50% chance of accessing safe drinking water compared to their urban counterparts".[364] In fact, in 2006, water coverage in urban areas was 65%, compared to 30% in rural areas.[365] Overall, despite Nigeria's improvement in providing safe water supplies, the result is well short of desired expectations, especially considering the situation in rural areas where the local government authorities lack the capacity to provide sustainable water supplies and improve resource management. This is why Nigeria still ranks among the countries with the lowest safe water coverage in the world.[366] Satisfying expectations under the SDG framework would require a review of current sector investment levels and trends, and the use of results from the review to strategically allocate resources that meet water supply priorities of the citizenry across the six geopolitical regions. In addition, the government – at the federal and state levels – ought to mobilize civil and political commitments towards addressing the high burden of demand in the water and sanitation sector. Nigeria's performance on sanitation is explored subsequently in more detail. Furthermore, it is essential to reiterate that Nigeria is among countries with the lowest water and sanitation coverage rates in the world.[367]

Angola was the worst performer of the four countries studied with only a 6.5% improvement in access to safe drinking water between 1990 and 2015. This may explain why Angola has the highest rate of diarrheal diseases in the world, with 114 years of life lost to diarrheal-associated illnesses per 1,000 people.[368] Persistent national conflict has been largely responsible for the stagnation in its water sector. The country experienced four decades of conflict which damaged most of its infrastructure, including WASH infrastructure. However, with the passage of the General Water Law and

---

364 Water & Sanitation Monitoring Platform (WSMP), "Nigeria: Water & Sanitation Summary Report," Factsheet 2008. Accessed from: https://www.unicef.org/nigeria/ng_media_Water_sanitation_summary_sheet.pdf [22 September 2017].

365 WHO/UNICEF Joint Monitoring Programme for Water Supply and Sanitation, 2008 Report.

366 UNICEF, Nigeria: "WaSH Country Summary Sheet 2008." Accessed from: https://www.unicef.org/nigeria/NG_resources_washsummary.pdf.

367 *Ibid.*

368 USAID, "Angola: Water & Sanitation Profile, Factsheet 2014". Accessed from: http://pdf.usaid.gov/pdf_docs/Pnado925.pdf [21 October 2017].

capital investment by the government in the sector, it is hoped that water supply coverage would improve under the SDG framework.

Access to Basic Sanitation

This indicator measures how much of a population has access to safe and hygienic sanitation facilities – public sewers, bathing facilities, pour/flush toilets, pit latrines with slabs, etc. It is a way to gauge the standard of living in a country and the health status of its citizens. For instance, poor sanitation facilities can lead to the spread of waterborne diseases such as cholera.

The results show that Angola achieved the most improvement with regards to access to basic sanitation facilities. Nigeria, on the other hand, recorded the worst performance with a substantial decrease in access to such facilities.[369] The rural areas account for this result as access to basic sanitation facilities is better in urban areas. This observation, yet again, mirrors the disparity in access to water supply between the urban and rural areas. Another factor that contributed to this poor result is the ongoing conflict in North Eastern Nigeria. According to the United Nations Humanitarian Response Plan (HRP) for North East Nigeria, "the Boko Haram insurgency in North East Nigeria has rendered over 2 million people internally-displaced, coupled with 8 million people facing food insecurity".[370] One sector that has been most affected by this conflict is the WASH sector. The UN estimates that 6.2 million people in the region lack access to safe water and hygienic sanitation facilities.[371] It indicates that an estimated US$21 million is required to address this need,[372] highlighting the scale of the WASH problem in Nigeria.

Access to Basic Sanitation Facilities, 1990 and 2015

Country	*1990*	*2015*	*Change*
Nigeria	38%	29%	-23.7%
South Africa	51%	66%	+29.4%
Kenya	25%	30%	+20.0%
Angola	22%	52%	+136.4%

World Bank

[369] World Bank, "Nigeria: Access to improved sanitation facilities". Accessed from: https://data.worldbank.org/indicator/SH.STA.ACSN?locations=NG [11 October 2017]

[370] United Nations, "Nigeria: Humanitarian Response Plan (HRP) for the North East," Policy Brief (2016). Accessed from: https://reliefweb.int/sites/reliefweb.int/files/resources/nigeria_2016_hrp_11012016.pdf [22 October 2017].

[371] *Ibid.*

[372] *Ibid.*

Change in Proportion of Population with Access to Basic Sanitation Facilities, 1990-2015 (%)

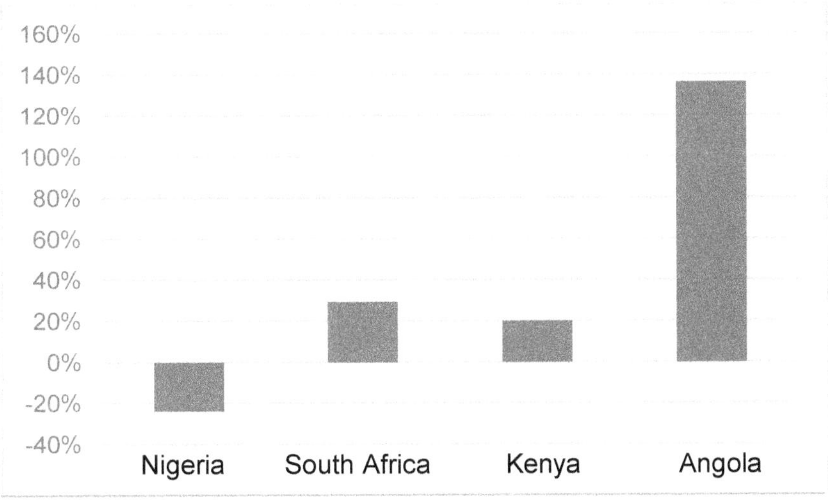

Nigeria has a vision of achieving 100% access to basic water supplies and sanitation facilities by the year 2030, with a fundamental emphasis on the rural areas. According to Sanitation and Water for All, an NGO, the country would require an estimated US$2 billion in capital investments yearly to achieve this target.[373]

It is also necessary to note that the WASH sector in Nigeria is guided by the National Water Resources Policy (2016-2030). This policy of the Federal Government – acting through the Federal Ministry of Water Resources – places a priority on eliminating open defecation in Nigeria by 2015, coupled with achieving universal access to safe drinking water and basic/hygienic sanitation facilities by 2030.[374] Achieving this target carries far-reaching implications for child health in Nigeria, especially considering that the majority of child deaths are attributable to unsafe water and poor sanitation, to which children are more vulnerable.[375] The effects of poor water

---

[373] Sanitation and Water for All, "Nigeria overview: Water, sanitation and hygiene," Briefing Note (2017). Accessed from: http://sanitationandwaterforall.org/wp-content/uploads/download-manager-files/2017%20Nigeria%20Overview_final.pdf.

[374] Federal Ministry of Water Resources, "National Water Resources policy (2016-2030)". Accessed from: http://www.waterresources.ng/wp-content/uploads/2017/02/Download.pdf [15 October 2017].

[375] Ezeh, O.K., Agho, K.E., Dibley, M.J., Hall, J., and Page, A.N., "The impact of water and sanitation on childhood mortality in Nigeria: Evidence from demographic and health surveys, 2003-2013," *International Journal of Environmental Research & Public Health*, 11 (2014): 9256-9272.

and sanitation as a leading cause of childhood diarrhoea and cholera have long been established.[376] Consequently, improving access to basic water and hygienic sanitation facilities is key to improving child health outcomes in Nigeria.

[376] Feyehun, O.A., “Household environmental health hazards and child survival in Sub-Saharan Africa”. DHS Working Papers, *Demographic & Health Research* 74 (2010). Accessed from: http://dhsprogram.com/pubs/pdf/WP74/WP74.pdf [11 August 2017].

CHAPTER 12

GLOBAL PARTNERSHIP FOR DEVELOPMENT

Introduction

This chapter discusses Nigeria's performance on MDG8, which deals with the need to develop a global partnership for development. The Millennium Declaration is, in effect, such a partnership. For all countries to achieve the MDGs, there is a need for developed countries to satisfy their official development assistance (ODA) obligations, besides debt relief and fair trade rules. The global partnership for development aims to reduce inequalities in development and access to development funding for developing countries. ODA levels continue to increase despite the global financial crisis; however, aid falls short of expectations and Africa continues to be short-changed.[377]

In recent times, significant progress has been made in reducing the underlying disparities between developed and developing countries. Aid is ever more focused on the poorest countries, with the least-developed countries receiving about a third of donors' aggregate aid flows. Developing countries are increasingly gaining access to the markets of developed countries, and the proportion of developed countries' imports from developing countries has been rising.[378] Furthermore, least-developed countries now enjoy tariff decreases from developed countries, giving them greater access to foreign markets. The tariffs of developed countries on imports of agricultural commodities, textiles and clothing have stayed high, but least-developed and developing countries seem to increasingly benefit from preferential tariffs, especially on agricultural products.[379]

Another area that the global partnership for development seeks to address is the heavy debt burdens on developing countries. Progress has been achieved in this regard; some countries, such as Nigeria, have had a significant

[377] Belgian Federal Public Service, Foreign Affairs, Foreign Trade and Development Cooperation, Global Partnership for Development: "Millennium Development Goal 8" (Directorate General of Development Cooperation, 2005).
[378] *Ibid.*
[379] Least-developed and developing countries enjoy about 1.6% tariff reductions.

portion of their foreign debt reduced and, in some cases, completely cancelled. For instance, 40 countries qualified for debt relief under the heavily-indebted poor countries (HIPC) initiative. Of these, 35 have had future debt repayments decreased by an estimated US$10 billion, and 28 have received further assistance of US$25 billion under the multilateral Debt Relief Initiative.[380] Despite these welcome developments, some of these debt relief initiatives are reaching the end of their tenure, and some low and middle-income countries remain at risk of debt distress.

Another area that the global partnership for development seeks to address concerns the access of developing countries to information and communication technology (ICT). Internationally, about 4 billion individuals had access to mobile phones by the end of 2009. Growth in mobile telephony remains strongest in developing countries where mobile penetration had exceeded 50% by the end of 2009.[381] In Sub-Saharan Africa, where only 1% of individuals have access to fixed telephone lines, more than 30% now have access to mobile phones. Linked to the growth in mobile telephony is the access to the internet.[382] Although internet penetration has improved in developing countries over the past few years, the majority of people still lack access to it. According to the United Nations MDGs Department, 23% of the world's population had access to the internet as at 2010.[383] In developed countries, the percentage remains higher than in developing countries, where only 1 in 6 individuals have access to the internet. In Oceania, Sub-Saharan Africa and South Asia, only 6% of the population had access to the internet.[384]

Global Partnership for Development: Nigeria's Perspective

Per capita official development assistance to Nigeria witnessed an upward trend over the last decade of the MDGs, despite marginal decreases in 2008 and 2009 owing to the global financial crisis. Prior to that, an 80% increase in ODA in 2004 can be attributed to the debt relief granted to Nigeria. What this shows is that the debt burden limits ODA inflows and points to the need for reductions in external borrowings by the governments of developing countries.

Furthermore, ODA allocations to critical sectors in 2005-2014 also witnessed an upward trend. The sector that has received the most ODA is the health sector. The percentage of aggregate sectoral ODA that accrued to the health sector in 2012, 2013 and 2014 was 66.5%, 97%, and 75% respectively. These increased ODA inflows were responsible for the some of the progress

---

[380] United Nations, "MDGs Fact Sheet" (2010).

[381] *Ibid.*

[382] *Ibid.*

[383] *Ibid.*

[384] *Ibid.*

achieved under the indicators for health-related goals. Another sector that has received substantial ODA inflows is agriculture. This sector is highly labour-intensive in Nigeria and accounts for a significant portion of the country's labour force. Consequently, improvements in agriculture are likely to lift a significant portion of the population out of poverty.

Official Development Assistance to Key Sectors in Nigeria, 2005-2014 (million US$)

Sector	*2005*	*2006*	*2007*	*2008*	*2009*	*2010*	*2011*	*2012*	*2013*	*2014*
Agriculture	2.4	1.1	0.9	0.8	6.3	0.4	20.6	9.8	1.0	34.2
Civil Society								0.1	0.05	0.7
Education								10.6		2.7
Health	2.4	3.0	3.5	4.9	7.2	7.9	11.3	179.2	256.8	480.0
Energy/Environ-ment			0.2	0.4	5.4	0.9	0.9	0.5	0.1	5.7
Governance								0.3	0.3	22.0
Government			0.1	0.9	0.2	0.8	1.4	12.5		37.7
Human Rights								0.2	0.2	
Political System							1.3	1.3	1.3	1.3
Poverty Alleviation							0.1	0.04	4.2	2.2
Women's Empowerment							0.1		0.6	4.2
Total (USD)	4,8	7.1	4.7	9.1	19.0	22.1	32.8	269.4	265.0	648.2

Notes: Figures are rounded. Totals for some years include ODA not included in sectors mentioned.

National Planning Commission, 2015

One of the main factors driving the rising per capita ODA to Nigeria is the commitment by global governments to achieving the MDGs. At this point, it is essential to highlight some of the challenges associated with MDG8, including the formulation and implementation of policies tied to its indicators. In Nigeria, policy implementation is weak and this makes it difficult for expected outcomes to feed through to the local level. One of the expectations under MDG8 is that the governments of developing countries will control internal and external borrowing. Nigeria appears not to have learnt from the experiences of operating under a huge debt burden even after the debt forgiveness of 2004. The country's debt profile has continued to rise at both the federal and state levels; this poses threats to ODA inflows required to meet local and international development expectations. Nigeria's rising debt profile can be attributed to the failure of the government, especially at the federal level, to establish and enforce set borrowing limits for state governments and federal MDAs. The Fiscal Responsibility Act[385] is supposed to address this; however, enforcement by the Federal Ministry of Finance and the Federal Ministry of Budget and National Planning has been weak.

MDG8: Goal-Specific Performance

This section analyses Nigeria's performance on 'the global partnership for development' goal. The indicators used to assess Nigeria's performance on MDG8 are as follows:

- Per capita ODA to Nigeria
- Fixed telephone lines per 100 people
- Cellular (mobile) phone subscribers per 100 people
- Internet users per 100 people

Per Capita ODA

The 'per capita ODA' indicator represents net disbursements for ODA at market prices to countries on the Development Assistance Committee (DAC) list. This indicator can be used to assess the economic well-being of citizens in a country as ODA inflows are supposed to have a positive effect on the local economy.

The following data shows Nigeria with highest ODA per capita of the four countries, followed closely by South Africa, while Angola witnessed a drop. Official development assistance is key to financing development needs, and is supposed to bridge the funding gap for development projects. While ODA can be useful for improving the well-being of the recipient country, there have been concerns about its actual impact on development outcomes.

Per Capita ODA (US$ billion)

Country	*1990*	*2015*	*Change*
Nigeria	2.7	13.4	+396%
South Africa	5.8	25.8	+345%
Kenya	37.9	52.4	+38%
Angola	14.1	13.6	-4%

World Bank

[385] This act is meant to provide for prudent management of Nigeria's resources, ensure long term macro-economic stability and secure greater accountability and transparency in fiscal operations within the Medium Term Fiscal Policy Framework. It creates the Fiscal Responsibility Commission to promote and enforce Nigeria's economic objectives and related matters.

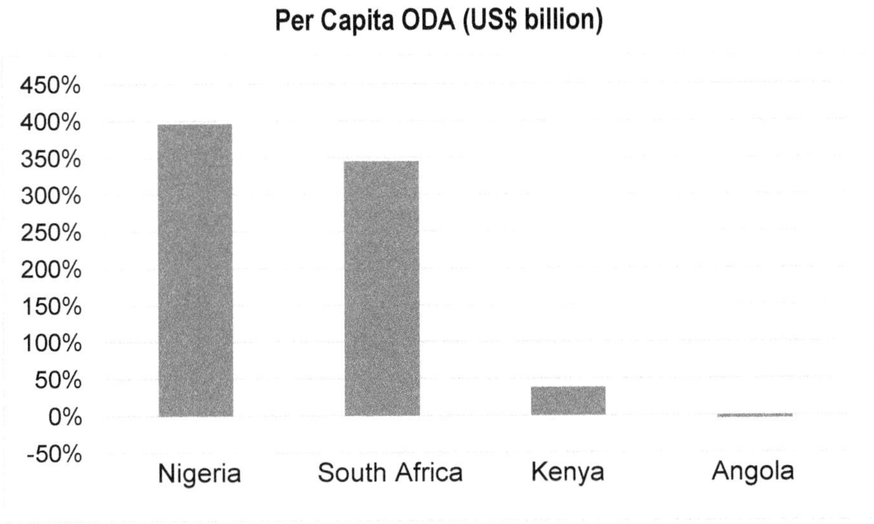

World Bank

for improving the well-being of the recipient country, there have been concerns about its actual impact on development outcomes.

Nigeria presents a useful case study for exploring the effects of ODA, considering the abundance of human and material resources in the country and Nigeria's role as one of the largest exporters of crude oil in the world. Concerns about the impact of development assistance are varied. Some studies indicate that it has a negative impact on development outcomes.[386] This view is premised on the suggestion that such assistance drives consumption more than investment in the recipient country. As indicated, Nigeria's per capita ODA rose from US$2.7 billion in 1990 to US$13.4 billion in 2015;[387] however, little has occurred in the way of industrialization and modernization of the economy. Nigeria's economy remains largely import-dependent despite inflows of ODA and FDI over the past 20 years. Proshare, an investment advisory firm, notes that Nigeria is the 52nd largest importer in the world, with imports of commodities such as wheat, dairy products, sugar, rice and frozen meat valued at about US$20 billion annually.[388]

---

[386] Burnside, C., and Dollar, D., "Aid, policies and growth," World Bank Policy Research Working Paper No.1777 (1997).

[387] World Bank, "Net official development assistance". Accessed from: https://data.worldbank.org/indicator/DT.ODA.ALLD.CD?locations=NG [12 August 2017].

[388] Proshare, "Nigeria as an import-dependent economy: Outlook for commodities and impact on ordinary people," Working Paper, January 2017. Accessed from: https://www.proshareng.com/news/NIGERIA%20ECONOMY/Nigeria-As-An-Import-Dependent-Economy---Outlook-for-Commodities-and-Impact-on-Ordinary-People-/33432 [11 July 2017].

Other literature considers ODA beneficial in providing budget support to low-income countries, such as Malawi and Botswana. Certain studies also suggest that when development assistance is complemented by sound, growth-focused macroeconomic policies, it can have a positive impact on development outcomes.[389] Under the current administration of President Muhammadu Buhari, the Economic Recovery and Growth Plan (ERGP) was launched with the following policy priorities: lifting Nigeria out of the economic recession, job creation, food sufficiency through agricultural growth, infrastructure development and industrialization.[390] While the ERGP has been hailed as a useful roadmap for reviving Nigeria's economy and positioning it to meet the needs of a population that is growing exponentially, concerns remain about its implementation. The fear is that it would end up abandoned like previous government economic policies, such as the Transformation Agenda of the previous administration of Goodluck Jonathan.

Despite significant inflows of ODA to Nigeria, concerns remain as to the degree to which they improve the lives of citizens, especially as the ODA is often channeled through MDAs that are characterized by corruption and bureaucracy. As noted earlier, policy implementation is the bane of MDG8.

Fixed Telephone Lines per 100 People

This indicator looks at the number of active analogue fixed telephone lines, voice-over-IP subscriptions, fixed wireless local loop and fixed public pay phones per 100 people. The quality of an economy's infrastructure, especially in information and communication technology, is key to attracting FDI inflows. The more access people have to means of communication, the more their lives are improved, considering that effective and seamless communication reduces transactional costs for small and micro businesses.

Fixed Telephone Lines per 100 People

Country	*1990*	*2015*	*Change*
Nigeria	0.302	0.102	-66%
South Africa	9.01	7.723	-14%
Kenya	0.747	0.183	-75%
Angola	0.677	1.249	+84%

International Telecommunications Union

389 Burnside, C., and Dollar, D., "Aid, the incentive regime, and poverty reduction," World Bank Policy Research Paper, No. 1937 (1998).

390 PricewaterhouseCoopers, "The Economic Recovery and Growth Plan (ERGP): 2017-2020," Policy Brief (2017). Accessed from: https://www.pwc.com/ng/en/assets/pdf/economy-alert-april-2017.pdf.

Change in Fixed Telephone Lines per 100 People, 1990-2015 (%)

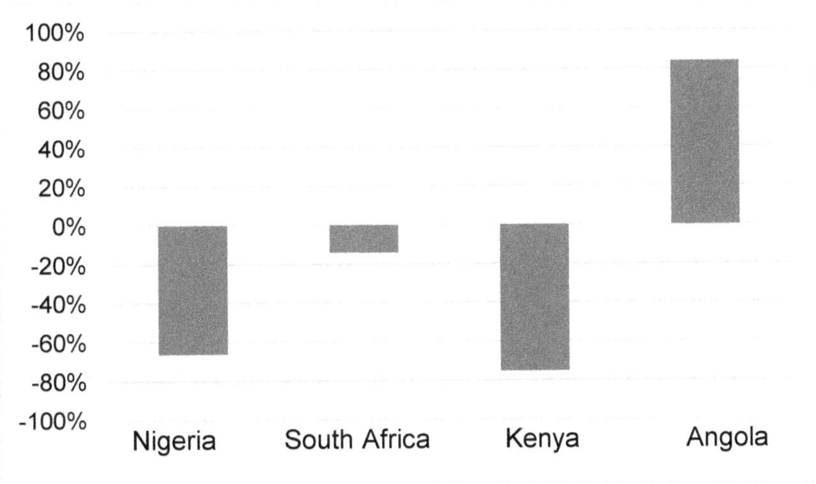

International Telecommunications Union

Based on the data shown here, Angola is the only country that recorded an increase in fixed-line telephone users per 100 people, with an 84% increase. The other countries, including Nigeria, recorded decreases in fixed-line telephone users between 1990 and 2015. Nigeria recorded a 66% decrease. This does not necessarily imply limited access for the majority of the population to ICT, as the data must be considered in conjunction with the number of cellular (mobile) phone users.

Cellular Phone Subscribers per 100 People

The number of cellular (mobile) phone users is another useful means of assessing the level of access to ICT, as these phones have become increasingly popular around the world and have been progressively displacing the use of fixed-line telephones in a number of countries.

Cellular Phone Subscribers per 100 People

Country	***1990***	***2015***
Nigeria	0	82
South Africa	0	165
Kenya	0	81
Angola	0	61

World Bank, International Telecommunications Union

Cellular Phone Subscribers per 100 People, 2015

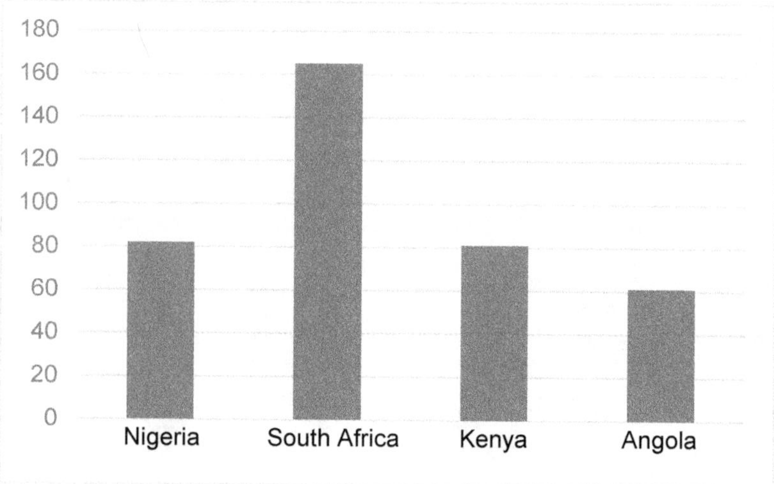

World Bank, International Telecommunications Union

For cellular phones, South Africa has the highest number of users, followed by Nigeria with 82 subscribers per 100 people in its population. Nigeria's figure suggests that the country has a high tele-density. In view of this, one would expect that Nigeria would also have high internet density. One of the reasons for Nigeria's high mobile phone subscriptions is the deregulation of the telecommunications sector in 1999, which saw the emergence of mobile telecommunications operators such as MTN, Etisalat, N-Tel, Airtel, etc. The International Telecommunications Union notes that Nigeria's mobile telecommunications market grew by 5% annually between 2010 and 2016. In fact, the sector contributed 8.83% to Nigeria's GDP in 2016.[391] This is evidence of the growth in mobile phone subscribers since the deregulation of the sector. Another factor contributing to the growing number of cellular phone subscribers is massive investment by the licensed telecommunications operators into improving infrastructure, *i.e.* increasing the spread of masts to cover rural areas, laying fibre-optic cables to improve the availability of data, etc. These investments are expected to bring down the cost of calls and data services further. Consequently, the number of active cellular phone subscribers is expected to increase over the next decade.[392]

---

[391] International Telecommunication Union, "Telecommunication/ICT markets and trends in Africa, October 2017". Accessed from: https://www.itu.int/ITU-D/ict/statistics/material/af_report07.pdf [14 October 2017].
[392] *Ibid.*

Internet Users per 100 People

This indicator measures the number of internet users. Access to the internet, as referred to here, involves devices such as computers, mobile phones, digital TV, etc. Currently, the world is in the midst of a digital revolution and ICT is increasingly plays a role in our daily lives. For instance, financial or bank transactions are increasingly conducted online. Again, this indicator is useful in gauging a country's level of development as access to information is critical to empowering citizens and lifting them out of poverty.

As shown in the tables below, South Africa has the highest number of internet users per 100 people with 51.9, followed by Nigeria with 47.4. These results validate the results obtained in the previous indicator. The implication is that there is a positive correlation between cellular phone subscribers and internet users – the growth in internet users is largely attributable to the growth in mobile phone users. The National Bureau of Statistics notes that 49% of internet connections in Nigeria are made through mobile phones.[393]

Internet Users per 100 People

Country	*1990*	*2015*
Nigeria	0	47.4
South Africa	0	51.9
Kenya	0	45.6
Angola	0	12.4

World Bank

Internet Users per 100 People, 2015

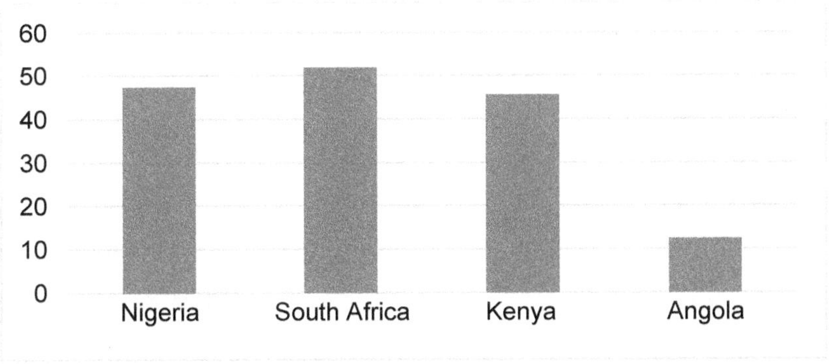

World Bank

[393] National Bureau of Statistics, *Nigeria T elecommunications (Services) Sector Report* (Abuja: NBS, 2016).

SECTION 3

PARTNERSHIP FOR DEVELOPMENT

CHAPTER 13

THE UN DEVELOPMENT AGENDA AND NIGERIA

Introduction

The Post-2015 Development Agenda is the global development framework which will inform international development for the next 15 years. As already highlighted, this framework is meant to build on achievements recorded during the MDG period whilst addressing gaps encountered. It comprises UN Secretary General-led initiatives, such as the work of the UN System Task Team on the Post-2015 Development Agenda and the High Level Political Forum (HLPF) on Sustainable Development, combined with the intergovernmental process of creating a set of Sustainable Development Goals (SDGs) to replace the MDGs.

The Millennium Development Goals provided the opportunity for Nigeria to commit to addressing the broad range of its development challenges. Based on the results obtained, Nigeria performed satisfactorily under some of the goals and fared less well under others. For instance, under MDG4, Nigeria recorded a 49% decrease in under-five mortality and a 45% decrease in infant mortality between 1990 and 2015.[394] This indicates considerable progress compared to where Nigeria was in the 1990s. Despite these impressive results, there were also cases where Nigeria performed below par. For instance, HIV prevalence among pregnant women aged between 15 and 24 years rose by 44% between 1990 and 2015 compared to Kenya's 49% decrease over the same period.

The analysis done in Section 2 highlights certain gaps in Nigeria's performance and its efforts to achieve the MDGs. One area that is of particular interest is the rate of poverty in Nigeria. Poverty remains a development problem in the country and hampers efforts to create an environment for self-directed development, especially as it relates to providing the tools and environment for people to lead healthy, fulfilling and productive lives. To put this observation into proper perspective, results from the analysis of Nigeria's performance under MDG1 indicated that the proportion of those living on less than US$1 per day decreased from 65% in 1990 to 40% in 2015. While this

[394] UNICEF, "Levels and trends in child mortality, 2015".

result is positive, it is still below expectations and it allows the propensity for civil unrest to persist.

This chapter discusses the global development agenda and also considers the way forward for Nigeria. Several observers view the Millennium Declaration as a critical consideration for charting the course for the post-2015 development agenda. What is clear is that a post-2015 development framework that emerges from a participatory, inclusive and bottom-up process will vary from one that is shaped by a group of experts and technocrats. The post-2015 development agenda will benefit from considering the inputs and concerns of a broad-range of stakeholders, *i.e.* a bottom-up approach. The voices of target beneficiaries must be considered to prevent a situation whereby the post-2015 development process becomes excessively technocratic or donor-focused in its nomenclature/design and implementation. This is vital for the success of the Sustainable Development Goals.

Global targets help focus the attention on human development and human rights, which are areas of universal concern that apply to all countries. These targets are meant to stimulate efforts and resources towards improving human living standards through inter-sectoral and inter-disciplinary work that gravitates beyond income-poverty. Considering that all development is endogenous – and never influenced by international resource transfers – global targets mean more than the mobilization of official development assistance (ODA). While they stimulate all nations to speed up progress in different thematic areas, their applicability can only be judged within the country-specific context.

The post-2015 development agenda needs to be bold and ambitious if the world is to make considerable progress towards drastically reducing poverty in all its forms and in realizing sustainable development. Consequently, it is expected that the SDGs – which are central to the post-2015 global development agenda – must not just compete with the unfinished benefits of the UN MDGs, but go a step further by ensuring that no one is left behind. There is a danger that many nations, including Nigeria, may fail to participate in the 4th revolution, *i.e.* the digital revolution. It is necessary to understand that human development goes beyond just lifting people out of poverty; it is more about making their escape from poverty permanent and supporting them in fulfilling their aspirations. This can be achieved through inclusive and effective governance, equity, human rights and the rule of law.

Multilateralism will come under considerable pressure in the post-2015 development environment, considering the growing resistance of some countries towards signing or ratifying global treaties and agreements.[395] A

[395]Vandemoortele, J., "Advancing the global development agenda post-2015: Some thoughts, ideas, and practical suggestions." Paper presented by the UN System Task Team on the Post-2015 Development Agenda. Accessed from http://www.un.org/millenniumgoals/pdf/jan_vandemoortele_Aug.pdf.

case in point is the United States, whose current president has taken steps to pull out of the Paris Climate Change agreement. Furthermore, creating peaceful and cohesive societies and the rule of law are seen as controversial in some quarters, especially in countries that have dictatorships. The ongoing resistance by some to the full empowerment and equality of women, for instance, to sexual and reproductive health rights, is disturbing. The problem of early marriage in Northern Nigeria presents a challenge to fulfilling key aspects of the SDGs.

Sustainability in the Post-2015 Development Landscape

The post-2015 development agenda occurs at a time of transition for much of the business community. A global movement is underway, transforming markets from within. In an increasingly connected world, it has become clear that success works *pari pasu* with social and environmental responsibility; hence, the private sector is expected to play a considerable role in the realization of the SDGs, especially in developing nations. The limited involvement of the private sector in the MDG era cannot be allowed to happen with the SDGs. Environmental, social and governance challenges affect the bottom line. Market disturbances, social unrest and ecological devastation carry far-reaching negative implications for business *vis-à-vis* supply chains, capital outflows and employee productivity.[396]

As traditional boundaries between public and private goods and services have become blurred in a globalized landscape, private-sector organizations are increasingly expected to do more in areas that were, in the past, the preserve of the public sector. As resources become scarcer, it is increasingly clear that the governments in many countries cannot address development challenges alone. The private sector is expected to demonstrate involvement and commitment to improving the well-being of human beings, as it does not operate in a vacuum.[397] Happenings in its external environment can impact its bottom line. A key means of making significant progress towards the realization of targets under the SDGs is for governments to offer incentives to business organizations that align their corporate social responsibility (CSR) programs to the SDG framework. Going forward, more and more firms are expected to view themselves as critical stakeholders in the development process, considering that they cannot succeed if the societies in which they operate fail.

Progress in the MDGs has been uneven across countries and continents of the globe and among social groups. Many African countries, including Nigeria, have fared less well than South East Asian countries and

---

[396] United Nations Association-UK, *Global Development Goals: Partnership for Progress*, (London: UNA-UK, 2016).
[397] *Ibid.*

China, which have achieved considerable progress in reducing poverty. Furthermore, African leaders appear to be taking the back seat in shaping the post-2015 development agenda. The implication of this is that the continent risks being foisted with a development framework that is retrogressive, less responsive to country-specific contexts, and which promotes the interests of developed nations through multilateral and bilateral agencies.

Meanwhile, there has been the emergence of new risks to global development and indeed global stability, such as climate change, terrorism and growing inequality, which were not addressed in the MDGs. For instance, global warming is causing drought and flash flooding across the world with the most significant impact being felt in Africa, even though the continent contributes the least to global emissions. While developing nations are responsible for only 20% of global greenhouse emissions, they face 75 to 80% of the potential damage resulting from natural disasters, mostly affecting rural communities. Though the international community has made significant funding available for adaptation and mitigation against climate change in many African countries, very limited resources have been channeled to sub-national levels. Consequently, the post-2015 development agenda will have to consider local mitigation and adaptation measures to address this global issue.

Furthermore, Africa does not possess the technological capacity required to fully participate in the global economy; raw materials form the largest exports from the continent. Again, terrorism is now the most significant threat to national security, peace and stability. Africa also has the unwholesome record of being the largest reservoir of unemployed youth; this is one of Africa's greatest challenges and the continent's lack of development makes it all the more difficult – it cannot create the jobs needed to absorb the burden. The African Outlook, published by the AFDB, OECD, UNDP and UNECA, indicated that 22 million out of 40 million African job seekers have become jobless and fearful of their future aspirations.[398] This is why many of them take significant risks – even to their lives – to seek greener pastures elsewhere. In Nigeria, the situation is critical. According to the National Planning Commission, youths under the age of 30 form over 50% of the Nigerian population.[399] Furthermore, the unemployment rate in the country is growing rapidly, and youth unemployment is three times the general unemployment rate.[400] In fact, Nigeria's spiraling youth unemployment levels are partly responsible for the social unrest in parts of the country – the Boko Haram insurgency in the North East and the Niger Delta militancy in the

---

[398] *African Economic Outlook, Promoting Youth Unemployment* (OECD, UNDP, & UNECA, 2012).

[399] National Population Commission, *Population Data for Nigeria.* (Abuja: National Population Commission, 2009).

[400] Doreo Partners, *The Nigerian Unemployment Challenge* (Africa Report Features. 2013).

Southern region. One implication of high levels of youth unemployment in Africa is that in another one or two decades, most of the youth will be parents in their mid-life years, with little or no adequate skills to compete in a large economy.[401] The potential unrest stemming from this situation could plunge the continent into a vacuum of prolonged low- or middle-income status.

Considerations for the Post-2015 Global Development Agenda

In shaping the post-2015 global development agenda, there is a need to consider the failings or challenges experienced during implementation of the MDGs. This is critical to ensuring that the SDGs build on the successes achieved under the MDGs. While the MDGs are seen as being among the most critical UN ideas that transformed the world, they devoted excessive attention to social needs at the expense of considering the role of inequality in perpetuating conditions that encourage underdevelopment.[402] Excluding MDG3, which focused on girls' education, no significant effort was devoted to dealing with the growing rate of inequality among social groups. By excessively focusing on the symptoms and effects of poverty, the MDGs failed to address the structural causes of poverty such as unequal access to resources and opportunities, discrimination and lack of representation. Women, children and youth, indigenous persons, rural populations, persons living with disabilities, the elderly and other marginalized groups are usually the most disadvantaged. These groups are more at risk of being poor, yet the MDGs operated on the premise that they would be impacted directly from aggregated economic growth through trickle-down effects.

Another area not addressed by the MDGs concerns the inequitable or unfair distribution of resources between central governments and state/local governments, which stifles rural development. Nigeria is a valid case in point for this particular observation. In Nigeria, the Federal Appropriation Act stipulates the following revenue sharing formula: the Federal Government collects 51% of all revenues generated across the federation and 49% is shared between the states and local governments.[403] Considering that Nigeria has 36 states and 774 local government catchment areas, it is clear that this formula is insufficient to address the country's development challenges, especially at the rural level. What makes the situation all the more difficult is that local

---

[401] Salami, C.G.E., "Youth Employment in Nigeria: A Time for Creative Intervention," *International Journal of Business & Marketing Management*, 1 (2013): 18-26.

[402] Decentralization and Local Governance (DeLoG), "Post-2015 Global Development Agenda: Making the Case for Decentralization and Local Governance," DeLoG Working Paper 2, February 2013.

[403] Ukaigwe, G.A., "Evolving an Ideal Revenue Sharing Formula: Nigerian Issues, Problems and Prospects," Master's Thesis, University of Nigeria, Nsukka, 2012).

governments are deprived full access to what is due to them by the state governments. This situation has informed recent growing calls for restructuring across the six geopolitical regions of the country. One of the main drivers of the restructuring call stems from the need to reduce items in the Exclusive List of the Constitution of the Federal Republic of Nigeria so that additional revenue can accrue to the states and local governments.[404] There is a widespread belief across the country that restructuring the system of governance – especially reducing the central power – will aid in stimulating economic growth and development across the six regions.

While the case for restructuring Nigeria makes sense in the context of diffusing economic growth and development across the 36 states, there are still concerns about the degree to which state governments can prudently and efficiently deploy the increase in revenues that would accrue to them from such a move. Political governance in Nigeria is widely seen as imperfect, especially considering the high levels of corruption among public officials. State governments in Nigeria do not receive the same scrutiny as the federal government, hence there are genuine fears that ceding more control to state authorities may encourage more corruption at the state and local government levels. Consequently, for restructuring to work – especially as it relates to improving the lives of citizens – there is a need to institutionalize effective checks and balances to ensure that state and local government authorities do not misappropriate public resources.

There are a number of critical considerations that must be addressed if the Sustainable Development Goals are to achieve global expectations for growth. For the purpose of this study, attention will be focused on the following considerations: inequality, health, poverty and gender equality/development.

Inequality in the Post-2015 Development Environment

As we have mentioned, under the MDGs there was an excessive focus on the social sector at the expense of some more salient considerations such as inequality. To initiate discussions on the importance of considering inequality when shaping the post-2015 development agenda, there is a need to cite the United Nations Millennium Declaration, Paragraph 2:

> We have a collective responsibility to uphold the principles of human dignity, equality, and equity at the global level. As leaders, we have a duty therefore to all the globe's people,

[404] El-Rufai, N.A., and Okolo, J., "What is restructuring and does Nigeria need it?" Chatham House, Africa Programme Meeting, 21 September 2017.

> especially the most vulnerable and, in particular, the children of the world, to whom the future belongs.[405]

In this citation, the need to improve human dignity and promote equity indicates the forward-looking standpoint of the MDGs, something not properly addressed because of the excessive focus on providing social needs. Despite many of the successes achieved by the MDGs, they have not managed to integrate all the principles outlined in the Millennium Declaration, including inequality. This discussion does not in any way diminish the importance of "social needs" in development; however, the position adopted in this study is that there is a need to consider the precursors of underdevelopment. One of these precursors is inequality.

The MDGs focus on national and global averages, and progress can conceal much slower progress or even rising disparities at the state and local levels and among specific populations. To the degree that accelerating progress towards certain targets is easier when public resources are focused among the better off or elite class, the MDG period may have inadvertently led to significant resources being channeled away from the poorest population groups or from those that are already at a disadvantage because of the impacts of discrimination based on gender, ethnicity, disability or residence. At the very least – and with the exception of MDG3, which has a target for girls' education – they have not provided sufficient direction for policy makers and governments to positively address inequalities.

The availability of data disaggregated by wealth quintile, sex and residence offers sufficient evidence on how the mixture of these variables has led to uneven progress towards achieving the MDGs. Young children in the poorest households are three times more likely to die from malnutrition.[406] For instance, despite Nigeria's vast mineral resources, 37% of children from the poorest households, or 6 million children, are stunted (*i.e.* chronic malnourishment), more than half of them severely. Furthermore, 18% of children suffer from wasting (*i.e.* acute malnutrition), and 50% of this group suffer from severe malnutrition.[407]

Gender disparities still persist in many countries and contexts despite successes recorded from the MDGs. Considering what is accessed by the MDG targets and indicators, decreased rates of secondary education enrolment (especially in Oceania, South Asia, and sub-Saharan Africa), poor representation in national parliaments, broad gaps in access to meaningful

---

405 United Nations, *UN MDGs* (New York: UN, 2000).

406 UNICEF, "Child Info: Disparities in Child Survival". Accessed from: http://wwww.childinfo.org/mortality_disparities.html [25 September 2017].

407 UNICEF, "Nutrition: Malnutrition Rates in Under-5 Children in Nigeria," Factsheet. Accessed from: https://www.unicef.org/nigeria/factsheets_NUTRITION_low.pdf [20 September 2017].

employment, and the gendered approach to addressing the HIV pandemic, all indicate the urgency of dealing with the problem of gender inequality. Inequalities and discrimination based on income, location, disability and ethnicity intersect with gender and are usually mutually reinforcing.

Income inequality is also a critical consideration for shaping the post-2015 Global Development Agenda. Income inequality is not only a problem for developing countries; it also affects developed countries. An estimated two thirds of countries with available data experienced a rise in income inequality between 1990 and 2015, despite globally robust economic growth.[408] In fact, in 2015, just 62 people had as much wealth as the poorest half of humanity, and the richest 1% owned more wealth than the rest of the world combined. At the same time, the poorest individuals are being denied their fair share; since the turn of the century, the poorest half of the globe's population has received just one percent of the aggregate rise in global wealth. Some countries, including high, low and middle-income ones, have experienced jobless economic growth, with the result that those at the top end of the income distribution have benefitted far more than people at the lower end of the pyramid.[409] For instance, in the United States, a study shows a widening wealth/income gap between ethnic groups. From 2005 to 2009, inflation-adjusted median wealth decreased by 66% among Hispanic households and 53% among African-American households, compared with just 16% among white households.[410]

In Nigeria, the scale of economic inequality has assumed extreme proportions, and it can be clearly observed in the daily struggles of most of the population in the face of the accumulation of enormous amounts of wealth by a minute percentage of the population. Corrupt politicians or public officials make up the bulk of this minute percentage. To put the extreme levels of inequality in Nigeria into proper perspective, a study conducted by Oxfam indicated that the amount of money that the richest Nigerian can earn each year from his wealth is sufficient to lift 2 million Nigerians out of poverty for one year. The study went further to indicate that lifting all Nigerians living below the poverty line out of poverty will cost an estimated US$24 billion.[411] This amount of money is lower than the aggregate wealth controlled by the five richest Nigerians in 2016, which was an estimated US$29 billion.[412]

[408] Ferreira, F.H.G., and Ravallion, M., "Global Poverty and Inequality: A review of evidence," World Bank Policy Research Working Paper 4623 (2008).

[409] Pew Research Center, "Wealth gaps rise to record highs between whites, blacks, Hispanics". Accessed from: http://www.pewsocialtrends.org/2011/07/26/wealth-gaps-rise-to-record-highs-between-whites-blacks-hispanics/.

[410] *Ibid.*

[411] Oxfam, "Inequality in Nigeria: Exploring the drivers". Accessed from: https://www.oxfam.org/sites/www.oxfam.org/files/file_attachments/cr-inequality-in-nigeria-170517-en.pdf [15 September 2017].

[412] *Ibid.*

Moreover, poverty in Nigeria has been rising in the context of an expanding economy.

Economic and gender inequality are interconnected and reinforce each other. The lives of Nigerian women are negatively impacted by discriminatory traditional and socio-cultural practices that place them at a disadvantage in some areas. Most employed women have casual, low-skilled, low-paid informal jobs. Furthermore, women in Nigeria are less likely than men to own land and 75% of the poorest women have never been to school, compared to 28% of the richest women. This observation highlights the importance of tackling the precursors of poverty. Consequently, for significant progress to be achieved in the post-2015 Global Development Agenda, there is a need for governments and development partners to address the conditions that propagate inequality among populations. Addressing these conditions, especially among marginalized groups, is key to helping the majority of the world's population to live meaningful lives and achieve their aspirations.

The Case for Addressing Inequality in the Post-2015 Global Development Landscape

The need to address inequality is borne out of global treaty obligations and human moral perspectives. Increasingly, it is becoming unacceptable to lose children who die from preventable diseases before they reach the age of five, or that we lose women during childbirth. Nevertheless, fiscal austerity and resource scarcity makes it difficult to make a case for focusing on the needs of the worst-off. Having said this, there is still a case for addressing inequality in the post-2015 development landscape. Firstly, there are human rights principles that are supposed to be considered when formulating macro-economic policies. Some of these principles are outlined below:

- The obligation of progressive realization and non-retrogression, which means that governments must move as expeditiously and effectively as possible to realize economic and social rights, and should not take steps backwards.[413]
- Non-discrimination and equality, which means that governments owe it to their citizens to ensure that conscious, targeted measures are established to obtain considerable

[413] Balakrishnan, R., and Heintz, J., "Making the International Monetary Fund Accountable to Human Rights". Available from: https://www.huffingtonpost.com/radhika-balakrishnan/making-the-international_b_549976.html [20 September 2017].

equality and that people have an equal opportunity to enjoy their rights.[414]

- The principle of maximum available resources, which implies that governments, even when confronted with limited resources, must utilize the maximum resources available to address the economic and social rights of all citizens irrespective of gender, race, ethnicity, sexuality, etc.[415]

On a second note, the rising levels of inequality are not just bad for people who become disadvantaged, but for society as a whole. Societies with high levels of inequality tend to grow more slowly than those with low income inequality. Furthermore, such countries are less effective in sustaining growth over prolonged periods of time and recover more slowly from economic downturns. Allowing inequality to persist affects large segments of the population. It can spur social unrest and political instability. Inequality only worsens current levels of crime, disease and environmental problems globally. This situation may thwart progress in realizing the goals of the SDGs.

Critical Health Issues for the Post-2015 Development Agenda

Health-related concerns were properly covered by the MDGs, with three out of the eight goals focused on health. Despite this, health remains a key issue as many low and middle-income countries still fell short of expectations under the MDG framework. For instance, HIV prevalence among pregnant women in Nigeria aged between 15 and 24 increased between 1990 and 2015,[416] as did under-five mortality between 2007 and 2011.[417] These results, together with the poor state of public health facilities more generally, typify the challenge. This has encouraged Nigerians to spend an estimated US$1 billion yearly on medical tourism abroad;[418] putting this into perspective, the Federal Ministry of Health's budget proposal for 2016 was US$1.3 billion.[419] These figures highlight a couple of concerns: the budget is insufficient to meet the basic health needs of the population; and the country loses sufficient resources to foreign health systems at the expense of its local health infrastructure.

---

[414] *Ibid.*

[415] *Ibid.*

[416] USAID, HIV/AIDS in Nigeria.

[417] National Population Commission and ICF Macro, *Nigerian Demographic and Health Survey 2008* (Abuja: ICF Macro and Calverton, 2009).

[418] Nigeria Sovereign Investment Authority, "Reversing Medical Toursim in Nigeria." In PricewaterhouseCoopers, "Restoring trust to Nigeria's Healthcare System" (2016). Accessed from: https://www.pwc.com/ng/en/assets/pdf/restoring-trust-to-nigeria-healthcare-system.pdf.

[419] 2016 proposed appropriation bill. Accessed from: www.budgit.com.

Health challenges – especially for low & middle-income countries – are critical considerations for the post-2015 development agenda. Health remains a precondition and indicator of progress in sustainable development. While there is no doubt that health must occupy a position in the next generation of development, a convincing case needs to be made for the manner in which health goals are framed. Consequently, there are three main issues that need to be addressed going forward:

- Sustaining Gains and Protecting Investments

In many low and middle-income countries, progress has been achieved in fulfilling some of the MDG goals, particularly against AIDS, malaria and tuberculosis, but there is still a need to sustain these gains and ensure further progress. Furthermore, the post-2015 health agenda is one for which sufficient advocacy is required to get governments to commit to health targets and adhere to funding expectations for the health sector.[420] Health in the post-2015 development landscape will also require investments in national and global processes or frameworks for tracking results and resources.

- The Evolving Global Health Agenda

A critical consideration for the post-2015 health agenda is increasing access to basic healthcare such as sexual and reproductive health services, vaccinations and affordable medicines. The global agenda for health is changing in ways that determine how development priorities are shaped in the future. One of the major changes concerns acknowledgement of the socio-economic effects of non-communicable diseases (NCDs). This observation does not in any way suggest that efforts to tackle NCDs replace other health priorities. Rather, more attention should be devoted to improving access to basic health services while considering the socio-economic and environmental determinants of health, not just the biomedical causes of sickness.

In contrast to the current set of health-related MDGs, there is now increased recognition of the need to devote sufficient attention on 'means' together with 'ends', considering that health is a human right and that governments have an obligation to protect the health security of their citizens. Health security can be improved by strengthening health systems and making them more responsive to the evolving health needs. Whilst highlighting the importance of securing government commitments to health needs, the challenge lies in defining how health can be characterized in a way that addresses most health concerns and generates much-needed political traction.

[420] The Abuja Declaration, involving ECOWAS member states; recommended US$5 billion yearly as a standard for the health budget with a progressive increase subsequently.

- The Sustainable Development Context of Health

One key question here concerns defining how health is perceived under the SDGs. Discussions provide added clarity on how health is perceived by policy makers around the world. These should inform directions for health policy in both developed and developing countries.[421]

In addition to the fact that healthy people possess stronger cognitive and physical abilities and, as a result, make more productive contributions to society, health policy contributes to reducing poverty through the financial protection implicit in universal health coverage. Changes in age structures, the distribution of people and population growth rates have correlations with national and international global health challenges.[422] Furthermore, health is also related to policies in a broad range of other sectors such as transport, energy and urban planning. And health data points can assess progress across the socio-economic and environmental pillars of sustainable development. Consequently, health metrics, in the post-2015 environment, are expected to become important measures of economic progress.

In summarizing this section, it is essential to note that health is a precondition, outcome and indicator for building sustainable societies and should be adopted as a universal value, a collective social objective and a political objective for all. It appears that the SDGs are weak when considering health from this particular paradigm. What is missing is that the drivers of major health risks and their potential as a systemic risk which can lead to economic breakdown are not properly considered. The World Economic Forum has identified positive relationships between global risks.[423] For instance, the recent ebola outbreak had negative macro-economic effects. Liberia was the second most affected country in terms of fatalities, *i.e.* 3,826 deaths. The impact on its GDP was US$187 million.[424] This shows that addressing the health risks, such as pandemic situations, is key to creating sustainable societies both on the social and economic fronts. Disease burdens can derail economic progress and can cause further impoverishment of the people, especially at the rural level. Risks of disease outbreaks and public

---

[421] World Health Organization, "Positioning health in the post-2015 development agenda". Discussion paper (2012). Accessed from: http://www.who.int/topics/millennium_development_goals/post2015/WHOdiscussionpaper_October2012.pdf.

[422] *Ibid.*

[423] World Economic Forum, "The Global Risks Report 2015". Accessed from: http://www3.weforum.org/docs/WEF_Global_Risks_2015_Report.pdf.

[424] United Nations Development Group, "Socio-economic Impact of Ebola Virus Disease in West African Countries: A call for national and regional containment, recovery and protection". Discussion Paper (2015). Accessed from: https://reliefweb.int/sites/reliefweb.int/files/resources/ebola-west-africa.pdf.

health emergencies ought to be considered by policy makers when shaping the direction of health policy.

Poverty Considerations in the Post-2015 Global Development Agenda

Having acknowledged that some degree of progress was achieved under the MDGs, there is still some way to go in dealing with the challenge of poverty. The general consensus appears to be on the need to move from reducing to ending extreme poverty, in all its forms. There is a need to ensure no person is left behind regardless of ethnicity, gender, race, physical condition or sexual orientation. Fighting the problem will largely depend on addressing the challenges faced by excluded or marginalized groups.

Addressing the challenge of poverty in the post-2015 development agenda will require a change in paradigm. This requires transforming economies for jobs and inclusive growth exemplified by improved economic opportunities to end extreme poverty and improve livelihoods. It implies a rapid shift to sustainable patterns of consumption and production – harnessing innovation, technology and the potential of the private sector to create added value and drive sustainable and inclusive growth. Diversified economies, with equal opportunities for all, can unleash the conditions for job growth and improved livelihoods, especially for young men and women. Creating jobs to meet the demands of a growing youth population is critical to managing the global risks of social unrest and political instability.

Creating jobs is key to achieving the overriding expectations of the SDGs as they relate to improving the well-being of all humans. Central to this is ensuring that people have the means and skills to satisfy their basic needs.[425] In addition, poverty can readily be addressed by improving access to quality education, clean water, basic healthcare, transport, electricity, etc. When people have access to these, they are likely to become more productive, thus increasing economic growth and development.[426] Governments ought to also create the basic economic conditions required to start viable businesses and secure meaningful jobs.

The paradigm shift to address the problem of extreme poverty requires addressing the drivers of poverty, especially in developing countries. Poor governance is central to the problem of poverty in these countries. This problem can effectively be addressed by an emphasis on building peaceful, open and accountable public institutions. With a per capita income that is 50%

---

[425] High-Level Panel of Eminent Persons on the Post-2015 Development Agenda, *A New Global Partnership: Eradicate Poverty and Transform Economies through Sustainable Development* (New York: United Nations, 2013).
[426] *Ibid.*

less than that of the next poorest region, Sub-Saharan Africa's growth has lagged since independence some 50 years ago.[427] One of the reasons for the region's slow economic growth and development stems from bad governance that has been exemplified by a long list of dictators, undemocratic governance and state media control. Africa performed well in the early years of independence but subsequently failed to do so, and is now characterized by low economic growth rates, limited agricultural productivity, below-par industrial capacity, and growing domestic and local debt that is often unsustainable.[428] Furthermore, Africa is plagued by coups, civil unrest, ethnic violence and widespread bureaucratic corruption alongside inept institutions and high levels of administrative inefficiency.

There is a general agreement among economists, policy analysts and development partners that corruption is a global problem, but its impact is more debilitating in developing and emerging economies, such as those in Africa. Furthermore, development partners rank public sector corruption as a significant constraint that has negatively affected Africa's economic, political and social development. Transparency International estimates that corruption on the continent accounts for between 20% and 30% of illegal outflows from funds designated for the provision of basic services.[429] Furthermore, the United Nations estimates that the ruling elites have been responsible for US$200 billion in illegal outflows to foreign banks.[430]

These observations highlight the need for a change in paradigm when addressing poverty. This implies attacking the drivers and conditions that allow poverty to thrive, especially in Africa. Good governance is key to addressing this challenge. Experience illustrates that throwing money at the problem is not effective, especially in developing and emerging economies.

The paradigm shift for poverty eradication also ought to consider the importance of integrating poverty into a broader sustainability framework. While the MDG framework identified and addressed the challenge of poverty eradication, it failed to consider the sustainability dimension. It is essential to note that poverty reduction is a critical aspect of sustainable development, and not the other way round. A sustainable approach to addressing the challenge of poverty requires sustainable production and consumption, and the associated problems of inclusive and equitable economic growth and

---

[427] Mills, G., "Why is Africa Poor?" Center for Global Liberty and Prosperity, Briefing Paper (2010). Accessed from: http://www.thebrenthurstfoundation.org/workspace/files/dbp6.pdf [2 September 2017].

[428] Leon, T., "The State of Liberal Democracy in Africa: Resurgence or Retreat?" *Development Policy Analysis*, 12 (2010).

[429] Bisssessar N., "Does corruption persist in Sub-Saharan Africa?" *International Advances in Economic Research*, 15 (2009): 336-350.

[430] Campos, N., Dimova, R., and Ahmed, S., "Whither corruption? A quantitative survey of the literature on corruption and growth," *CEPR Discussion*, 8140 (2010).

improving economic opportunities for all.[431] It also requires managing the resource base and ecosystems on which economic and social development depend, while increasing resilience in the face of new and emerging problems.

Africa presents a good case study for exploring the causes and effects of poverty. Some of the information already highlighted in this section showcase Africa's dismal economic challenges, many of which appear to be self-inflicted – notably bad governance. Having said this, there is a need to ask what conditions have perpetuated poverty in Africa despite huge inflows of foreign aid and FDI. If Africa's poor economic performance can be narrowed down to bad choices, one has to ask: "What conditions have prompted African leaders to make bad choices?" Perhaps a key reason could be that Africans and the international community have permitted them to do so. The former – citizens and civil society – live under the belief that they lack the capacity to change the status quo. The misplaced resilience of Africans is largely responsible for the persistence of inept leadership and institutional stagnation. Citizens need to utilize existing systems to address the challenge

Critical Considerations for Addressing Poverty under the SDGs Framework

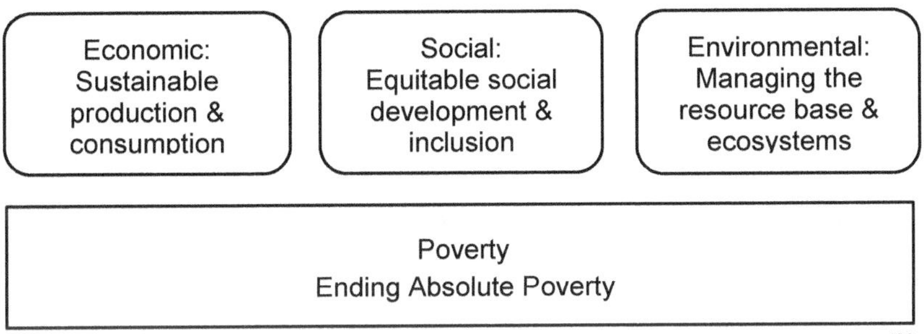

Center on International Cooperation [432]

of poor governance, such as by voting, understanding their rights, and demanding quality leadership from elected and appointed officials. Nigeria is making slow progress in this regard; however, the challenge of reviving public institutions and institutionalizing quality leadership and effective management of public resources has appeared insurmountable.

The media in Nigeria is constantly awash with news of embezzlement of public resources, collapsing infrastructure and gross mismanagement by public officials. Having said this, the 2015 general elections may be a watershed moment, especially as the incumbent political party lost to the

[431] Mills, G., "Why is Africa Poor?"

[432] Center on International Cooperation, "Goals in a post-2015 development framework: options and strategic choices". Working Report (2013). Accessed from: http://cic.nyu.edu/sites/default/files/cic_goals_in_a_post-2015_development_framework_a4_2.pdf [27 August 2017].

opposition party for the first time since Nigeria's return to democratic rule in 1999. This represents a step in the right direction as citizens voted *en masse* against an incumbent party which they perceived as 'corrupt'. The 2019 Elections will highlight the degree to which electoral institutions in the country are positioned to deliver 'free' and 'fair' elections to the citizenry.

Critical Gender Equality Considerations for the Post-2015 Development Agenda

Though there has been economic growth in the past two decades, the degree of inequality – especially between the rich and the poor – has broadened. An estimated 800 million people in the world are undernourished,[433] another 500 million people are obese and as much as 50% of the global food supply is wasted.[434] In presenting these grim statistics, it is essential to note that though women are directly responsible for producing 50% of the world's food, they account for majority of the globe's hungry.[435] In fact, women account for an estimated two-thirds of the estimated 1 billion people living in extreme poverty, and they make up 60% of the estimated 575 million working poor internationally.[436] Rural women and girls are even more vulnerable to poverty and hunger,[437] since they own less than 20% of land globally and as little as 5% in certain countries.[438]

The situation is worse in Africa, where archaic cultural systems limit women from owning property and restrict them from participating in productive activities. In Nigeria, poverty and illiteracy have contributed to perpetuating discriminatory property ownership rights against women. This condition traces its origins to the pre-colonial era, a time when women lived in subjugation and perpetual subordination. The situation has improved since the colonial era with the introduction of new patriarchal conceptions – by colonialists – of the social role of women.[439] Still, the majority of women

---

[433] Food and Agriculture Organization, *The state of food security in the world: Economic growth is necessary but not sufficient to accelerate reduction of hunger and malnutrition* (Rome: FAO, 2012).

[434] World Health Organization, "Nutritional challenges". Working Report (2013). Accessed from: http://www.who.int/nutrition/challenges/en/index.html [13 September 2017].

[435] Office of the High Commissioner for Human Rights, *Addressing gender equality in the Post-2015 Development Framework: the Contribution of the United Nations Human Rights System*. (Geneva: OHCHR, 2012).

[436] International Labour Office, *Global Employment Trends for Women* (Geneva: ILO, 2009).

[437] International Fund for Agricultural Development, *New realities, new challenges: new opportunities for tomorrow's generation* (Rome: IFAD, 2010).

[438] Food and Agriculture Organization, *The state of food security in the world.*

[439] Abdulraheem, N.M., "Rights of women in pre and post-colonial era in Nigeria: Challenges for today," *Journal of Public Law*, 3 (2010): 83-93.

traditionally have no rights to own land. This contravenes the dictates of the Nigerian Constitution, which states that:

> no citizen of Nigeria shall be subjected to any disability or deprivation merely by reason of the circumstances of his birth.[440]

Global conventions and declarations have offered legal frameworks for the protection and promotion of women's property rights. Nevertheless, Nigerian women are still confronted with serious discrimination regarding rights to property ownership, control, access and inheritance. This is common among the different major ethnic groups and across the six geopolitical regions of the country. In some ethnic groups, especially in the South East, some widows are not allowed to inherit land, and many are stripped of their husbands' possessions by their deceased husbands' relatives. This situation is largely responsible for the discrimination that women face in many ethnic enclaves.

- Gender Equality: Recent Developments

In 1992, the Global Congress of Women for a Healthy Planet, which comprised over 1,000 women from 83 countries and was led by the Women's Environment and Development Organization, produced a Women's Action Agenda 21 that generated suggestions on all the main concerns. These suggestions hinged on the belief that women's empowerment is key to realizing equity among and within nations. They proposed a universal code of ethics and global legislation designed to promote equity, respect for human dignity and cultural diversity.[441] The recommendations of the women's agenda identified a relationship between women's rights and economic development. In fact, this agenda indicated that improving women's rights has the potential to lift 30% of the world's extreme poor out of poverty.[442]

Concerns have been expressed about the degree to which the MDGs addressed the issue of gender equality. In fact, one key fact that emerged from the MDGs concerned 'gender mainstreaming' with no clear definition or explanation as to how this can deepen the impact of development interventions on the condition of women. Essentially, the fundamental relationship between women's rights, gender or power relations, ecology, the economy and the environment was being replaced by more popular topics or gender

---

[440] 1999 Constitution of the Federal Republic of Nigeria, Section 43.

[441] Women's Environment & Development Organization, "Women's Action Agenda 21". Advocacy Paper (1991). Accessed from: http://www.wedo.org [28 August 2017].

[442] *Ibid.*

mainstreaming methodologies for a weak growth framework.[443] This is understandable, considering that fewer women or women's groups were actively involved in developing the MDG framework. There are additional concerns that under the framework, gender appears to have been narrowly defined. For instance, MDG3 – which specifically focused on gender equality and women's empowerment – had only one target for education together with limited indicators on women's political participation and labour force involvement. In fact, concerning MDG3, Dr. Naila Kabeer offered the following remark concerning the need for deeper gender analysis, especially as it relates to the precursors of poverty:

> Gender analysis is about the capacity to establish relationships which are not always clear. One set of connections [is] between production and reproduction, between economic growth and human development. Another set of relationships concerns linking varying levels of analysis: the micro, meso, and macro levels. Public policy should play a critical part in supporting efforts aimed at tackling the norms, customs, and values that are discriminatory against women, and prevent them from meaningfully contributing to national economies.[444]

The aforementioned observation highlights the limited depth of analysis and consideration given to improving the socio-economic conditions of women under the MDGs. Furthermore, the MDG framework is characterized by little or no consideration of the gendered effects of the macro-economy despite the fact that global trends have in many ways undermined the potential benefits for women and girls. Women's rights advocates concede that some progress was achieved for women under the MDGs, especially in areas such as HIV/AIDS and malaria, and in narrowing the gender disparities in education. However, the main concern is that they failed to address the main causes of poverty. In fact, improving the socio-economic conditions can assist in a significant reduction of global poverty, especially in developing countries where most of those living in extreme poverty are domiciled.

The final report from an expert group meeting on the effects of the Beijing Platform for Action on the MDGs notes the negative effects of the

---

[443] Wichterich, C., *The future we want: a feminist perspective* (Berlin: Heinrich Boll Stiftung, 2013).

[444] Kabeer, N., "Gender equality, poverty eradication and the MDGs: Promoting women's capabilities and participation," *Gender & Development Series*, 13, Economic and Social Commission in Asia and the Pacific, 2003.

different challenges associated with people's livelihoods, and the access of people to basic social services such as health, education, food, water, etc.[445] This group indicated that the economic growth paradigm that has dominated international production is largely driven by deregulation – which focuses on short term gain – as opposed to long-term sustainable growth. Consequently, it recommended that the Beijing Platform for Action be used to transform local and national strategies to support gender equality and women's empowerment as key to achieving the MDGs.[446]

- Gender Equality Gaps in the MDGs Framework

With respect to gender equality, the MDG framework is characterized by certain omissions and commissions, and some key actors have expressed a number of concerns that need to be addressed. One is that the MDGs appear to have diluted the overarching objectives of the Millennium Declaration, as their structure failed to consider the comprehensive goals and targets of the UN Conferences of the 1990s whose methodologies were centered on the realities of people's expectations in different regions and nations. One critical gap was in the area of sexual and reproductive health and rights.[447]

The MDGs did not sufficiently address the interconnected nature of the risks and vulnerabilities faced by the target beneficiaries. These risks and vulnerabilities tend to arise out of poor governance, socio-economic inequalities, and environmental and demographic factors. As a result, the MDG framework ended up with a set of goals that became silos in themselves. A recurring criticism against the MDGs is that they failed to address the inequalities and imbalances in power relations that perpetuate gender discrimination and poverty.[448] It is not sufficient to just create goals, it is equally important to identify or develop the modalities – processes, tools and methodologies – for the realization of each goal. This may highlight some inherent gaps in the framework design, as was the case with the MDG framework, which looked more like a technocratic or bureaucratic exercise than one that was supposed to be participatory in nature. The limitations of the MDG framework – especially in relation to instituting the conditions for improved gender parity – must be addressed under the SDGs; otherwise, the SDGs may be lost to policy silos as was the case with their predecessors.

---

[445] United Nations, "Realizing the future we want. UN System Task Team on the Post-2015 Development Agenda: Report to the Secretary General," 2012.

[446] DAWN, *Breaking through the development silos: SRHR, MDGs and Gender Equity: Experiences from Mexico, India & Nigeria* (e-book, 2013). Accessed from: http://issuu.com/dawnfeminist/docs/breakingsilos [11 September 2017].

[447] Vandemoortele, J., "Advancing the global agenda post-2015: Some thoughts, ideas and practical suggestions". Background Paper prepared for the Experts Group Meeting to support the advancement of the Post-2015 UN Development Agenda. New York (2012).

[448] *Ibid.*

• Gender Equality in the Post-2015 Development Agenda

Gender equality and women's empowerment is at the core of the SDGs, or what may also be referred to as the "2030 Agenda". They are addressed both in SDG5, which deals with realizing gender equality and empowering all females, and via mainstreaming it under other goals and targets. This approach shows that under the SDGs, gender equality is now viewed as an objective in itself, as well as a prerequisite for realizing all development goals. In fact, paragraph 20 of the 2030 Agenda states:

> Achieving gender equality and improved women empowerment is critical for making sufficient progress across all the goals and targets under the different SDGs.[449]

UN Women is the UN's entity responsible for promoting gender equality and women's empowerment. In June 2013, UN Women released a report entitled "A Transformative Stand-Alone Goal on Achieving Gender Equality, Women's Rights, and Women's Empowerment: Imperatives and Key Components", which outlined UN Women's vision for a stand-alone SDG devoted to gender equality and women's empowerment.[450] It identified three main issues to be targeted with a view to tackling the structural causes of gender-based discrimination and to best position this stand-alone SDG to bring about an improvement in women's socio-economic conditions:

- Gender-based violence
- Gender equality in the distribution of capabilities
- Increased representation of women in decision-making positions in the public and private sectors.

For each of the aforementioned areas, the UN Women's report suggested specific targets and indicators to assess progress nationally and internationally. Whilst having a stand-alone goal, and associated targets, for gender equality and empowerment, it is supposed to ensure that sufficient commitment is devoted to addressing issues affecting women. The SDGs go a step further by mainstreaming gender considerations under other goals.[451]

---

[449] Economic & Social Commission for Western Asia, "The 2030 Agenda for Sustainable Development: a new roadmap to achieve gender equality and the empowerment of women and girls," Committee on Women, 7th Session, 20-21 January 2016. Accessed from: https://sustainabledevelopment.un.org/content/documents/9783ESCWA_2030%20Agenda%20for%20Sustainable%20Development-Gender%20Equality.pdf.

[450] UN Women, *A Transformative Stand-Alone Goal on Achieving Gender Equality, Women's Rights and Women's Empowerment: Imperatives and Key Components* (New York: UN Women, 2013).

[451] *Ibid.*

For instance, target 3.7 in SDG3 is concerned with ensuring or promoting universal access to sexual reproductive health services, especially family planning. Target 4.5 in SDG4 focuses on eliminating inherent gender disparities in education. Furthermore, the targets connected with SDG5 address concerns not addressed under MDG3: ending discrimination against women and girls (target 5.1), eliminating all forms of gender-based violence (target 5.2), eliminating harmful practices, including forced marriage and female genital mutilation (target 5.3), etc. These targets reveal that gender equality was given substantial attention in developing the SDGs.

Although there is broad agreement that the SDGs addressed the issue of gender equality sufficiently compared to the MDGs, concerns have been raised by some women's groups about its failure in addressing the issue of rights-based development. For instance, the Women's Major Group (WMG) – one of the major groups involved in negotiation processes for the SDGs – indicated that sexual and reproductive health targets do not go far enough.[452] Furthermore, the WMG noted that under the SDGs, sufficient attention was not devoted to addressing the role of women in promoting peace and justice. Basically, in order to not repeat the mistakes of the MDGs, there is a need to gravitate beyond a mere focus on goals and targets to the structural and policy constraints that are an impediment to the realization of women's rights, gender equality and women's empowerment.

---

[452] UN Women, "Accelerating gender equality through the Post-2015 Development Agenda". Accessed from: https://unwomen.org.au/wp-content/uploads/2015/10/Accelerating-Gender-Equality-through-the-Post-2015-Development-Agenda.pdf [2 September 2017].

CHAPTER 14

THE SUSTAINABLE DEVELOPMENT GOALS

Introduction

The Sustainable Development Goals (SDGs), the development agenda succeeding the MDGs, are supposed to build on the progress achieved from implementation of the MDGs. In September 2015, 192 UN member states came together at the institution's headquarters in New York to chart a course for sustainable development. Given the lessons learnt from implementation of the MDGs, the SDGs are designed to shift the development focus towards a more sustainable path for the world.[453] Following a series of consultations at this gathering, the UN member states adopted a new Global Development Agenda committed to people, to the planet, to promoting peace and stability and to lifting more members of the population from poverty to prosperity by 2030.[454]

The SDGs came into effect in January 2016 and will guide actions required to achieve their targets over the next fifteen years. The 2030 Agenda consists of 17 Sustainable Development Goals (SDGs), with a total of 169 targets, for the period 2015 to 2030. They are geared towards a universal, integrated and transformative vision for an improved world. The SDGs provide an opportunity for many countries, especially Nigeria, to address performance gaps recorded under the MDGs.

One such area is poverty. Despite some progress, Nigeria experienced a major economic recession in 2017 stemming from the sharp decline in commodity prices, especially crude oil, which accounts for 80% of its foreign exchange revenues. Consequently, when crude oil prices fell from a high of US$100 in 2015 to US$40 in 2016, the country's economic vulnerability was exposed. This situation contributed to the following challenges: the inability of state governments to meet their monthly recurrent expenditure

[453] Brazil Ministry of Planning, Development & Management, "Voluntary National Review on the Sustainable Development Goals, July 2017". Accessed from: https://sustainabledevelopment.un.org/content/documents/15806Brazil_English.pdf [27 October 2017].
[454] *Ibid.*

requirements;[455] the loss of jobs;[456] the closure of many businesses, especially factories relying on raw material imports;[457] and the inability of the federal and state governments to finance development programmes. In fact, the federal government had to borrow to support the implementation of the 2017 budget. The impact of the recession is broadly felt and is likely to have increased the number of people living in poverty.[458]

Another area where Nigeria has made significant progress is in primary school enrolment.[459] Despite this progress, the country performed poorly when it came to primary school completion rates.[460] This is compounded by the low enrolment and completion rate for girls.[461] Still another area where Nigeria recorded some significant improvement is in under-five mortality.[462] The 2030 Global Agenda provides an opportunity for the Nigerian government to correct the mistakes of the MDG era and improve in areas where performance gaps were identified.

Each country is faced with particular difficulties when it comes to implementing activities that support the realization of the SDGs. The most vulnerable countries – especially low-income countries and many African countries – require special support. Some middle-income countries also have serious challenges. The scale and ambition of the new agenda demand a revitalized global partnership to support efficient and effective implementation of goal-directed activities by UN member states. In reaching a resolution to adopt the SDGs, the member states acknowledged the need for greater and meaningful collaboration between governments, NGOs, CSOs,

---

[455] The state governments were bailed out in 2016 by the federal government. The Federal Ministry of Finance provided funding to some state governments to enable them meet their monthly salary obligations.

[456] The banking sector in Nigeria was one of the worst hit by the recession. The mop up of government funds from the banks – funds which accounted for a significant portion of banking liquidity – resulted in pay cuts and signficant job losses in the sector.

[457] The 2017 economic recession was compounded by the fall in the value of the Nigerian Naira relative to the dollar. This led to the Central Bank of Nigeria (CBN) placing restrictions on access to foreign exchange in a bid to stem the decline in the Naira's value. The situation made it challenging for manufacturers to access foreign currency required to purchase raw materials and contributed to the closure of many factories. The Lagos Chamber of Commerce reported that the CBN's foreign exchange restrictions contributed to a 30% loss of capacity in the manufacturing sector.

[458] National Bureau of Statistics, "Nigerians living in poverty grows to 61%". Accessed from: http://www.bbc.com/news/world-africa-17015873 [14 August 2017].

[459] UNICEF, "At a Glance: Nigeria, 2008-2012". Accessed from: https://www.unicef.org/infobycountry/nigeria_statistics.html.

[460] *Ibid.*

[461] British Council, "Girls' Education in Nigeria: Issues, Influencers, and Actions".

[462] UNDP, OSSAP-MDGs and DFID, "Millennium Development Goals: End-point Report for Nigeria, September 2015". Accessed from: http://www.ng.undp.org/content/dam/nigeria/docs/MDGs/Nigeria_MDG_Report%202015%20Full%20Report.pdf [22 August2017].

the private sector and other relevant stakeholders in developing strategies and implementing goal-oriented activities.[463]

Considering that many developing countries face funding challenges coupled with public finance weaknesses and capacity gaps, the 2030 Agenda acknowledges the need for broader collaboration to bridge these gaps. The Agenda recognises the critical role of the private sector in addressing funding challenges and encourages governments to create the appropriate regulatory environment to attract private-sector interest and funding for development projects. In many developing countries, the private sector tends to be reluctant to invest in public-sector projects that contribute to addressing development challenges.

Before outlining some of the challenges stifling inflows of private-sector resources for the financing of development projects, it is essential to identify and discuss the role of the private sector in the implementation of the SDGs. The private sector is a key player in the 2030 Agenda, especially considering SDG12 – which deals with sustainable consumption and production – and some cross-cutting targets of SDG8 and SDG9. Sustainable consumption and production are increasingly seen as necessary to encourage resource efficiency and provide sustainable infrastructure to the citizenry.[464] Furthermore, the private sector will play a key part in improving access to basic services, reducing youth unemployment and improving the standard of living for a significant part of the population.

One of the challenges that made it difficult for many countries, including Nigeria, to meet aggregate performance expectations for the MDGs is the limited involvement of the private sector as it relates to financing and technical support. In many developing countries, there appears to be a disconnect between the public and private sectors. This disconnect has created entry barriers for the private sector in development financing. One of the problems is the absence of adequate incentives to attract private investment in development.[465] This is understandable, considering that private-sector

---

[463] United Nations, "Transforming our world: The 2030 Agenda for Sustainable Development". Working Paper A/RES/70/1 (2016). Accessed from: https://sustainabledevelopment.un.org/content/documents/21252030%20Agenda%20for%20Sustainable%20Development%20web.pdf [28 September 2017].

[464] Ibrahim, A., "The role of private sector in implementing the Sustainable Development Goals (SDGs) in Bangladesh". Presentation at the Workshop on the "Realization of the SDGs," Metropolitan Chamber of Commerce & Industry, Dhaka, and the Citizens Platform for SDGs, Bangladesh, 2 October 2016. Accessed from: http://cpd.org.bd/wp-content/uploads/2016/10/Role-of-Private-Sector-in-SDGs-Implementation.pdf [12 November 2017].

[465] United Nations, "Challenges in raising private sector resources for financing sustainable development". Working Paper produced by the UNTT Working Group on Sustainable Development, July 2016. Accessed from:

organizations are largely driven by the need to make profits.[466] Consequently, there is a need for development partners, especially governments, to develop a model that balances the expectations of private-sector partners with development outcomes. So far, an acceptable model that takes into consideration ethical concerns and best practices has yet to be developed.

Other reasons for the limited active involvement of the private sector in development financing include regulatory concerns, poor governance and investors' concerns. Regulatory uncertainty and poor governance structures on a national level make development financing a "high risk" prospect for private financial institutions. These factors present structural impediments – such as imperfect information and other market failures – that threaten investment principal and expected returns from funding development projects. In Nigeria, for instance, it is more a case of the financial institutions preferring to lend directly to the government and then the government can use such funds to finance development programs across the country. At the moment, there is no methodology for direct financing of development projects by commercial banks and other financial institutions.

Challenges in the Implementation of the MDGs

One of the challenges with the MDGs was their perceived limited attention to the concerns of women. Graduate Women International (GWI), an NGO, noted that the MDGs were not 'en-gendered'.[467] Essentially, this implied the lack of gender mainstreaming in the development and implementation of the MDGs. Gender mainstreaming would have resulted in equal rights and equal opportunities for women through the achievement of all the MDGs and not just MDG3 and MDG5. GWI further notes that when it comes to the number of people living below the poverty line, for instance, there were more women than men. This is understandable, considering that there are cultural practices and societal barriers in some countries, like Nigeria, that restrict women's access to land.

Another problem with the MDGs is that they were more macro-level goals that sometimes did not reflect intra-country challenges. The MDGs were limited when it came to contextualizing and adapting them to the unique

---

https://sustainabledevelopment.un.org/content/documents/2106Chapter%203-challenges%20in%20raising%20private%20sector%20resources.pdf [22 November 2017].

[466] Many private-sector entities see the development landscape as more of an aid-driven initiative than a profitable one, hence the incentive to allocate resources to financing development projects is lacking.

[467] Graduate Women International, "Challenges and achievements in the implementation of the Millennium Development Goals for gaps and lessons learned," March 2016. Accessed from: http://www.graduatewomen.org/challenges-achievements-implementation-millennium-development-goals-women-girls-gaps-lessons-learned-csw-58/ [13 September 2017].

situation of each country. This is a mistake that ought not to be repeated under the SDGs. Adapting the MDGs to local situations would have provided the opportunity to ensure that the most vulnerable are targeted by development interventions under each goal. Doing this with the SDGs presents an added challenge because of their breadth.

The limited involvement of the private sector in the implementation of the MDGs is partly responsible for the poor performance recorded by many developing countries, especially in Africa.[468] Without significant private sector involvement – especially by way of resource reallocation or development financing – in the implementation of the SDGs, many countries are likely to perform below expectations upon assessment in 2030. The position adopted in this work for improving private sector involvement in the SDGs implementation consists of two critical considerations:

1. The need to develop a development financing model that balances medium- and long-term development outcomes with the profit or investment-return expectations of private financing institutions, *i.e.* aligning private sector incentives with public goals.
2. Governments in both developed and developing countries must create an appropriate regulatory environment that removes risks from development financing. This entails strengthening the legal, policy and regulatory framework in a way that creates an enabling environment for investing in development projects. The propensity for political instability and high levels of uncertainty in many developing countries, such as Nigeria, remains a significant impediment to attracting private funding inflows into programs and projects targeted at the realization of the SDGs.

It appears more fitting to conclude this section by discussing another major challenge in the implementation of the MDGs: high levels of corruption in developing countries that is largely responsible for the below-par performance of many, especially in Africa. Corruption in the utilization of resources designated for the implementation of development projects affects the sustainability of the projects and also restricts the number of people benefitting from them. A quote by Ban Ki-Moon, the United Nations Secretary-General, aptly captures the effect of corruption on the realization of set development targets:

468 United Nations, "Challenges in raising private sector resources for financing sustainable development".

> When public money is stolen for private gain it means fewer resources to build schools, hospitals, roads and water treatment facilities.

The aforementioned statement highlights the negative effect of corruption on the realization of the MDGs – and potentially the SDGs. Nigeria presents a useful case study for exploring the impact of corruption on the implementation of the MDGs. In 2016, the Global Fund to Fight Aids and Malaria suspended disbursements of funds for malaria, HIV/AIDS and tuberculosis interventions in Nigeria after a detailed financial audit uncovered large-scale fraud by government officials responsible for managing them. One of the main findings of the audit – which covered an estimated US$880 million of Global Fund grants – was that systemic weaknesses in participating government ministries, departments and agencies and collusion between project officials and vendors resulted in the illegal diversion and embezzlement of about US$3.8 million.[469] Furthermore, the audit uncovered unretired and unverifiable expenditure to the tune of US$20 million by the National Agency for the Control of AIDS, one of the government agencies that benefitted from Global Fund grants.[470] Nigeria's failure to meet some of the targets for malaria, HIV/AIDS and tuberculosis could be attributed to the large-scale misappropriation of Global Fund grants by public officials.

The Sustainable Development Goals

These observations indicate that corruption can potentially derail the capacity of countries to satisfy the expectations of the 2030 Agenda. Full implementation of the SDGs started in January 2016 following their adoption by UN member states in September 2015. The SDG goals cover a broad range of traditional and contemporary development issues, such as poverty, hunger, health, education, gender inequality, infrastructure, resource management (*i.e.* sustainable production and consumption), climate change, and peace and security. The 17 goals are listed on the next page.[471]

---

469 Ogundipe, S., Obinna, C., and Olwale, G., "Global Fund uncovers fraud in malaria, tuberculosis, HIV/AIDS grants to Nigeria," *Vanguard*, 6 May 2016. Accessed from: https://www.vanguardngr.com/2016/05/global-fund-uncovers-fraud-malaria-tb-hivaids-grants-nigeria/ [22 November 2017].

470 *Ibid.*

471 Catholic International Development Charity, "Sustainable Development Goals: Action towards 2030," September 2015. Accessed from: https://cafod.org.uk/content/download/27011/266522/version/2/file/CAFOD_SDG_Action_Towards_2030_%20Single.pdf [13 October 2017].

1. End poverty in all its forms everywhere by 2030.

2. End hunger, achieve food security and improved nutrition and promote sustainable agriculture.

3. Ensure healthy lives and promote well-being for all at all ages.

4. Ensure inclusive and equitable quality education and promote life-long learning opportunities for all.

5. Achieve gender equality and empower all women and girls.

6. Ensure availability and sustainable management of water and sanitation for all.

7. Ensure access to affordable, reliable, sustainable and modern energy for all.

8. Promote sustained, inclusive and sustainable economic growth, full and productive employment and decent work for all.

9. Build resilient infrastructure, promote inclusive and sustainable industrialization and foster innovation.

10. Reduce inequality within and among countries.

11. Make cities and human settlements inclusive, safe, resilient and sustainable.

12. Ensure sustainable consumption and production patterns.

13. Take urgent action to combat climate change and its effects.

14. Conserve and sustainably use the oceans, seas, and marine resources for sustainable development.

15. Protect, restore and promote sustainable use of terrestrial ecosystems, sustainably manage forests, combat desertification, and halt and reverse land degradation and halt biodiversity loss.

16. Promote peaceful and inclusive societies for sustainable development, provide access to justice for all and build effective, accountable and inclusive institutions at all levels.

17. Strengthen the means of implementation and revitalize the global partnership for sustainable development.

Each of these goals are introduced and discussed briefly in the pages that follow with a view to understanding what development outcomes are expected by the year 2030. Before doing this, it is essential to highlight two critical qualities that distinguish them from the MDGs: "universality" and "integration of the need for sustainable development". From the standpoint of universality, the SDGs edge out the MDGs when it comes to their broad applicability. The MDGs placed added emphasis on driving action in low-income countries; in fact, only MDG7 (environmental sustainability) & MDG8 (global partnership for development) involved developed countries. The SDGs are more encompassing in that they are equally applicable with challenging targets for both developed and developing countries. Furthermore, the SDGs provide an opportunity for CSOs and NGOs to advocate for a more equitable development approach that is focused on tackling the fundamental causes of poverty and unsustainable development. From the standpoint of integrating sustainable development, the SDGs were developed with due consideration for environmental, social and economic variables.

As noted earlier, the SDGs encompass 169 targets. For the purposes of this study, the discussion of each goal includes some of their respective targets.

Goal 1: End Poverty in All its Forms Everywhere by 2030

This is indeed an ambitious target that would require the concerted and cooperative efforts of all to achieve it. This goal is broader than MDG1 in that it refers to the varying dimensions of poverty, *i.e.* education, nutrition, jobs and health. SDG1 consists of clearly framed and quantifiable targets that can be used to benchmark implementation progress in UN member states. The targets for SDG1 are outlined below:[472]

Target 1.1: "eradication of extreme poverty for all people living everywhere, currently measured as people living on less than US$1.25" per day. Concerns have been expressed about this poverty benchmark, with some indicating that it does not sufficiently capture the true picture of those living in extreme poverty. Given these concerns, it is expected that between 2015 and 2030, this target will undergo some review. Consequently, purchasing power parity considerations may lead to an upward or downward adjustment of the benchmark.

---

[472] United Nations Development Programme, "Sustainable Development Goals (SDGs)", Corporate Booklet, October 2016. Accessed from: http://www.undp.org/content/dam/undp/library/corporate/brochure/SDGs_Booklet_Web_En.pdf [2 November 2017].

Target 1.2: to "reduce by a minimum of 50% the proportion of men, women, and children of all ages living in poverty in all its dimensions according to national definitions". In this target, one can observe the difference between the MDGs and the SDGs as it allows countries to adapt SDG1 to their unique national circumstances. Cutting poverty in all its dimensions is a cross-cutting target in that it connects with other SDGs such as SDG2 (which deals with hunger), SDG3 (which deals with education), SDG4 (which deals with health) and SDG6 (water and sanitation), etc.

Target 1.3: to "implement suitable national social protection mechanisms and measures for all, and by 2030 realize significant coverage of the poor and vulnerable". This target is geared towards getting government to invest in social protection systems, *i.e.* social safety nets for the most vulnerable such as the elderly, persons with disabilities, unemployed youths, women, etc. Developing and implementing social safety nets are key to reducing poverty and vulnerability, as they provide temporary relief to people living in extreme poverty. Acknowledging the importance of establishing effective safety nets, the Nigerian government is already working with the World Bank to develop a Social Protection System for vulnerable segments of its population. At present, this is largely concentrated at the federal level, but it is expected that state governments will increasingly buy into this plan to ensure that the adopted framework actually reaches target beneficiaries.

Target 1.4: to "have equal rights to economic resources, as well as access to basic services, ownership, and control over land and other types of property, inheritance, natural resources, innovative technology and financial services". It is essential to note that all the dimensions of poverty are addressed by this indicator, especially income poverty. The indicator also presents an opportunity for mainstreaming gender in poverty eradication programs. For instance, customary practices that limit access to property and land is a major problem inhibiting women's empowerment in parts of Nigeria. Target 1.4 presents an opportunity for dealing with this challenge.

Target 1.5: to "build the resilience of the poor and those in vulnerable situations, and decrease their exposure and vulnerability to climate-related extreme conditions, and other environment and socio-economic shocks and disasters". This target is supposed to encourage governments to create social protection systems that offer relief to those affected by environmental/natural disasters (*i.e.* earthquakes, droughts) and economic crises (*i.e.* recessions).[473]

---

[473] Loewe, M., and Rippin, N., "The Sustainable Development Goals (SDGs) of the Post-2015 Development Agenda: Comments on the OWG and SDSN Proposals, 26 February 2015". Accessed from: https://www.oecd.org/pcd/DIE__Comments__on__SDG__proposals__150226.pdf [21 August 2017].

Goal 2: Ending Hunger and Achieving Food Security

SDG2 is mainly concerned with "ending hunger, achieving food security and improved nutrition, and promoting sustainable agriculture". This goal was set up to deal with global concerns about hunger. Over the past two decades, the world has made significant progress in combating the scourge of hunger. In fact, hunger has been cut by about 50%, according to the United Nations Development Programme. Despite this achievement, hunger still remains a global problem, considering that 1 in 9 people go to bed hungry every night.[474] This goal consists of critical components such as strengthening food security and meeting the nutritional requirements of the most vulnerable in society, especially pregnant and lactating women (PLAWs) and children under five years old.

Key to meeting target expectations for hunger by the year 2030 is promoting food sufficiency through increased emphasis on 'sustainable farming methods'.[475] Agricultural is at the core of SDG2, hence its emphasis on an agricultural, food-based and rural-centered approach. In recognition of the importance of agriculture in the realization of the targets for SDG2, the Nigerian government – under the administration of President Muhammadu Buhari – is currently taking steps to stimulate the growth and modernization of the agriculture sector with a view to achieving food sufficiency by 2020 based on "the Green Alternative" document.[476] Among the policies taken by the administration to achieve this target is a ban on the importation of rice. Prior to the ban, Nigeria spent an estimated US$2 billion on rice imports annually.[477]

The targets for SDG 2 are as follows:[478]

Target 2.1: to "end hunger and ensure access by all people, especially the poor and the people in vulnerable situations including infants, to safe, nutritious and sufficient food all year round". This target stresses the need for improved access to safe and nutritious food for vulnerable populations. This is key to improving child and maternal health outcomes in developing countries. Essentially, the target is concerned with getting governments to

---

[474] United Nations Development Programme, Sustainable Development Goals".

[475] *Ibid.*

[476] "The Green Alternative (2016-2020)" is the agricultural promotion policy launched in 2016 by the Federal Ministry of Agriculture and Rural Development to boost output in the sector. This policy also serves as fulcrum for reviving the sector and diversifying the economy away from its dependence on crude oil exports.

[477] Dangote, A., "Rice Importation Costs Nigeria US$2bn Annually," *Vanguard Newspapers*, 15 February 2015. Accessed from: https://www.vanguardngr.com/2017/02/rice-importation-costs-nigeria-2bn-annually-dangote/ [12 October 2017].

[478] United Nations Development Programme, "Sustainable Development Goals".

implement measures aimed at empowering the majority of the citizenry to live active and healthy lives.

Target 2.2: to "end all types of malnutrition, including realizing globally-accepted targets on stunting and wasting in under five children and addressing the nutritional requirements of adolescent girls, pregnant and lactating women (PLAWs), and the elderly by 2025". This target focuses on the problem of malnutrition, which is more prevalent in developing countries, especially in Africa. To put things into proper perspective, the North East conflict has resulted in an estimated 400,000 children facing severe acute malnutrition (SAM) in the region.[479] Also affected by the conflict are PLAWs, children and the elderly, many of whom have been displaced or ejected from their communities. Malnutrition in Nigeria is not only concentrated in the North Eastern part; it is a national problem. On the national level, about 2 million children suffer from SAM. Essentially, achieving SDG2 requires the implementation of initiatives that complement activities for hunger, food security and nutrition.

Target 2.3: to "double the agricultural productivity and the incomes of small-holder farmers, especially women, indigenous people, pastoralists and fishermen, including secure access to land, inputs, and other productive resources, such as technology, financial services and non-farm employment". This target is key to improving food sufficiency in developing countries, especially low and middle-income countries. It will help in improving access to food for farmers and other vulnerable groups in rural communities, as well as producing a positive aggregate improvement in food availability. This particular target is critical for sub-Saharan Africa, where agricultural output has not increased in line with population growth. To achieve this particular target, UN member states must commit to keeping food prices under control as this is key to broadening access to safe and nutritious food. Furthermore, the capacity of many countries to achieve this target is reliant on diversifying production and income, including monitoring and managing climate change risks. America's recent withdrawal from the Paris Climate Change Agreement threatens to derail progress in achieving this target.

Target 2.4: to "ensure sustainable food production systems and implement resilient agricultural practices that raise productivity and production, that aid in maintaining ecosystems, that improve capacity for adaptation to extreme climate change conditions, and progressively enhance land and soil quality". This target encourages governments to invest in promoting sustainable consumption and production techniques with a view to strengthening food security and resilience in target countries.

Target 2.5: requires that states, by 2020, "maintain genetic diversity of seeds, cultivated plants, farmed and domesticated animals and their associated wild species, including through soundly managed and diversified

[479] UNICEF, "400,000 children in North-East Nigeria at risk of severe acute malnutrition".

seed and plant banks at national, regional, and global levels, and ensure access to and fair and equitable sharing of benefits emanating from the use of genetic resources and associated traditional knowledge, as internationally agreed".

Goal 3: Ensure Healthy Lives and Promote Well-being for All at All Ages

SDG3 focuses on the need for governments to commit and take action towards promoting healthy lives and improving the well-being of all, irrespective of age. This is a really ambitious goal, considering the threat of pandemics, excessive population growth and scarcity of resources. However, as an aspirational goal, it is intended to get governments to think and act boldly with regards to improving the general well-being of citizens. This goal is related to other goals such as SDG4 (health is essential for people to have the capacity to be educated), SDG6 (the need to limit the spread of diseases);[480] and SDG8 (increasing the economic well-being of citizens, especially youth, through job creation). The targets for this particular goal are as follows:[481]

Target 3.1: to "reduce the global maternity mortality ratio to less than 70 per 100,000 live births". There is a need to adapt this particular target to different countries. It builds on the maternal and child health targets of the MDGs. There is also a need to strengthen data collection and management systems in developing countries – such as maintaining accurate data on the number of births and deaths – so as to correctly capture progress in this target.

Target 3.2: to "end preventable deaths of newborns and under 5 children". To achieve this target, there is a need to mobilize resources for developing countries, especially in Africa, where child and maternal health indicators are below expectations.

Target 3.3: to "end the epidemics of AIDS, tuberculosis, malaria, and neglected tropical diseases and combat hepatitis, water-borne diseases and other communicable diseases".

Target 3.4: to "reduce by one-third premature mortality from non-communicable diseases (NCDs) through preventive measures and adequate treatment, and promote mental health and well-being".

Target 3.5: to "strengthen the prevention and treatment of substance abuse, including narcotic drug abuse and alcohol abuse". More advocacy-type

---

[480] Globalization has made it easy for the transmission of diseases from one part of the world to another. The ebola pandemic which led to the loss of over 10,000 lives highlights this possibility. [See: Saker, L., Lee, K., Cannito, B., Gilmore, A., and Campbell-Lendrum, D., "Globalization & Infectious Diseases: A Review of the Linkages," *WHO Special Topics*, 3 (2004)].

[481] United Nations Development Programme, Sustainable Development Goals".

projects are required in this area. In Nigeria, for instance, an estimated 2 million youths in Northern Nigeria suffer from substance abuse.[482] Given Nigeria's high youth population, this particular target is key for the country, given the saying that "the youths of today are the leaders of tomorrow".

Target 3.6: to "cut by 50% global deaths and injuries from road traffic accidents". This global target is very ambitious, hence there is a need to adapt it to national contexts. It is key for Nigeria, where over 15,000 lives were lost in fatal road accidents between 2006 and 2013.[483] The Federal Road Safety Cooperation, a federal government parastatal entity charged with the mandate of maintaining safety on Nigerian roads, is largely responsible for meeting this target.

Target 3.7: to "ensure universal access to sexual and reproductive healthcare services".

Target 3.8: to "achieve universal health coverage (UHC) including financial risk protection, access to quality essential healthcare services, and access to safe, effective, quality, and affordable essential medicines and vaccines for all".

Target 3.9: to "significantly decrease the proportion of deaths and illnesses resulting from exposure to harmful chemicals and air, water, and soil pollution and contamination". This target is of particular importance to Nigeria, where environmental pollution stemming from oil exploration activities have damaged the ecosystem in the Niger Delta region and, in the process, destroyed livelihoods in the area. Ogoniland, a community in the Niger Delta region of Nigeria, which was renowned for its biodiversity and was once a source of significant fish stock in Southern Nigeria, is one that has been severely affected by this problem.

Goal 4: Ensure Inclusive and Equitable Quality Education

SDG4 is mainly concerned with the need to "ensure inclusive and equitable quality education and promote lifelong learning opportunities for all". This goal is borne out of the need to stem the effects of conflict, poverty and the low standards of education that keep many children out of school. The UNDP notes that in developing countries, children from the poorest households are four times more likely to be out of school than those of the richest households. While this statistic highlights the dismal nature of

---

[482] Baiyewu, L., "Senate probes codeine abuse in the North," *Punch Newspapers* [online], 11 October 2017. Accessed from: http://punchng.com/senate-probes-codeine-abuse-in-north/ [22 December 2017].

[483] Ukoji, V.N., "Trends and patterns of fatal road accidents in Nigeria (2006-2014)," *Nigeria Watch* [online], 28 November 2014. Accessed from: http://www.nigeriawatch.org/media/html/WP6VitusV6Final.pdf [16 October 2017].

education in developing countries, such as Nigeria, some achievements were recorded for the MDGs. For instance, the primary school enrolment rate in developing countries has reached 91% globally.[484] In Nigeria, the net primary school enrolment ratio increased by more than 18% between 1990 and 2015.[485] While this represents some progress, it is still insufficient considering that there are about 10.5 million out-of-school children in Nigeria.[486] This makes Nigeria one of the countries with the most out-of-school children in the world. This target is particularly important to satisfying the development aspirations of its citizenry and includes adult literacy considerations.

SDG4 goes beyond a focus on enrolment and completion rates – as emphasized by MDG2 – by concentrating on educational/learning outcomes and cognitive skills. The "life-long learning" component of the goal stresses the need to create skilled workers who can contribute their quota to the growth of their country's economy. The main targets for SDG4 are outlined below:

Target 4.1: to "ensure that all girls and boys complete free, equitable, and quality primary and secondary education leading to relevant and effective learning outcomes". It is meant to increase access to primary and secondary education irrespective of class or economic status. However, concerns remain about the degree to which quality education can be provided for free. In Nigeria, the Universal Basic Education Act of 2004 provides for compulsory and free primary education, yet challenges still remain considering the hidden costs associated with educating a child through the five to six years of primary education. Furthermore, there have been concerns that the UBE scheme, while well-intentioned, has done little to improve the standard of education in Nigeria.

Target 4.2: to "ensure that all girls and boys possess access to quality early childhood development care and pre-primary education so that they are prepared for primary education". In addition to providing primary and secondary education, there is also an emphasis on supporting early childhood development. Some developing countries, including Nigeria, may find it difficult to achieve this target given that many of them already struggle to provide quality primary and secondary education let alone supporting early childhood development. For these countries, devoting resources to early childhood development – which is somewhat alien to some of them – may further worsen the quality of primary and secondary education. Consequently, some degree of national adaptation is needed in the application of this target.

---

[484] United Nations Development Programme, Sustainable Development Goals".

[485] UNDP, OSSAP-MDGs and DFID, "Millennium Development Goals: End-point Report for Nigeria, September 2015".

[486] British Broadcasting Corporation, "Nigeria has 'largest number of out-of-school children' in the world," Africa Report, 25 July 2017. Accessed from: http://www.bbc.com/news/world-africa-40715305 [13 September 2017].

Essentially, funding early childhood development initiatives may not be a priority for many developing countries, considering that many of them face public finance challenges.

Target 4.5: to "ensure equal access for all women and men to affordable quality technical, vocational, and tertiary education". The vocational component of this target is particularly important to Nigeria considering the low supply of technical skills. Furthermore, strengthening vocational education in Nigeria is key to making significant numbers of the population self-reliant, thereby reducing youth unemployment. The previous and current administrations have established partnerships with international organizations such as UNIDO and the British Council to implement projects for such education across the six geopolitical regions of the country.

Target 4.7: to "ensure that all learners gain knowledge and skills required to promote sustainable development through education for sustainable development and encouraging/incentivizing people to live sustainable lives, upholding human rights, improving gender equality, promoting a culture of peace and non-violence, encouraging global citizenship, and increased appreciation of the part that 'cultural diversity' plays in sustainable development". This target is key to building a national culture and approach to the issue of 'sustainable development'. Fulfilling it would include strengthening resource management, especially in resource-rich countries like Nigeria.

Goal 5: Achieve Gender Equality and Empower All Women and Girls

While acknowledging that the world has made considerable progress in lifting a significant number of people out of poverty, the economic well-being and situational conditions of women have not met desired expectations. This problem cuts across both developed and developing nations. In developed countries, there is an ongoing debate about wage disparities between men and women even when both genders do the same job. In fact, a study conducted by the Institute for Women's Policy Research indicated that there is a 19.5% gender wage gap between the earnings of full-time male and female employees in the United States.[487] In addition to entrenched societal and cultural stereotypes about women in many societies, low growth in real wages has made it challenging to narrow this gap in many countries. SDG5 is all about achieving gender equality and empowering women and girls. The main aim of this goal is to create equal opportunities for women, *i.e.* equitable

[487] Institute for Women's Policy Research, "The gender wage gap 2016: Earnings differences by gender, race, and ethnicity". Research Report (2016). Accessed from: https://iwpr.org/publications/gender-wage-gap-2016-earnings-differences-gender-race-ethnicity/ [12 November 2017].

economic opportunities and the opportunity to participate in political governance. While the world, and indeed Nigeria, has made some progress towards narrowing gender disparities in education (especially in terms of improving girls' enrolment and completion rates at the primary and secondary levels), there is still more that needs to be done to narrow the gender gap across the world, particularly in developing countries where there is the problem of deeply entrenched socio-cultural norms. At this point, it is essential to note that SDG5 is a cross-cutting goal considering its relationship to education and health outcomes. For instance, improving girls' education outcomes would have a significant impact on narrowing gender disparities, including wage disparities. Key targets of SDG5 are as follows:[488]

Target 5.1: to "end all forms of discrimination against women and girls everywhere by 2030". This can be said to have been achieved when the socio-economic needs of all women – both in developed and developing countries – have been met. It is a bold target, especially for Nigeria where entrenched norms and attitudes perpetuate discrimination against women. There are ethnicities in Nigeria that place barriers to women engaging in economic activities. Earlier, we cited the case of limited access to land for women as one of the factors restricting women from fulfilling their roles as significant economic agents. These negative cultural norms and societal attitudes must be attacked if significant gender parity is to be achieved in Nigeria. Consequently, policy advocacy is central to realizing this target.

Target 5.2: this target requires UN member states to "eliminate all forms of violence against women and girls in public and private spheres, including trafficking and sexual and other forms of exploitation". This is yet another bold target, especially for developing countries and in particular Nigeria, where violence against women is rife. The 'conflict dimension' of violence against women is a critical consideration for fulfilling this target.[489] To date, conflict studies that have considered the gender dimension have been limited. The patriarchal nature and structure of most societies – especially in Africa – is partly responsible for this situation. The Boko Haram insurgency in the North East presents a useful case study for exploring the impact of conflict of women, as they have been impacted the most; some have lost husbands and children; some have lost property; some have been sexually

---

[488] United Nations Development Programme, Sustainable Development Goals".

[489] George, T., "Lethal violence against women". IFRA Working Paper Series, 15 January 2015. Accessed from: http://www.nigeriawatch.org/media/html/WP7George.pdf [22 September 2017].

assaulted, both by the insurgents and members of the Nigerian military, etc.[490] The abduction of women and girls (especially the Chibok School girls who were kidnapped from their school as they prepared for their final exams) by Boko Haram in 2015 captured the attention of the world and drew attention to Nigeria for the wrong reasons.[491] The Rohingya situation in Myanmar is another situation that has captured the attention of the world, considering the level of violence unleashed against women.[492] Consequently, stemming the effects of conflict on women and girls is central to achieving this target.

Target 5.3: to "eliminate harmful practices, such as child, early and forced marriage and female genital mutilations". This target is closely related to target 5.2 given that these harmful practices – especially female genital mutilation (FGM) and early marriage – can also be interpreted as violence against women. This target is particularly relevant for developing countries, especially Nigeria, where FGM, early marriage and other harmful practices still occur, notably in the South East and parts of the South West. Where it is practiced, it is believed that it reduces women's propensity for promiscuity. Relative to its population, Nigeria accounts for the highest number of FGM cases in the world. UNICEF estimates that between 10 and 15 million girls in Nigeria have been circumcised.[493] Early marriage is another serious issue and shows a correlation with the poor education outcomes for girls. It is prevalent in Northern Nigeria, where 48% of girls are married by age 15;[494] the rate is highest in the North West, where it reaches 70%.[495]

Target 5.4: to "recognize and value unpaid care and domestic work through the provision of public services, infrastructure and social protection policies, and the promotion of collective responsibility within the household and the family as nationally fitting".

Target 5.5: to "ensure women's full and effective participation and equal opportunities for leadership at all levels of decision-making in political, economic, and public life".

Target 5.6: to "ensure universal access to sexual and reproductive health (SRH) and reproductive health rights as agreed in accordance with the Programme of Action of the International Conference on Population and

---

490 Agnes, O.-N., and Princewill, C., "Consequences of Boko Haram Terrorism on Women in Northern Nigeria," *Applied Research Journal*, 1 (2015):101-107. Accessed from: http://arjournal.org/files/2015/05/ARJ-V.1n.3.101-107.pdf [16 September 2017].

491 *Ibid.*

492 British Broadcasting Corporation, "Rohingya Crisis: UN Rights Chief Cannot Rule Out Genocide," Special Report, 5 December 2017. Accessed from: http://www.bbc.com/news/world-asia-42234469 [22 October 2017].

493 UNICEF, "Nigeria: Female Genital Mutilation," Fact Sheet, May 2007. Accessed from: https://www.unicef.org/nigeria/FGM_.pdf [9 October 2017].

494 UNFPA, "Nigeria: Child marriage country profile, 2012".

495 *Ibid.*

Development and the Beijing Platform for Action and the outcome documents of their review conferences".

FGM Statistics for Nigeria

Basic Statistics	
- Nigeria has a projected population of	126 million
- Total female population	61.5 million
- Female population 10years and above	44.9 million
- Female population married aged 10years and above	29.7 million
Prevalence of FGM among adult women by geo – political zones	
North East	1.3 per cent
North Central	9.6 per cent
North West	0.4per cent
South West	56.9 per cent
South East	40.8 per cent
South South	34.7 per cent
Source: Nigeria Demographic and Health Survey: 2003	

Target 5.4: to "recognize and value unpaid care and domestic work through the provision of public services, infrastructure and social protection policies, and the promotion of collective responsibility within the household and the family as nationally fitting".

Target 5.5: to "ensure women's full and effective participation and equal opportunities for leadership at all levels of decision-making in political, economic, and public life".

Target 5.6: to "ensure universal access to sexual and reproductive health (SRH) and reproductive health rights as agreed in accordance with the Programme of Action of the International Conference on Population and Development and the Beijing Platform for Action and the outcome documents of their review conferences".

Goal 6: Clean Water and Sanitation

SDG6 is concerned with "ensuring availability and sustainable management of water and sanitation for all". It goes beyond the water section of MDG7 – which seeks to cut by 50% the number of people around the world without sustainable access to safe water supply and sanitation – in different ways: it improves the standards and coverage for water supply and sanitation; and it adds other critical concerns associated with water resources management that were absent in the MDG framework, such as ensuring that available water is safe, improving treatment and reuse of water, and protecting water-related environments. The targets for SDG6 are as follows:[496]

[496] United Nations Development Programme, Sustainable Development Goals".

Target 6.1: to "achieve access to safe and affordable drinking water for all by 2030". This target goes beyond just increasing water supply. It stresses the need for safe and affordable access, and the need for improved management of water resources.

Target 6.2: to "provide access to sanitation and hygiene for all by the year 2030". This target focuses on the sanitation component of the WASH project. The emphasis of this target is increasing the number of people who have access to safe and hygienic sanitation facilities. This is particularly important to Nigeria, where most people lack access to safe and hygienic facilities and open defecation remains a major problem. Nigeria is one of the countries with the highest levels of open defecation, and UNICEF estimates that over 40 million people in Nigeria practice it.[497] This highlights the health risks posed to the populace. Studies have shown a correlation between sanitation and maternal/child health outcomes. The WHO further estimates that access to improved sanitation in Nigeria declined between 1990 and 2015,[498] clearly underperforming the MDG agenda.[499]

Target 6.3: to "improve the quality of water, cut by 50% the proportion of untreated wastewater and raise recycling and safe reuse globally by 2030".

Target 6.4: to "considerably improve the efficiency of water usage across all sectors and ensure sustainable withdrawals and supply of fresh water to deal with the problem of water scarcity and decrease the proportion of people affected by water scarcity".

Target 6.5: to "implement integrated water resources management at all levels, including through transboundary cooperation as fitting".

Target 6.6: to "protect and restore water-related ecosystems by 2020".

Goal 7: Sustainable Production and Consumption of Energy

SDG7 is basically concerned with ensuring access to affordable, reliable, sustainable, and modern energy for all by 2030. On the global level, the number of people with access to electricity increased by about 1.7 billion between 1990 and 2010.[500] While this is a welcome development, the demand for affordable and clean energy is projected to rise over the next decade,

---

[497] UNICEF and Federal Ministry of Water Resources, "Making Nigeria Open Defecation-free by 2025". Strategy Document, February 2015. Accessed from: https://www.unicef.org/nigeria/NATIONAL_ROAD_MAP_FOR_ELIMINATING_OPEN_DEFECATION_IN_NIGERIA.pdf [4 September 2017].

[498] World Health Organization, "Water & Sanitation Challenges in Nigeria". Working Paper, June 2014.

[499] World Bank, "Nigeria: Access to Improved Sanitation". Accessed from: https://data.worldbank.org/indicator/SH.STA.ACSN?locations=NG [11 August 2017].

[500] United Nations Development Programme, Sustainable Development Goals".

considering global population growth. This goal is particularly important to Nigeria, where an unreliable power supply – due to limited investments in existing energy infrastructure, a limited energy mix and corruption – has been cited as the bane of economic development despite the country's abundance of human and material resources. Electricity generation, transmission and distribution account for less than 1% of Nigeria's GDP and 50% of the share of utilities (*i.e.* electricity and water supply) in the GDP. The sector was deregulated in 2014; however, challenges still persist, especially as concerns have been raised about the transparency of the process for awarding power distribution licenses and the poor transmission infrastructure.[501] The main sources of energy in Nigeria are hydroelectric power and gas. However, the federal government has been partnering with donor agencies (*i.e.* the World Bank, the African Development Bank, the Japan International Cooperation Agency, the U.K. Department for International Development and the United States Agency for International Development) and has launched affordable energy supply initiatives to increase access to electricity, especially in rural areas.

At present, about 50% of the population have access to electricity; however, only 10% of this number are in rural areas. In view of the significant disparity in access to electricity supplies in rural and urban areas, the government initiated the Rural Electrification Program[502] as a means of getting more rural communities connected to the national grid.

The indicators for SDG 7 are as follows:

Target 7.1: to "ensure that all human beings have reliable access to affordable and modern energy services by 2030". While this target is ambitious, achieving it is key to improving aggregate development outcomes in developing countries. A significant improvement in this indicator would have multiplier effects on the other goals, especially those dealing with poverty, health and economic development. An improvement in electricity supply, for instance, would encourage the rapid industrialization of Nigeria's economy, thus creating more jobs and reducing poverty.

Target 7.2: to "increase substantially the share of renewable energy in the global energy mix by 2030".

---

[501] National Bureau of Statistics, "Electricity supply and demand". Briefing Document [online], June 2015. Accessed from: http://www.nigerianstat.gov.ng/pdfuploads/ELECTRICITY%20SUPPLY%20AND%20DEMAND.pdf [22 October 2017].

[502] The Rural Electrification Program was developed following the establishment of the Rural Electrification Agency. The Rural Electrification Agency was set up by Section 88 of the Electric Power Sector Reform Act 2005, and the board and management of the Agency were installed on 16 March 2006. Since its creation, it has been responsible for implementing the Federal Government of Nigeria's commitment to aggressive rural electrification.

Target 7.3: to "double the global rate of improvement in energy efficiency by 2030".

Energy Statistics for Nigeria

Variable	Amount
Aggregate Energy Consumption	1,259 TWhr per annum
Aggregate Electricity Production	19.78 TWhr per annum
Energy Consumption per capita	8.1 MWhr
Electricity Consumption	18.05 TWhr
Access to Electricity	51%
Access to Electricity – rural	10%
Installed Generation Capacity	10,000 MW
Transmission Capacity	7,000 MW
Peak Generation to Date	4,500 MW

Federal Ministry of Power[503]

Goal 8: Inclusive and Sustainable Economic Growth

The eighth SDG is concerned with "promoting sustained, inclusive and sustainable economic growth, full and productive employment and decent work for all", *i.e.* growth and job creation. This goal reinforces the need for governments to focus on achieving inclusive growth given its potential to reduce youth unemployment across the world, especially in developing countries. A critical aspect of economic growth is that individuals possess meaningful jobs that pay them adequately to meet their basic needs. Based on this goal, governments are expected to move beyond just achieving positive growth rates to ensuring that economic growth benefits a large segment of the population. Inclusive growth is key to lifting a significant portion of the population out of the poverty.

The world has made significant progress in reducing inequalities, considering the rise of the middle class. The UNDP notes that the middle class is growing globally, almost tripling in size in developing nations in the past

[503] Federal Ministry of Power, "Investment opportunities in the Nigerian power sector". Presentation at an Investment Summit Organized by the Ministry to outline investment opportunities stemming from the deregulation of the sector, August 2014. Accessed from: http://www.power.gov.ng/download/Investment%20Opportunities%20in%20the%20Nigerian%20Power%20Sector.pdf [22 September 2015].

25 years, to more than a third of the population.[504] However, progress has slowed significantly as income inequality appears to have widened since 2015. A number of factors account for this situation, such as economic shocks (*i.e.* recessions), a marked decline in job creation and corruption (especially in developing countries). As at 2015, the UNDP indicated that an estimated 200 million were unemployed globally. Inequality is a concern for both developing and developed countries.[505] In 2007, UNICEF reported that the wealthiest 20% of the global population enjoyed nearly 83% of the aggregate global income compared to the poorest 20%, which had exactly a single percentage point under the global accounting model.[506] More worrying is that the poorest 40% of the global population increased its share of the aggregate income by less than 1% between 1990 and 2007.[507]

This goal is also critical for Nigeria, considering the sharp increase in the gap between the 'haves' and the 'have nots'. Furthermore, youth unemployment continues to increase, leading to civil unrest and increased crime across the six geopolitical regions of the country. In Nigeria, over 50% of the population live below the poverty line while a small group of elites enjoys ever-growing wealth. Recently, Oxfam conducted a study on inequality in Nigeria. The scale of economic inequality has reached extreme degrees, and it finds expression in the daily struggles of most of the population in the face of the accumulation of enormous amounts of wealth by a small number of people. While more than 112 million people were living in poverty in 2010, the richest Nigerian man will take 42 years to spend all of his wealth at 1 million Naira (US$4,000) per day.[508]

The targets for SDG 8 are as follows:[509]

Target 8.1: to "sustain per capita economic growth in accordance with national circumstances and, in particular, at least 7% annual GDP growth in the least developed countries (LDCs)".

Target 8.2: to "achieve higher levels of productivity through diversification, technological upgrading and innovation, including through an emphasis on high-value added and labour-intensive sectors".

Target 8.3: to "promote development-oriented policies that support productive activities, decent job creation, entrepreneurship, creativity and

[504] United Nations Development Programme, Sustainable Development Goals".

[505] *Ibid.*

[506] Ortiz, I., and Cummins, M., "Global inequality: Beyond the bottom billion: A rapid review of income distribution in 141 countries," *UNICEF Policy & Practice*, April 2011. Accessed from: https://www.unicef.org/socialpolicy/files/Global_Inequality.pdf [18 October 2017]

[507] *Ibid.*

[508] Oxfam, "Inequality in Nigeria: Exploring the drivers".

[509] Loewe, M., and Rippin, N., "The Sustainable Development Goals (SDGs) of the Post-2015 Development Agenda".

innovation, and encourage the formalization and growth of micro, small and medium-sized enterprises, including through access to financial services".

Target 8.4: to "improve progressively, through 2030, global resource efficiency in consumption and production and endeavour to decouple economic growth from environmental degradation, in accordance with the 10-year framework of programmes on sustainable consumption and production, with developed countries taking the lead".

Target 8.5: to "achieve full and productive employment and decent work for all women and men, including for young people and persons with disabilities, and equal pay for work of equal value by 2030".

Target 8.6: to "substantially decrease the percentage of youth not in employment, education or training".

Target 8.7: to "take immediate and effective measures to eradicate forced labour, end modern slavery and human trafficking and secure the prohibition and elimination of the worst types of child labour, including recruitment and use of child soldiers, and by 2025 end child labour in all its types".

Target 8.8: this target is concerned with "protecting labour rights and the promotion of safety and security at the workplace". It is especially concerned with protecting labour rights in developing countries where public institutions are weak.

Target 8.9: to "devise and implement policies to promote sustainable tourism that creates jobs and promotes local culture and products by 2030".

Target 8.10: to "strengthen the capacity of domestic financial institutions to encourage and expand access to banking, insurance and financial services for all".

Goal 9: Building Resilient Infrastructure, Promoting Inclusive and Sustainable Industrialization, and Fostering Innovation

Technological progress helps us address complex global challenges, such as creating jobs and becoming more energy-efficient.[510] Technological advances – such as the role of the internet in the digital revolution – have deepened globalization and created jobs. SDG9 is critical to fulfilling some other goals, such as SDG8, which deals with the need to create meaningful jobs for the population. Technological advances provide an opportunity for countries to grow their economies and improve the general well-being of their citizens. However, there is a problem of access to affordable technology,

[510] United Nations Development Programme, Sustainable Development Goals".

especially for developing countries. This has stifled their growth and development.[511]

There is broad agreement that the globe is currently in the midst of a digital revolution; however, many developing countries have failed to benefit from it. We mentioned earlier that Nigeria is an import-dependent economy. To put this into proper context, it is notable that Nigeria – one of the largest crude oil producers – currently imports refined petroleum products. This causes a drain on the country's financial resources, as the country spends an estimated US$3 million daily to subsidize imports of refined petroleum products, especially premium motor spirit. Furthermore, the country spends an estimated US$2 billion annually importing rice despite having dwindling foreign exchange reserves, which were under US$30 billion in 2015.[512] One of the factors responsible for Nigeria's import-dependent economic status stems from limited access to modern and affordable technology required to improve productivity, especially in the oil and gas and agriculture sectors.[513] Furthermore, the agriculture sector in Nigeria is still largely labour-intensive and this is inadequate to achieve food sufficiency. Access to new and appropriate technologies should support steady improvement in living conditions, which can be lifesaving for the most vulnerable populations, and increase productivity gains which ensure growing incomes.[514] Consequently, developing countries need to integrate science, technology and innovation goals into public policy goals if they are to harness the potential of technological advances in improving productivity in critical sectors of their economy.

The targets for SDG 9 are as follows:

Target 9.1: to "develop quality, reliable, sustainable, and resilient infrastructure".

Target 9.2: to "promote inclusive and sustainable industrialization, and considerably increase industry's portion of employment and GDP by the year 2030".

---

511 United Nations, "UN Systems Task Team on the Post-2015 UN Development Agenda: Science, Technology and Innovation for Sustainable Development in the Global Partnership for Development Beyond 2015" (2015). Accessed from: http://www.un.org/en/development/desa/policy/untaskteam_undf/thinkpieces/28_thinkpiece_science.pdf [22 October 2017].

512 Dangote, A., "Rice Importation Costs Nigeria US$2bn Annually." *Vanguard Newspapers*, 15 February 2017.

513 Organization for Economic Cooperation, "Adoption of technologies for sustainable farming systems", Wageningen Workshop Proceedings, 2001. Accessed from: http://www.oecd.org/greengrowth/sustainable-agriculture/2739771.pdf [15 October 2017].

514 United Nations, "UN Systems Task Team on the Post-2015 UN Development Agenda".

Target 9.3: to "increase access of small-scale industrial and other enterprises, especially in developing countries, to financial services including affordable loans and their integration into market value chains". This particular target is critical to realizing SDG9 and other goals related to improved incomes/poverty reduction (*i.e.* SDG1). In the Nigerian agricultural sector, farming is largely labour-intensive as many farmers lack access to the capital required to acquire technology to boost their output. A recent survey conducted by a Nigerian NGO, Enhancing Financial Innovation and Access, revealed that 42% of the population in Nigeria have no banking relations.[515] Increased financial access is critical to fulfilling SDG9, considering that technological adoption is expensive.

Target 9.4: to "upgrade infrastructure and retrofit industries to make them sustainable, with increased efficiency in the use of resources and increased adoption of clean and environmentally sound technologies and industrial processes, all countries taking action in accordance with their respective strengths or capabilities".

Target 9.5: to "enhance scientific research, upgrade the technological capabilities of industrial sectors in all countries, especially developing countries, including by 2030 encouraging innovation and raising the number of research and development (R&D) workers per one million people and public and private R&D expenditure".

Goal 10: Reducing Inequality

SDG10 is mainly concerned with decreasing inequality within and among countries. Widening income inequality is a global issue that demands global solutions. Some of the solutions suggested for addressing it include: improved regulation of financial markets and institutions (here it is essential to note that excessive risk-taking by banks was at the heart of the financial crisis that rocked the global economy in 2008 and 2009); targeting development assistance to countries where it is most needed; reducing corruption; improving support to assist people to migrate safely (*i.e.* this should be accompanied by efforts among world leaders to address conflict, especially in developing countries), etc. Although progress has been achieved in reducing poverty, the progress in reducing inequality has been weak.

Inequality remains a global problem given its correlation to global unrest. Recently, many countries across the world have been experiencing one form or social unrest or another ranging from the food riots in Asia, Africa and Latin America to the 'Arab Spring' events and the 'Occupy' movement in the USA and some countries in Europe. Such unrest has been driven by

[515] Enhancing Financial Innovation and Access, "Access to Financial Services in Nigeria (A2F) 2016 survey" (2016). Accessed from: http://www.efina.org.ng/assets/A2F/2016/Key-Findings-A2F-2016.pdf [19 November 2017].

discontent with rising inequality and social exclusion. These observations indicate that social conflicts tend to emanate from inequitable distribution of resources and the balance of power in societies. Nigeria is currently experiencing civil unrest across the country – ranging from protests by trade unions to violent clashes between farmers and herdsmen over grazing and dwindling water sources – which many have attributed to growing inequality, high levels of youth unemployment, gross embezzlement of public resources by officials at all levels and nepotism within the current administration of President Muhammadu Buhari. Issues of the power balance, gender equity, nepotism and corruption must be treated if progress is to be made in narrowing income inequality. Furthermore, the international community – especially the developed countries – must show commitment to strengthening governance institutions in developing countries as this is key to achieving aggregate targets for SDG9. Specific targets for this goal are as follows:[516]

Target 10.1: to "progressively achieve and maintain income growth of the bottom 40% of the population at a rate higher than the national average by the year 2030".

Target 10.2: to "empower and promote the social, economic and political inclusion of all irrespective of age, sex, disability, race, ethnicity, origin, religion, or economic or other status". This target is aimed at getting UN member states to commit to ensuring a fair distribution of progress towards all SDG targets.

Target 10.3: to "ensure equal opportunity and decrease inequalities of outcomes, including through eliminating discriminatory laws, policies and practices and promoting suitable legislation, policies, and action in this regard".

Target 10.4: to "adopt policies, especially fiscal, wage and social protection policies, and progressively attain increased equality".

Target 10.5: to "improve regulation and monitoring of global financial markets and institutions and improve the implementation of such regulations".

Target 10.6: to "ensure enhanced representation and voice of developing countries in decision making in global international economic and financial institutions in order to deliver more effective, credible, accountable and legitimate institutions".

Target 10.7: to "facilitate orderly, safe, regular and responsible migration and movement of people, including through proper implementation

---

[516] Rippin, N., Keijzer, N., Loewe, M., and Schraven, B., "Goal 10: Reduce inequality within and among countries". SDG Working Report, October 2016. Accessed from: https://www.oecd.org/pcd/DIE__Comments__on__SDG__proposals__150226.pdf [22 November 2017].

of proposed and well-managed migration policies". The current increase in migration to Europe is being seen as the largest and most complex facing Europe since World War II. Since the beginning of 2014, an estimated 800,000 individuals have arrived at European Union (EU) borders through illegal routes, fleeing from the lack of economic opportunities, repression, and conflict/violence in their home countries.[517] The majority of this problem is largely attributable to conflicts in parts of the world (*i.e.* Syria), high levels of insecurity and political instability (*i.e.* Iraq, Libya, Afghanistan, etc.) and adverse economic conditions (*i.e.* Ivory Coast, Sierra Leone, Liberia, Democratic Republic of Congo, Central Africa Republic, Nigeria, etc.). These conditions are sharply driving up migration numbers as people seek safety and better economic opportunities in developed countries, especially Europe. The international community is complicit in the migration crisis. Their reluctance to address "front and centre" conflicts, violence and human rights violations in countries where the migrants are emanating from is partly responsible for the crisis. Essentially, initiatives aimed at addressing extreme poverty, high levels of inequality, poor governance institutions and climatic adaptability have been insufficient. One of the key steps in addressing this problem is for EU member states to adopt a clear, long term and comprehensive strategy that addresses both the causes and the consequences of the current influx, including as part of a broader global initiative to optimize the benefits and minimize the human and economic costs of international migration. EU and UN member states can no longer afford to sit by and allow instability and conflict to intensify without intervening. Conflict ranks highest as the push factor for the current Europe migrant crisis.[518]

Goal 11: Building Inclusive, Safe, Resilient and Sustainable Cities

SDG11 is concerned with "making cities and human settlements inclusive, safe, resilient, and sustainable". High rural-urban migration and the expanding middle class is putting pressure on the infrastructure of existing cities. Over 50% of the world's population now resides in cities, and this figure is expected to rise to about two-thirds of the world's population by 2050.[519] As cities expand, there is a need for governments to consider how they will allocate resources to sustainably meet the demands of such

[517] Metcalfe-Hough, V., *The migration crisis? Facts, challenges and possible solutions*, (London: Overseas Development Institute, 2015).

[518] Kingsley, P., "What caused the refugee crisis?" *The Guardian*, 9 December 2015. Accessed from: https://www.theguardian.com/commentisfree/2015/dec/09/what-caused-the-refugee-crisis-google [24 October 2017].

[519] United Nations, "Towards sustainable cities". Working Paper (2013). Accessed from: http://www.un.org/en/development/desa/policy/wess/wess_current/wess2013/Chapter3.pdf [13 November 2017].

expansion. Cities occupy just 3% of earth's land, but are responsible for 70% to 80% of all energy consumption and 75% of carbon emissions.[520]

In 1990, there were 10 mega-cities, each home to about 10 million individuals. This has risen since then to 28 mega-cities with about 450 million inhabitants.[521] Lagos State, the commercial hub of Nigeria, is home to about 21 million individuals – more than a 100% increase from 10 million in 2009 – making it the largest city in Africa. Given the exponential increase in urban populations, SDG11 behooves countries to rethink sustainable ways of dealing with the demands of this growth, especially as it relates to energy efficiency, infrastructure (*e.g.* roads), waste management, healthcare delivery, environmental protection, etc. What makes the situation more critical for cities is their limited land areas. Lagos occupies 1,000 square kilometres.[522] To cope with its expanding population, the Lagos State government has had to reclaim land, creating artificial islands for residential and commercial uses. While this is laudable, such land reclamation projects are increasingly seen as reserves for the middle class and the rich; this has had the unintended consequence of increasing slum areas, where infrastructure is either non-existent or dilapidated. The rise of slums in urban areas poses significant health and environment risks to the population.

Another consideration for building sustainable and safe cities concerns the issue of slum settlements around major cities, especially in developing nations. Slums are usually the result of poorly planned urbanization and represent a drag on a country's GDP. They are also crowded settlements that present a health risk to the cities that they envelop. UN-Habitat indicates that the population in slums almost doubled in sub-Saharan Africa between 1990 and 2010, rising from 103 million to 200 million.[523] Countries like Nigeria grapple with the spread of slum settlements, which are the harbingers of crime, disease, and poverty. Slums are home to the poorest of urban populations in Africa, and this is typified by the houses where they live. Such occupancies tend to be decrepit, structurally unsafe, overcrowded, and lack functional sanitation/refuse disposal systems. 75% of dwellings in urban areas in Nigeria are slums. This situation cuts across the six geopolitical regions where slums seem to be expanding as the rate of poverty increases.[524]

---

[520] United Nations, "Sustainable cities: Why they matter". Working Paper (2017). Accessed from: http://www.un.org/sustainabledevelopment/wp-content/uploads/2016/08/16-00055K_Why-it-Matters_Goal-11_Cities_2p.pdf [22 October 2017].

[521] *Ibid.*

[522] Lagos Bureau of Statistics, *Abstract of Local Government Statistics* (Ikeja: Ministry of Economic Planning and Budget, 2012).

[523] UN-Habitat, *Emerging futures in urbanization and development: World Cities Report* (UN Habitat: Nairobi, 2016).

[524] Bobadoye, S., and Fakere, A., "Slum prevalence in Nigeria: What role for architects?" *World Environment Journal*, 3 (2013): 45-51. Accessed from: http://article.sapub.org/pdf/10.5923.j.env.20130302.02.pdf [22 October 2017].

Slum Prevalence in Nigerian Cities

City	*Notable Slum Locations*
Lagos	Ajegunle, Makoko, Agege, Bariga, Badia, Ilaje, Ijeshatedo/Itire, Iwaya, Amukoko
Kano	Kurna Asebe, Sabon Gari, Nassarawa
Ibadan	Beere, Oje, Inalende, Mapo, Oke-Padi, Yemetu, Oniyanrin, Agbokojo, Akobo-Ojuirin, Bodija, Ojoo
Akure	Erekesan, Obanla, Isolo, Idiagba/Ijemikin
Kaduna	Angwar Kurmin Gwari, Television, Nassarawa, Angwar, Shanu
Jos	Bayan Rogo, Gangare, Katako, Angwan Rukuba
Enugu	Akwuke, Uwuaji, Abakpa, Emene, Akegbeugwu
Port Harcourt	Njemanze, Igbo-Etche, Bundu Waterside, Mile 1, Eleme
Ado-Ekiti	Oke-Isa, Irona,Okeila
Abuja	Dutse-Alhaji, Karimu, Gwagwa, Kabusa, Kuchi Bena
Minna	Tudun Fulani, Kpakungu, Angwan Biri, Dutse Kura
Makurdi	Wadata, Agwan Jukun, Idye, Logo
Zaria	Parts of Samaru, Hagin Dogo

Federal Ministry of Housing

The photograph on the next page depicts the nature of slum settlements and the health risks they pose to surrounding areas. Consequently, SDG11 is a key target for Nigeria, given the need to improve the well-being of citizens, as it relates to addressing the high rate of poverty in the country.

The targets for this particular goal are presented here:[525]

Target 11.1: this target is to "ensure access for all to adequate, safe and affordable housing and basic services and upgrade slums". It speaks to the issue of slum settlements as a critical consideration for building safe and sustainable cities. Addressing the problem of slum settlements in developing countries would require the following actions, amongst others: provision of improved low-cost housing to address the housing needs of those at the lower end of the economic strata; improved planning of land use and non-secure land tenure; and strengthening development controls in urban areas (*i.e.* identifying and evicting illegal settlements that are against the urban development plan for concerned cities).

Target 11.2: to "provide access to safe, affordance, accessible, and sustainable transport systems for all, improving road safety by the year 2030".

[525] Rippin, N., Keijzer, N., Loewe, M., and Schraven, B., "Goal 10: Reduce inequality within and among countries".

As urban areas expand in population, transport infrastructure will have to improve to meet growing demands. The need to sustain the growth and development of human settlement and their economies, among other things, makes it necessary for the transport sector to be very responsive to varying forces that impact transport planning, operations and management. Some of

Makoko Slum Settlement in Lagos State

Lagos State Government

these forces include: the ownership and control structure of transport infrastructure and services; the degree of investment in different transport modes (*i.e.* maritime, roads, air, rail and inland waters); the level of inter-modal coordination; and the rate of response to technological changes, particularly with respect to developments in global transport technology.[526] Basically, governments must invest in improving transport infrastructure in response to rising urban populations so that productivity can increase.

Target 11.3: to "enhance inclusive and sustainable urbanization and capacities for participatory, integrated and sustainable human settlement planning and management in all countries".

---

[526] Augustus, 1., "An evaluation of transport infrastructure in Lagos State, Nigeria," *Journal of Alternative Perspectives in the Social Sciences*, 5 (2013): 477-494. Accessed from: http://www.japss.org/upload/2.%20Atubi.pdf [18 October 2017].

Target 11.4: to "strengthen efforts to protect and safeguard the world's cultural and natural heritage". Supervision of this target is under the purview of the United Nations Education, Scientific, and Cultural Organization (UNESCO), which is responsible for identifying and protecting world heritage sites.

Target 11.5: to "considerably decrease the proportion of deaths and the proportion of affected people and reduce the economic losses relative to GDP caused by disasters, including floods, with an emphasis on protecting the poor and individuals who find themselves in vulnerable situations".

Target 11.6: to "decrease the adverse per capita environmental effect of cities, including by paying special attention to air quality, municipal, and other waste management by the year 2030".

Target 11.7: to "provide universal access to safe, inclusive and accessible, green and public spaces, especially for women and children, the elderly and persons living with disabilities".

Goal 12: Sustainable Consumption and Production

SDG12 is mainly concerned with the need for countries to pursue sustainable consumption and production (SCP) patterns, given concerns about the need to protect the environment. Basically, this goal focuses on changing production and consumption patterns towards sustainable levels that remain within the capacity of the planet. The idea behind SCP is that there is a relationship between economic processes and the natural environment.[527] Essentially, production activities – such as crude oil exploration, gas flaring, emissions from automobiles, etc. – have an impact on the environment, and this should be addressed to reduce the damage to the atmosphere. During discussions and negotiations on the post-2015 development agenda, there was broad agreement that the current and future social, environmental and economic challenges are interlinked and must be dealt with through an integrated approach.[528] Governments should mainstream poverty reduction in resource management. Furthermore, they should pursue policies that change production and consumption behaviour. Such policies should result in high resource efficiency to minimize effects on human beings and reduce the pressure on the ecosystem. The targets for SDG12 are presented below:[529]

---

[527] United Nations Environment Programme, "Sustainable consumption and production indicators for the future SDGs". Discussion Paper (2015). Accessed from: https://sustainabledevelopment.un.org/content/documents/2301SCP%20indicators.pdf [23 August 2017].

[528] *Ibid.*

[529] Rippin, N., Keijzer, N., Loewe, M., and Schraven, B., "Goal 10: Reduce inequality within and among countries".

Target 12.1: this target reinforces the need to implement the "10-Year Framework of Programmes on Sustainable Consumption and Production (10YFP), all countries taking action, with developed countries taking the lead, considering developing countries' capacity".

Target 12.2: to "achieve sustainable management and efficient use of natural resources by the year 2030".

Target 12.3: the aim of this target is to "cut by 50% the per capita global food waste at the retail and consumer level, and decrease food losses along production and supply chains including post-harvest losses by the year 2030".

Target 12.4: to "achieve environmentally sound management of chemicals and all wastes throughout their life cycle with respect to agreed global frameworks and considerably decrease their release to air, water, and soil to reduce their adverse effects on the environment and human health".

Target 12.5: to "sufficiently decrease waste generation through prevention, reduction, recycling, and reuse".

Target 12.6: this target is concerned with "encouraging firms, especially multinational corporations, to adopt sustainable practices and to integrate sustainability information into their reporting cycle". With respect to this target, it is essential to note that information on sustainability practices is a key prerequisite for conscious consumer decisions, thereby transforming consumption trends.

Target 12.7: this target is concerned with "promoting procurement practices that are sustainable in accordance with national policies and priorities".

Target 12.8: to "ensure that people everywhere possess the relevant information and awareness for sustainable development and lifestyles in harmony with nature".

Goal 13: Action on Climate Change and Its Effects

SDG13 is concerned with generating and sustaining a global response to climate change and its effects, *i.e.* climate change mitigation and climate change adaptation. Climate change is mainly the result of CO2 emissions. It affects natural and human systems internationally through the rise in the average surface temperature, adverse weather events, rising sea levels and acidification.[530] When these events occur, the safety and livelihoods of people tend to be affected. Combatting climate change is increasingly seen as a cross-

---

[530] SDG Compass, "Take urgent action to combat climate change and its impacts," *Policy Brief*, April 2016. Accessed from: https://sdgcompass.org/wp-content/uploads/2016/04/Goal_13.pdf [13 November 2017].

cutting theme – especially as it relates to poverty – considering its effects on livelihoods.[531]

The degree to which this goal can be realized has been called into question as some countries – especially developed countries – are reluctant to consent to global climate change agreements. Only recently, the United States of America pulled out of the Paris Climate Change Agreement. Firstly, this has been interpreted by some analysts as an attack on multilateralism; a situation with the potential to weaken other countries' commitment towards the pact.[532] Such a situation could derail the progress that has been made towards decarbonisation. It would be disastrous for developing countries as they contribute a minute percentage of global CO2 emissions. The Paris Agreement provides a useful framework for achieving SDG13. It is intended to strengthen the global response towards the dangers of climate change by getting governments to commit to reducing greenhouse (GHG) emissions over a set period of time.[533] Essentially, parties to the agreement agree to meet nationally determined contributions, which are periodically revised. Under the agreement, developed countries are expected to support developing countries in meeting emissions targets.

Nigeria has felt the effects of climate change, notably with the 2012 floods across parts of the country. The immediate effects included the destruction of homes and properties, leading to the displacement of millions of people and the erosion of livelihoods.[534] The medium- to long-term effects of the disaster are the destruction of the ecosystem and environment in the affected areas.[535] Following the floods, the World Bank, the Federal Ministry of Environment, the UNDP and the EU jointly carried out a Post-Disaster Needs Assessment. Some of the findings include: 363 people killed; 5,850 people injured; and 3.8 million people displaced.[536] The aggregate value of

---

[531] Bauer, S., Brandi, C., Chan, S., and Mathis, O.L., "Take urgent action to combat climate change and its impact". OECD Discussion Paper (2016). Accessed from: https://www.oecd.org/pcd/DIE__Comments__on__SDG__proposals__150226.pdf [22 October 2017].

[532] Oxford Institute for Energy Studies, "The significance of the US withdrawal from the Paris Agreement on Climate Change". Discussion Paper (2017). Accessed from: https://www.oxfordenergy.org/wpcms/wp-content/uploads/2017/06/The-Significance-of-the-US-Withdrawal-from-the-Paris-Agreement-on-Climate-Change.pdf [12 November 2017].

[533] *Ibid.*

[534] Action Aid, "Floods in Nigeria: Revisiting state accountability on emergency response/preparedness and disaster risk reduction in Nigeria". Policy Brief, October 2012. Accessed from: https://reliefweb.int/sites/reliefweb.int/files/resources/POLICY%20BRIEF-2012.pdf [11 November 2017].

[535] *Ibid.*

[536] Federal Republic of Nigeria, World Bank, EU, UN, *et al.*, "Nigeria: Post-Disaster Needs Assessment of the 2012 Floods". PDNA Report, 2013. Accessed from:

destroyed physical and durable assets caused by the 2012 floods in the most affected states of Nigeria was estimated at US$9.5 billion.[537]

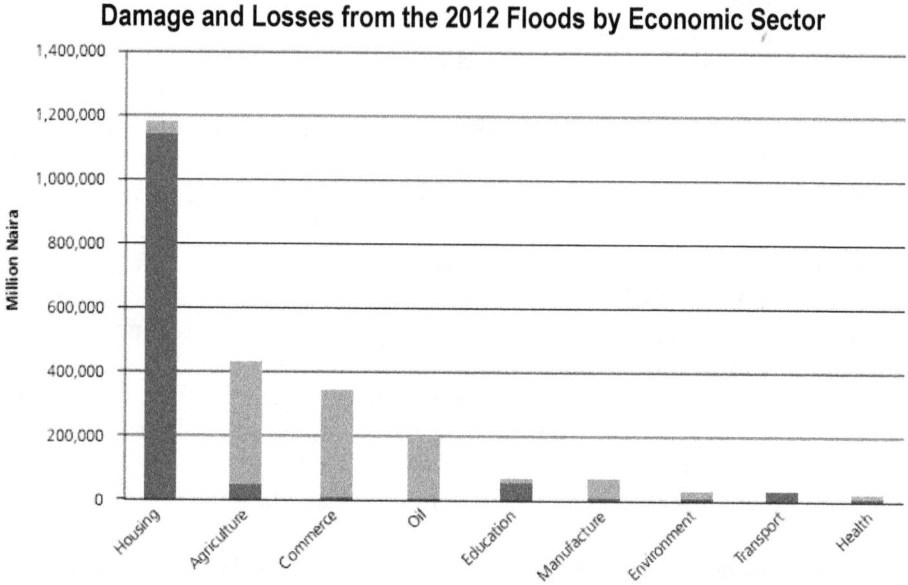

Post-Disaster Needs Assessment Report for the 2012 Floods

The 2012 floods in Nigeria and similar natural disasters in other developing countries reinforce the observation that developing countries are the most affected by global warming. Consequently, developed nations are expected to provide the needed leadership in reducing global CO2 emissions especially as they account for the most of them. The six largest emitting countries/regions in 2015 were: China (with a 29% share of the global aggregate); the United States (14%); the European Union (10%); India (7%); Russia (5%); and Japan (3.5%).[538]

The targets for SDG 13 are as follows:[539]

Target 13.1: to "strengthen resilience and adaptive capacity to climate-connected hazards and natural disasters in all countries".

---

https://www.gfdrr.org/sites/gfdrr/files/NIGERIA_PDNA_PRINT_05_29_2013_WEB.pdf [27 October 2017].

537 *Ibid.*

538 PBL Netherlands Environmental Assessment Agency, *Trends in Global CO2 Emissions: 2016 Report* (The Hague: Department of Environment, 2016).

539 Bauer, S., Brandi, C., Chan, S., and Mathis, O.L., "Take urgent action to combat climate change and its impact".

Target 13.2: to "integrate climate change measures into national policies, strategies, and planning".

Target 13.3: to "improve education, awareness raising and human and institutional capacity on climate mitigation, adaptation, impact reduction, and early warning".

Goal 14: Conservation and Sustainable Use of Marine Resources

SDG14 is concerned with getting UN member states to commit to conserving and sustainably using oceans, seas and marine assets for sustainable development. Oceans and seas, which make up three-quarters of the earth, are necessary for global and national sustainable development. They provide a veritable direct source of income for hundreds of millions of people around the globe through fishing, while over 3 billion people are dependent on marine and coastal diversity for their sources of income.[540] The ecosystem surrounding oceans and seas is vital for the survival of mankind. Furthermore, global ocean activity significantly contributes to the global economy, above all through global trade via the movement of goods by sea – marine transportation accounts for 90% of global trade.[541] Consequently, caring for ocean and sea assets is vital for the survival of mankind. This is the reason why the key indicator for measuring progress towards the realization of SDG14 is the "Ocean Health Index", which assesses 10 aspects of marine ecosystems and their utilization by human beings; among them are food provision, artisanal fishing opportunities, natural products, carbon storage, protection of coastal areas, provision of tourism opportunities, clean waters and biodiversity.

While the Ocean Health Index is a useful indicator for tracking progress in the realization of SDG14, it is a composite index; hence, it is not sufficient to separately track progress related to the different dimensions of ocean health, let alone ocean acidification. Consequently, there is a need to expand the indicator to address the long term impacts from habitat loss and climate change.

This goal was developed to deal with concerns about the exploitation of ocean and sea assets, excessive or unregulated fishing methods such as the use of industrial fishing trawlers and the deliberate targeting of endangered species. Another reason why this goal is important is the issue of global

---

540 United Nations Environment Programme, "Sustainable consumption and production indicators for the future SDGs".

541 Brandi, C., "Conserve and sustainably use the oceans, seas and marine resources for sustainable development". OECD Discussion Paper (2016). Accessed from: https://www.oecd.org/pcd/DIE__Comments__on__SDG__proposals__150226.pdf [October 2017].

warming/climate change. Unsustainable use of ocean and sea assets can damage the ecosystem, as 30% of carbon dioxide produced by human activity is absorbed by the seas and oceans.[542] The targets for SDG14 are outlined below:

Target 14.1: to "prevent and significantly decrease marine pollution of all kinds, especially from land-based activities, including marine debris and nutrient pollution". The Ocean Health Index provides a useful indicator for measuring progress here alongside other specific indicators addressing all issues connected with marine conservation.

Target 14.2: to "sustainably manage and protect marine and coastal ecosystems to prevent considerable extreme effects, including by strengthening their resilience, and take action for their restoration, to achieve healthy and productive oceans".

Target 14.3: to "reduce and address the effects of ocean acidification, including through enhanced cooperation at all levels".

Target 14.4: to "effectively regulate harvesting, and end overfishing, illegal, unreported and unregulated fishing and destructive fishing practices and implement science-based management plans, to restore fish stocks in the shortest time feasible at least to levels that can bring about sustainable yield as determined by their biological attributes".

Target 14.5: to "conserve at least 10% of coastal and marine areas, consistent with national and international law and based on best available scientific information". This particular target stresses the significance of marine biodiversity for ecosystem services and thus the future of humanity.

Target 14.6: to "prohibit particular types of fisheries subsidies which lead to overcapacity and excessive fishing, and remove subsidies that add to IUU fishing, and refrain from introducing new such subsidies, acknowledging that suitable and effective special and differential treatment for developing and least developed countries (LDCs) should be an essential part of the WTO fisheries subsidies negotiation".

Target 14.7: to "increase the economic benefits to Small Island Developing States (SIDS) and LDCs from the sustainable utilization of marine resources, including through sustainable management of fisheries, aquaculture and tourism".

Goal 15: Sustainable Use of Terrestrial Assets and Ecosystems

SDG15 is concerned with getting UN member states to commit to the sustainable utilization of land-based or terrestrial assets, including ecosystems and biodiversity, which are absolutely necessary for sustainable development. In the same vein as ocean and sea assets, land and soil are equally an essential

[542] United Nations Development Programme, Sustainable Development Goals".

aspect of the environmental agenda as human survival is also dependent on the quality of terrestrial assets. Sustainable use of land assets strengthens the resilience and adaptive capacity of both developed and developing countries to environmental stresses.

Considering that consumption and production are the leading drivers of the loss of terrestrial assets, ecosystems and biodiversity, there are significant overlaps with SDG12 (promoting sustainable consumption and production patterns), SDG13 (the need for UN member states to take swift action on climate change and its effects), and SDG14 (conservation of marine resources). Consequently, countries must consider these overlaps when seeking to achieve SDG15 to prevent duplication of efforts and resources. In a similar vein as the need to conserve marine-based ecosystems, the conservation of land-based assets – especially forests – is critical for human existence given that they play a vital role in climate change mitigation coupled with resilience to the effects of climate change.[543]

Humans and animals depend on land for food and survival. Plant life comprises 80% of the human diet, and forests make up 30% of the Earth's surface.[544] Plant life and forests play a key role in reducing carbon emissions, considering that during the process of photosynthesis plants absorb the carbon dioxide in the atmosphere and give off oxygen. The need for urgent action on the protection of terrestrial assets stems from the fact that arable land is disappearing 30 to 35 times faster than it has done historically.[545] In Africa, including Nigeria, desertification is putting pressure on terrestrial assets and this is spurring conflict as resources become scarcer. This pressure is exemplified by the current conflict between herders and farmers in Nigeria as the depletion of forage and land-based assets – especially around the Lake Chad Basin – is forcing herders to traverse the geography in search of foliage or grazing areas for their livestock. Often times, these herders encroach on farms, destroying crops, and in the process destroying the livelihoods of farming communities. This situation has resulted in violent clashes between farmers and herders, with the farmers on the receiving end in terms of loss of lives and crops. A recent report in *Premium Times*, one of the leading national dailies in Nigeria, indicates that Nigeria loses US$14 billion annually to the herdsmen-farmers clashes.[546] In view of this, the realization of SDG15 is

---

[543] Bauer, S., and Meijer, K., "Protect, restore and promote sustainable use of terrestrial ecosystems, sustainably manage forests, combat desertification, and halt and reverse land degradation and halt biodiversity loss". OECD Discussion Paper (2016). Accessed from: https://www.oecd.org/pcd/DIE__Comments__on__SDG__proposals__150226.pdf [22 September 2017].

[544] United Nations Development Programme, Sustainable Development Goals".

[545] *Ibid.*

[546] Ogundipe, S., and Oluwole, J., "Nigeria loses US$14bn annually to herdsmen-farmers clashes". Special Report, 15 April 2016. Accessed from:

increasingly seen as necessary for national cohesion in Nigeria, given the outrage that has trailed violent attacks by herdsmen on farming communities across Nigeria, especially the Middle Belt region.

The major targets for SDG 15 are as follows:

Target 15.1: to "ensure conservation, restoration, and sustainable utilization of terrestrial and inland freshwater ecosystems and their services, especially forests, wetlands, mountains and drylands, in accordance with obligations under international conventions by the year 2020". As highlighted earlier, this target bears significant relevance for Nigeria considering the ongoing herdsmen-farmers conflict and the damage to land and marine ecosystems caused by unregulated oil exploitation activities of multinational oil companies in the Niger Delta region.

Target 15.2: this target requires UN member states to "promote the implementation of sustainable management of all types of forests, halt desertification, restore degraded forests, and raise afforestation and reforestation globally by 2030".

Target 15.3: to "combat desertification, and restore degraded land and soil, including land affected by desertification, drought and floods, and increase efforts towards achieving a land-degradation neutral environment".

Target 15.4: to "ensure the conservation of mountain ecosystems, including their biodiversity, to improve or strengthen their capacity to yield benefits which are necessary for sustainable development by 2030".

Target 15.5: to "take urgent and considerable action to decrease degradation of natural habitat, stop the loss of biodiversity, and by 2020 protect and prevent the extinction of threatened species". This particular target emphasizes the protection of specific species.

Target 15.6: to "ensure fair and equal sharing of the benefits that arise from the use of genetic resources, and promote suitable access to genetic resources".

Target 15.7: to "take urgent action to end poaching and trafficking of protected species of flora and fauna, and address both the demand and supply of illegal wildlife products". This target is key for African countries, considering the steep decline in the population of elephants, which are considered endangered species. This the result of the illegal sale of elephant tusks or ivory, largely driven by demand in China and the United States. Elephant tusks are used for a variety of purposes such as carved statues, jewellery, billiard balls and piano keys. To truly appreciate the effects of elephant poaching, there is a need to present some dire statistics: In 1977, 1.3

---

https://www.premiumtimesng.com/news/headlines/201829-nigeria-loses-14-billion-annually-herdsmen-farmers-clashes-report.html [29 November 2016].

million elephants lived in Africa; by 1997, only 600,000 remained.[547] As at 2009, there were an estimated 40,000 elephants. Consequently, there is a need to take urgent action towards preventing the elephant and other endangered species from becoming extinct.

Target 15.8: to "initiate measures to stop the introduction and considerably decrease the effect of invasive alien species on land and water ecosystems, and control or eradicate priority species".

Target 15.9: this target requires UN member states by 2020 to "integrate ecosystems and biodiversity values into national and local planning, development processes and poverty reduction strategies, and accounts".

Goal 16: Peace, Justice and Strong Institutions

SDG16 is concerned with getting UN member states to commit to good governance (*i.e.* creating accountable, inclusive, transparent and participatory institutions and decision-making) together with just and peaceful societies. This goal was created in acknowledgement of the view that global sustainable development is impossible without progress in governance and peacebuilding. Essentially, where there is conflict and injustice, sustainable development initiatives are relegated to the background. Conflict and weak public institutions make it challenging – if not impossible – to achieve the different SDGs, considering the effects on lives, livelihoods and the economic well-being of the citizenry. In response, building responsive, accountable and strong public institutions is key to promoting functional health and education systems that lift the majority of the population out of poverty.

Developing countries such as Nigeria must improve human rights and promote the rule of law to create the appropriate environment for the realization of the SDGs. In fact, SDG16 is considered central to the realization of all the other SDGs, given that governance is at the core of focused government action towards achieving set targets. The main aim of the SDGs is to reduce all types of violence and propose that governments and concerned communities discover lasting solutions to conflict and insecurity.

There are concerns regarding Nigeria's capacity to achieve the SDGs, considering the rising spate of regional conflicts and violent crimes. The Boko Haram insurgency in the North East, the herdsmen-farmers conflict in the Middle Belt region and the rising spate of kidnappings and armed robbery in the South South region all point to the failure of leadership and public institutions and the erosion of core societal values that ought to promote peaceful co-existence among the different ethnicities and communities. Some

[547] Bagheera, "The Asian and African Elephant: An Endangered Species". Discussion Paper (2009). Accessed from: http://www.bagheera.com/inthewild/van_anim_elephant.htm [19 November 2017].

public affairs analysts have attributed these issues to signs of a failing state. In the case of the ongoing attacks by herdsmen on farming communities, which has resulted in the loss of over 1,500 lives,[548] the government has been ineffective in dealing with the problem; no one has yet to be brought to book for the killings and the destruction of property. This points to a failure of the "rule of law" in Nigeria as farming communities attacked by herdsmen have increasingly resorted to defending themselves in response to what they see as the failure of the federal government – especially security agencies – to protect them. When government fails in its chief responsibility of protecting lives and property, the result is likely to be chaos. Under such circumstances, it becomes almost impossible to make any meaningful progress towards achieving the SDGs in Nigeria.

The main targets of SDG16 are as follows:

Target 16.1: requires UN member states to "commit to reducing violence and associated deaths everywhere".

Target 16.2: to "end abuse, exploitation, trafficking and all types of violence and torture against children".

Target 16.3: to "promote the rule of law at the national and global levels, and ensure equitable access to justice for all".

Target 16.4: to "decrease illicit financial and arms flows, strengthen recovery and return of stolen assets, and combat all types of organized crime by the year 2030". This particular target is critical for Nigeria as the widespread circulation of arms has encouraged the spread of violent crimes and conflict across the country. For instance, investigations have revealed that the herdsmen employ sophisticated weapons such as rocket launchers and AK-47s when they raid farming communities. To put this into proper context, a Small Arms Survey put the number of illegal small arms and light weapons in Nigeria at between 1 and 3 million.[549] In furtherance of this, there are concerns that the ongoing conflict between farmers and herdsmen could lead to an arms race in the Middle Belt region as farming communities seek to protect themselves, given the failure of security agencies in curbing the conflict.

On the issue of recovery of assets, civilian administrations in Nigeria have been making efforts to recover stolen assets by some officials of past

[548] Ogundipe, S., and Oluwole, J., "Nigeria loses US$14bn annually to herdsmen-farmers clashes".

[549] Amaza, M., "Nomadic conflict: Nigeria's next security challenge is at a tipping point and could be as deadly as Boko Haram". Special Report (2016). Accessed from: https://qz.com/670768/nigerias-next-security-challenge-is-at-a-tipping-point-and-could-be-as-deadly-as-boko-haram/ [14 November 2017].

military administrations. The current administration of President Muhammadu Buhari is currently negotiating with the Swiss government to recover an estimated US$321 million looted by General Sani Abacha, a former military head of state.[550] The government recently recovered US$85 million – proceeds from the illegal and controversial Malabu oil deal – following negotiations with the UK authorities.[551] Illicit financial outflows, largely stemming from corruption, is the bane of economic development as it stifles the Nigerian government at all levels from having resources to improve the economic well-being of the citizenry. Addressing the problem of illicit financial flows from Africa is key to promoting good governance and addressing underdevelopment in the region. A report published by Global Financial Integrity notes that between 1970 and 2010, an estimated US$1.8 trillion was illegally moved out of the continent to tax havens and foreign accounts in developed countries such as the United Kingdom, the United States and Switzerland.[552] In 2007, Governor Ndungu of the Central Bank of Kenya made an apt observation about the problem and the effects of illicit financial flows from the African continent:

> The costs of this financial haemorrhage have been significant for African nations. In the short term, significant capital outflows and drainage of national savings have undermined growth by stifling private capital formation. In the medium to long term, delayed investments in support of capital formation and expansion have caused the tax base in most African countries to narrow over the years. Naturally and to the degree that capital flight may encourage external borrowing, debt service payments also grew and further complicated public investment prospects. In addition, capital flight has had adverse welfare and distributional effects on [the] majority of the population – especially the poor – in many African countries in that it heightened income inequality and jeopardized employment prospects.

---

[550] Premium Times, "US$321mn Abacha loot: Nigeria concludes negotiation with Switzerland". Special Report, 26 October 2017. Accessed from: https://www.premiumtimesng.com/news/top-news/247432-321-million-abacha-loot-nigeria-concludes-negotiation-switzerland.html [10 November 2017].

[551] *Ibid.*

[552] Global Financial Integrity, "Illicit financial flows from Africa: Hidden resource for development". Working Paper (2008). Accessed from: http://www.gfintegrity.org/storage/gfip/documents/reports/gfi_africareport_web.pdf [2 December 2017].

This observation highlights the scale of the problem of good governance facing the governments of African countries and casts the spotlight on Africa's capacity to achieve the SDGs.

Target 16.5: to "significantly decrease corruption and bribery in all its forms". Again, this particular target is key for Nigeria, considering that corruption – especially in the public sector – is at the core of poor governance and the failure of public institutions. As noted earlier, Transparency International gave Nigeria a poor ranking in its Corruption Perception Index. This index can be an effective indicator for measuring progress toward this target.

Target 16.6: to "develop effective, accountable and transparent institutions at all levels of governance".

Target 16.7: to "ensure responsive, inclusive, participatory, and representative decision-making at all levels".

Target 16.8: to "broaden and strengthen the participation of developing countries in the institutions of global governance".

Target 16.9: to "provide legal identity for all including birth registration by 2030".

Target 16.10: to "ensure public access to information and protect fundamental freedoms, in accordance with the national legislation and global agreements". The Nigerian government has made significant progress in this regard by passing the Freedom of Information (FOI) Act.[553] As a means of promoting transparency in political governance, the administration of former President Goodluck Jonathan signed the FOI Act into law in 2011. This law is supposed to give the public access to information, especially as it concerns responses to information requests by government ministries, departments and agencies. While this was hailed as a landmark achievement towards promoting transparency and accountability in governance at the time, the FOI Act has been bedeviled by weak implementation as it is still challenging to obtain certain information from public institutions, especially information related to their finances, *i.e.* income, budgets and expenditures.

Goal 17: Partnerships for the Goals

In a similar vein as MDG8, SDG17 stresses the importance of cooperation among UN member states to achieve desired progress for the post-2015 development agenda. The world is increasingly more connected than ever through globalization and the digital revolution; hence, there is increased need for cooperation between countries to record significant results under the SDGs. SDG17 stresses the need to strengthen the means of

[553] The FOI Act guarantees the right to information within the control of public institutions to all Nigerians, regardless of age, class, or occupation.

implementing and revitalizing the global partnership for sustainable development. While it is presented as one goal, it consists of multiple aims and sets the aggregate framework for achieving the post-2015 development agenda. Again, SDG17 seeks to revitalize MDG8, which is now formulated as the "global partnership for sustainable development". This partnership encourages cooperation between UN member states in capacity building (*i.e.* strengthening the capacity of developing countries in governance issues, especially policy and systemic issues) and trade (*i.e.* the need for developed countries to give increased market access to developing countries).

The main targets for SDG 17 are as follows:

Target 17.1: to "strengthen domestic resource mobilization, including through international support to developing countries to improve domestic capacity for tax and other revenue collection".

Target 17.2: this target demands developing countries to "implement fully their Overseas Development Assistance (ODA) commitments, including to offer 0.7% of GNI in ODA to developing countries of which 0.15% to 0.20% to least developed countries".

Target 17.3: to "mobilize additional financial resources for developing countries from diverse sources".

Target 17.4: to "assist developing countries in attaining long-term debt sustainability through coordinated policies aimed at improving debt financing, debt relief and debt restructuring, as appropriate, and address the external debt of highly indebted poor countries (HIPC) to decrease debt distress".

Target 17.5: to "adopt and implement investment promotion regimes for LDCs".

Target 17.6: to "enhance North-South, South-South and triangular regional and international cooperation on and access to science, technology and innovation, and enhance knowledge sharing on mutually agreed terms, including through improved coordination among existing mechanisms, especially at the UN level, and through a global technology facilitation mechanism when agreed".

Target 17.7: requires UN member states to "promote development, transfer, dissemination and diffusion of environmentally sound technologies to developing countries on favourable terms, including on concessional and preferential terms, as mutually agreed".

Target 17.8: requires UN member states to "fully operationalize the technology bank and STI (*i.e.* science, technology, and innovation) capacity building mechanism for LDCs by 2017, and strengthen the use of enabling technologies, especially ICT".

Target 17.9: requires UN member states to "strengthen global support for implementing effective and targeted capacity building in developing countries to support national plans to implement all sustainable development goals, including through North-South, South-South, and triangular cooperation".

Target 17.10: to "promote a universal, rules-based, open, non-discriminatory and equitable multilateral trading system under the WTO including through the conclusion of negotiations within its Doha Development Agenda".

Target 17.11: to "increase considerably the exports of developing countries, especially with a view to doubling the LDC share of global exports by 2020".

Target 17.12: requires UN member states to "realize timely implementation of duty-free, quota-free market access on a long term basis for all LDCs consistent with WTO decisions, including through ensuring that preferential rules of origin applicable to imports from LDCs are transparent and simple, and contribute to support market access".

Target 17.13: requires UN member states to "enhance global macroeconomic stability including through policy coordination and policy coherence".

Target 17.14: to "strengthen policy coherence for sustainable development".

CONCLUSION:

RESULTS, RECOMMENDATIONS AND OUTLOOK

The conclusions presented here are largely based on the identification and discussion of Nigeria's development challenges, and on the analysis of Nigeria's performance under each MDG. They explore Nigeria's preparedness to fulfil the expectations of the Post-2015 Development Agenda and propose recommendations for positioning the country to fulfil them, drawing on the assessment of Nigeria's performance under the 8 MDGs relative to its peers.

Development Challenges in Nigeria

The first objective of this research concerns identifying and summarizing Nigeria's development challenges, which break down into five thematic areas: poverty, education, gender equality and women's empowerment, health, and environmental issues.

Poverty

Over the past ten years, living standards in Nigeria have continued to decline, affecting the quality of life of the majority of the citizenry, and approximately 50% of Nigerians live below the poverty line.[554] Poverty is the major challenge to development in Nigeria as it deprives people of the capacity to satisfy their basic needs. In conducting this review, past poverty eradication programmes were identified and discussed, and reasons for their failure can be broadly categorized into two groups: (1) those connected with their design and implementation, and (2) those connected with policy acceptability among the populace.[555] For the first group, there was poor policy dialogue and stakeholder engagement at the formulation stage of the policies – they were created without properly understanding the needs and expectations of the target beneficiaries. Furthermore, corruption and poor performance management hampered their effective implementation. For the

[554] National Bureau of Statistics, "Nigeria Poverty Profile" (2010).

[555] Forae, O., and Benedict, A., "An appraisal of poverty alleviation programmes in Nigeria".

second group, unacceptability and lack of ownership of the policies among target beneficiaries also contributed to their failure.

The problem of poverty in Nigeria is closely associated with its low human development indicators, as reflected in the country's poor ranking in the UNDP's Human Development Index. The extent of this poverty is paradoxical: as noted earlier, Nigeria is blessed with abundant natural resources but its standard of living and life expectancy have sharply declined over the last decade. While there has been significant annual GDP growth, unemployment levels have risen and the number of people living below the poverty line has continued to increase. This highlights structural problems within Nigeria's economy that make it difficult for an improvement in GDP to translate into improved standards of living. As we have noted, the causes of Nigeria's poverty include corruption, weak leadership, neglect of the agriculture sector, weak infrastructure, a high debt burden and uncontrolled population growth.

Education

The challenges with education in Nigeria can be traced to a complex mix of socio-economic and socio-political reasons. Poorly planned and inadequately implemented programmes are among factors that have contributed to the deteriorating state of Nigerian education.[556] Despite the 10-year national educational development plan launched in 2006 and other efforts aimed at reforming the sector, education in Nigeria is still plagued by the problems noted earlier – low student achievement, low enrolment rates, inadequate infrastructure, unfit curriculum at all levels of education, poverty, poor parenting/guidance, poorly qualified teachers, inadequate funding, etc.[557]

The UBE Scheme was launched as part of efforts to address the problem of high illiteracy in Nigeria. Prior to its launch, the government's education policy had led to distortions, high dropout rates, inadequate curriculum, and poorly qualified and unemployable graduates. While the UBE initiative is a positive development for education, it is not without its challenges. As noted earlier, these include inadequate funding that has limited the ability of UBEC to fulfil its mandate, and politicized and incorrect data for planning that has led to poor implementation of education development projects.[558]

---

[556] Jisse, S.R., "The dropout crisis in Nigeria's education".

[557] Ajaga, K.B., "Problems of evaluation in Nigeria's secondary school".

[558] Tahir, G., "The Universal Basic Education Programme: Issues and Challenges".

Gender Equality and Women's Empowerment

Gender disparities remain a problem in Nigeria and deny the country the benefits of harnessing the economic potential inherent in women. One area where gender disparity in Nigeria is prevalent is the political space. There are prevailing barriers such as religious and cultural bias against the participation of women in politics at the federal, state, and local government levels. Low women's membership of political parties and limited participation in the decision-making structures of these parties are largely responsible for the limited involvement of women in politics in Nigeria. The aggressive and masculine nature of Nigerian politics also limits women's participation and perpetrates power imbalances in the political space.

There is also an economic dimension to the challenge of gender inequality and low women's empowerment in Nigeria. One of the variables is women's limited access to economic assets. In Africa, the majority of the work that women do is in the informal sector and the dominance of masculinity in national cultures is largely responsible for this. In Nigeria, women are restricted from engaging in economic activities that would otherwise make them independent. They are denied equitable access to decent employment and are faced with occupational segregation despite having the same qualifications and academic credentials as their male counterparts.

Health

Despite the global decline in under-five mortality, Nigeria has not recorded a significant improvement in this area, and at present it is one of the five countries that account for 50% of the world's under-five deaths.[559] There are regional disparities within Nigeria when it comes to the under-five mortality rates, with Northern Nigeria accounting for the highest number of such deaths per 1,000 live births.

Although some progress has been made towards improving maternal care globally, Africa continues to lag on maternal mortality indicators. Almost 75% of women who die prematurely in Africa would be alive if they had access to interventions that prevent pregnancy and reduce complications associated with childbirth. Poverty, demographic challenges and insufficient funding in public healthcare contribute to poor maternal health outcomes in Nigeria. Furthermore, the women who survive pregnancy and childbirth must also contend with compromised health as inadequate health facilities, the cost of services, the distance to healthcare facilities and cultural norms discourage pregnant and lactating women from accessing modern healthcare services.

---

[559] National Population Commission and ICF Macro, *Nigerian Demographic and Health Survey 2008.*

Environmental Issues

Water resource management and access to safe drinking water are key environmental issues in Nigeria. Poor management of the environment more generally is partly responsible for the country's high rate of poverty. Nigeria's population growth has been accompanied by insufficient investment in infrastructure, natural resource management and development. The implications of this include increased waste generation coupled with poor waste management; limited access to decent water, sanitation, and hygiene facilities (WASH); insufficient supplies of water; poor land use; limited availability of decent and affordable housing, leading to increased slum dwellings; poor land use; and high rural-urban migration. The lack of environmental sustainability in Nigeria is evidenced by the low quality of life of the majority of citizens.

Results from the Assessment of Nigeria's MDG Performance

The second and third research objectives are concerned with examining Nigeria's performance under the eight MDGs in relation to selected peer countries: South Africa, Kenya and Angola. Both objectives are at the core of this review as they provide the basis for an in-depth appreciation of Nigeria's development challenges across key thematic areas. Results from the analysis also provide viable pointers that can be used by the government to efficiently allocate resources towards realizing the expectations of the Post-2015 Development Agenda.

MDG1: Eradicating Poverty and Hunger

MDG1 concerns "eradicating poverty and hunger". Under MDG1, Nigeria made some progress towards eradicating poverty, especially with respect to reducing poverty prevalence, although it fell short of the target. Together with South Africa, which also made significant progress, it failed to halve the proportion of those living below US$1 per day by 50%. Angola and Kenya, by contrast, failed to make any progress on this particular indicator as the number of those living in poverty increased significantly. Nigeria's inability to meet the set target is partly responsible for the growing inequality in the country. On the issue of the proportion of under-five children who are underweight, Nigeria recorded a reduction from 35.7% in 1990 to 25.5% in 2015 but fell short of this target as well. The other countries also recorded declines in the prevalence of underweight children.

A number of factors account for the persistence of Nigeria's high poverty prevalence. One is that poverty is extreme in rural areas, where there is poor infrastructure and inadequate public service delivery. Another problem is that productivity in the agricultural sector is low despite accounting for 60%

of the workers.[560] Acute mismanagement of public resources and corruption by public officials are largely responsible for Nigeria's inability to meet basic development expectations despite being the most populous nation in Africa.

In addition to its failure in achieving poverty alleviation targets, Nigeria also failed to meet child nutrition targets. In addition to growing social inequality, the conflict in the North East region of the country has scaled back any progress achieved in this area. The situation worsened between 2015 and 2017 as more children faced severe acute malnutrition in North East Nigeria. To put things into proper perspective, UNICEF estimated that 400,000 children – the majority of whom are under the age of five – face acute malnutrition in the North East.[561] It is essential to note that there is an interplay between poverty and malnutrition, especially as extremely poor families account for the largest proportion of malnourished children. A number of suggestions have been provided to deal with the high levels of poverty in the country. One is to develop a robust social protection system that supports inclusive economic growth, *i.e.* translating economic growth into improved standards of living.

MDG2: Achieving Universal Primary Education

MDG2 concerns achieving universal basic education, the target being "to ensure that all boys and girls complete a full course of primary schooling". In Nigeria, the literacy rate was 59.6% in 2015, *i.e.* 59.6% of the population aged 15 and over can read and write.[562] The implication of this is that approximately 40% of the population can neither read nor write, and are likely to be left out as the digital revolution takes hold.

To address the low levels of literacy, the Federal Government introduced the Universal Basic Education scheme, which involves six years of tuition-free primary education and three years of free junior secondary education, translating into nine years of free uninterrupted education geared towards addressing the problem of illiteracy.

While the UBE scheme has improved the net enrolment of primary school children, there are still concerns as to whether it has improved qualitative education in Nigeria. The mass education planned by the programme would not produce the desired results if the issues of quality, efficiency and relevance are not dealt with. On the issue of relevance, for instance, there are concerns about the usefulness of the curriculum in imparting the skills required to produce economic growth in a rapidly evolving global economy. On the issue of quality, there are concerns about the quality of teachers being recruited to teach in primary and secondary schools. Some

[560] U.S. Central Intelligence Agency, "World Factbook: Nigeria".
[561] UNICEF, "400,000 children in North East Nigeria at riskof severe acute malnutrition."
[562] U.S. Central Intelligence Agency, "World Factbook: Nigeria".

of the teachers enrolled on the program lack the teaching skills and qualifications required to properly inculcate the appropriate skills in the students. The dismissal of over 10,000 teachers by the Kaduna government in 2017 following their abject performance on basic aptitude tests underscores the 'quality challenges' that bedevil effective implementation of the UBE, especially at the state level. A number of factors account for poor education outcomes in Nigeria. Poor planning has affected net enrolment rates in primary schools. Weak management structures within the education system have propagated the negative trends in education outcomes such as literacy levels and net enrolment rates.[563] In addition, poor management of an insufficient education budget has also affected the capacity to meet expectations for universal basic education in Nigeria.

While Nigeria, like South Africa, made some progress in improving net enrolment ratios under MDG2, the improvement is insufficient to meet the illiteracy burden in the country. On the primary school completion indicator, Nigeria's performance fell far short of expectations. The number of those who graduated or completed primary school declined from 82% in 1990 to 71% in 2015. Angola was the highest performer on this indicator with a significant improvement in the number of those completing their primary education. Nigeria's performance here weakens any progress achieved in the net enrolment ratio.

MDG3: Gender Equality and Women's Empowerment

This goal was established to address issues of gender equality and women's empowerment. In Nigeria, one in seven girls is married before they reach 15 years of age, with some child brides as young as age nine.[564] Furthermore, while women make up more than 40% of the workforce in the agriculture sector, only 3% of them own or have access to land for farming. These statistics indicate that Nigeria is not harnessing the opportunities inherent in empowering women.

Gender-based discrimination is largely responsible for low levels of gender equality in Nigeria, as in many other countries. This is evident in low health and socio-economic development outcomes for women in Nigeria as buttressed by some of the statistics highlighted earlier. Negative perceptions of women in Nigeria only reinforce female poverty and limit the country's economic potential. Nigeria's failure to act locally on Article 1 of the Convention on the Elimination of All Forms of Discrimination against Women has limited efforts to emancipate women in the country, affecting the effective implementation of the National Gender Policy, which is supposed to improve conditions for Nigerian women, especially as it relates to their

---

[563] Maduagwu, S., *Development of education in Nigeria: Past, present and future.*
[564] *Ibid.*

participation in political governance, education, and private enterprise. Secondly, the nomenclature of Nigeria's society and culture is another factor that has stifled women empowerment in Nigeria, especially from a political and economic standpoint. Nigeria operates a patriarchal society which is highlighted by its high masculine and power distance scores based on Geert Hofstede's Cultural Dimensions.[565] The implication of a high power-distance score is that less powerful and vulnerable members of society, such as women and girls, accept that power is distributed unequally.

Nigerian culture sees women as inferior to men and this is why more preference is placed on boys by households, thus restricting women to the stereotyped role of domestic chores, child bearing, child rearing etc.[566] This negative stereotype prevents women from reaching their full potential as most parents prefer to invest more in their male children. Local customs, traditional practices and customary law also serve to subjugate women in Nigeria.

Nigeria recorded the highest level of improvement when it comes to increasing the ratio of girls to boys in secondary school; however, as with Angola's ratio, it remains low when compared to South Africa. This must change if gender parity in Nigeria is to be improved.

Nigeria also underperformed in the proportion of seats held by women in the national parliament. A comparison of the 2007 and 2011 general elections showed an impressive rise in the number of women seeking elected office; however, progress appears to have diminished considerably going by the dismal statistics obtained from the 2015 general election.

MDG4: Child Mortality

MDG4 deals with reducing child mortality. All four countries examined here made some progress, although Nigeria and Angola failed to meet the target for SSA, and Nigeria is still considered to have a high child mortality rate. On the other hand, South Africa and Kenya surpassed the target. Poor funding of the health sector, poor WASH conditions in rural areas, inadequate PHCs, a lack of qualified health workers and poor education outcomes for women are among the factors responsible. Nigeria can replicate some of the steps taken by Kenya, outlined earlier, to reduce child mortality.

Broken down more specifically, Nigeria made some significant progress on the infant mortality indicator, from 126 deaths per 1,000 live births in 1990 to 69 deaths per 1,000 live births in 2015. Despite this, Nigeria failed to achieve the MDG4 target reduction of 50%, while South Africa and Kenya respectively had 34 and 36 infant deaths per 1,000 live births.

---

[565] Geert Hofstede, "Nigeria: Cultural dimensions."

[566] Ifemeje, S., and Ikpeze, O., "Global trend towards gender equality".

MDG5: Maternal Health

MDG5 deals with the commitment to improve maternal health. A key measure, maternal mortality, is a serious problem in Nigeria where underlying socio-cultural and socio-economic inequities in access to quality healthcare services lead to significant fatalities from pregnancy and childbirth-related complications. With respect to the maternal mortality ratio, Angola recorded the greatest reduction in maternal deaths, followed by Nigeria. Although Nigeria failed to meet the target for MDG5, this progress is worthy of note. South Africa had an increase, but despite this result the actual number of maternal deaths was much lower than in the other countries.

Another indicator for measuring maternal health is the proportion of births attended by a skilled health worker. Here again, Angola recorded a sharp improvement while Nigeria's smaller but still significant improvement was similar to that of the other countries studied.

MDG6: Combating HIV/AIDS, Malaria and Other Diseases

MDG6 focuses on combatting the scourge of HIV/AIDS, malaria and other diseases. With an estimated 2% of the Nigerian population infected by HIV, significant progress has been achieved in reducing mother-to-child transmission in Nigeria through initiatives such as voluntary counselling and testing. ARV prophylaxis has also been effective in reducing infection rates and deaths from the disease. Still, for reasons cited earlier, Nigeria failed to meet its target for MDG6 as it relates to controlling HIV/AIDS.

Malaria remains a risk for most of Nigeria's population. It accounts for 25% of infant deaths and 30% of childhood mortality in the country, and an estimated 50% of the population experience an episode of malaria annually. The peer comparison shows that although all four countries achieved decreases in malaria incidence rates, Nigeria's decline was the smallest.

As for tuberculosis, only Kenya achieved a decrease in the incidence rate. Angola and South Africa registered increases, while Nigeria's rate was stable. As noted earlier, the TB burden in Nigeria is largely HIV-driven. The implication of this is that controlling HIV/AIDS will have a significant effect on controlling TB. Consequently, the lack of progress in reducing the TB incidence rate in Nigeria is understandable as less than significant progress was achieved in reducing the HIV prevalence rate.

MDG7: Ensure Environmental Sustainability

MDG7 addresses the issue of environmental sustainability. On the "access to safe drinking water" indicator, Nigeria recorded the greatest improvement among its peers. Despite this, it remains well short of the target of 75% of the population having access to safe drinking water. Furthermore, the significant disparity remains between water coverage in urban and rural areas.

With respect to the "access to basic sanitation" indicator, which looks at the proportion of the population with access to safe and hygienic sanitation facilities, Nigeria recorded the worst performance among the four countries examined, with the only decline. Angola achieved the most improvement although South Africa and Kenya also had significant gains. Once again, the rural areas accounted for this result in Nigeria, with access to basic and hygienic sanitation better in urban areas. Another factor that contributed to this poor result is the ongoing conflict in North Eastern Nigeria.

MDG8: Global Partnership for Development

MDG8 deals with the need to develop a global partnership for development. One of the expectations under MDG8 is that the governments of developing countries will control internal and external borrowing, but Nigeria's debt profile continues to rise at both the federal and state levels; this poses threats to official development assistance inflows required to meet local and international development expectations. Nigeria recorded the highest rise in ODA per capita of the four countries, followed by South Africa. Of the four countries only Angola witnessed a drop.

While ODA can be a useful mechanism for improving the well-being of the recipient country, certain studies indicate that development assistance has a negative impact on development outcomes in the recipient country.[567] This view is premised on the suggestion that such assistance mainly drives consumption as opposed to investment in the recipient country. Nigeria's per capita ODA assistance rose from US$2bn in 1990 to US$13bn in 2015;[568] however, little has occurred by way of the industrialization and modernization of the economy. Nigeria's economy remains largely imported-dependent despite inflows of ODA and FDI into the country over the past twenty years.

Regarding cellular/mobile phone subscribers per 100 people, South Africa has the highest number at 165. This is followed by Nigeria and Kenya at about half of that level, which is nonetheless quite high. One of the reasons for Nigeria's high mobile subscriptions is the deregulation of the telecommunications sector in 1999, which saw the emergence of licensed telecommunications service providers. Nigeria's mobile market is regarded as one of the fastest growing in the world. The ITU notes that Nigeria's mobile telecommunications market grew by 5% annually between 2010 and 2016, and that the sector contributed 8% to Nigeria's GDP in 2016.[569]

---

567 Burnside, C., and Dollar, D., "Aid, policies and growth".

568 World Bank, "Net official development assistance".

569 International Telecommunication Union, "Telecommunication/ICT markets and trends in Africa, October 2017".

In 2015, South Africa had the highest number of internet users per 100 people with 51.9, followed by Nigeria with 47.4. Essentially, the growth in internet users in Nigeria is largely attributable to the growth in mobile phone users.

Recommendations

In this section, suggestions for addressing inherent gaps in performance under the eight MDGs is provided. These recommendations can be taken on board by the Nigerian government in developing an effective roadmap for meeting the expectations of the post-2015 development Agenda.

MDG1: Eradicating Poverty and Hunger

Some of the measures that can be taken by the government to address the pervasive problem of poverty and hunger are as follows:

- Formulate a social safety net system for the most vulnerable in society, such as unemployed people, the elderly and persons living with disabilities. This is one of the most effective ways of achieving inclusive growth in Nigeria, *i.e.* translating economic growth into improved standards of living. A coherent and consistent social protection policy should assist the government – especially at the federal and state levels – in effectively identifying vulnerabilities and reacting to them in a more systematic way.
- Invest in improving access to public services. "Access" is synonymous with "affordability". This entails targeting certain public services, especially health and education. Effective coordination between the different arms of government is required to address the problem. In the healthcare sector, cost is a major barrier to improving access, and the Primary Healthcare Framework can be improved to ensure that people in rural and remote locations have equitable access to quality basic healthcare services.
- Strengthen the relationship between citizens and the government as part of the social contract. This is required to reduce the incentive to engage in corrupt practices, especially as corruption is one of the critical drivers of poverty in Nigeria. Furthermore, there is a need to make corruption a development issue, in which case government at the federal, state, and local levels should devote attention to social provisioning as a disincentive for citizens to engage in corrupt practices. Building on this, anti-corruption agencies – such as EFCC and ICPC – must be properly funded and encouraged to establish programmes of robust documentation, including creating a reliable and consistent database on corruption.

MDG2: Achieving Universal Primary Education

The following recommendations have been formulated as a means of improving access to basic education:

• One of the challenges to quality universal basic education in Nigeria concerns poor planning. To ensure that education programmes succeed, there is a need for accurate data on enrolment and participation in primary education. To this end, the National School Census should be conducted on an annual basis so that results can influence budget allocations to the education sector and support effective implementation of projects identified by the Federal Ministry of Education in its annual budget proposals to the National Assembly. This approach will assist the government to accurately forecast human and material requirements for the sector.

• Funding to the education sector has diminished over the past decade and this has affected outcomes at the primary level. This trend needs to be reversed if desired changes are to be realized for universal basic education outcomes. Funding for the education sector must be prioritized in annual budget appropriations and the private sector must be involved to improve access to basic education. The government can offer tax incentives, for instance, to companies that fund educational institutions as a way of attracting organized private sector funding for the education sector.

• Again, poor girls' education outcomes remain a problem in Nigeria, especially in Northern Nigeria. Consequently, in addition to improving funding for the sector, there is a need for increased investment in improving WASH infrastructure in primary and secondary schools. Making schools gender-friendly is key to improving net school enrolment and completion rates, especially for girls.

MDG3: Gender Equality and Women's Empowerment

• Nigeria grossly underperformed on the indicator dealing with the representation of women in the national parliament. The electoral system and structure in Nigeria – which is influenced by the discriminatory nature of the Nigerian constitution – is partly responsible for the low involvement of women in politics. Given the high masculine nature of Nigerian society, one of the effective ways of radically transforming women's representation in the political space is through "gender quotas". Such quotas, backed by legislation, are the most rapid and effective way of bringing this about. It takes longer for people to transform or change their paradigm on issues, especially deeply-held views. Furthermore, increased advocacy and sensitization by civil society and development partners, which proved successful in the 2011 electoral cycle, should be replicated for the 2019 electoral cycle.

• Governments at all levels – especially state governments – must pass the Child Rights Act as a means of adapting the CEDAW convention to local situations. Passage of this law is key to addressing the high levels of gender-based violence in Nigeria.

• Education has been proven to be an effective vehicle for lifting families out of poverty and breaking the barriers that prevent women from realizing their full potential. A lack of quality education is a strong barrier to the meaningful participation of women in the formal economy, *i.e.* wage employment in the agriculture and non-agriculture sectors. To this end, the government should initiate policies and implement programmes designed to increase female enrolment in education at all levels. Investing in girls' education would also require changes in certain traditional practices – such as early or forced marriage – in rural communities. Without comprehensive education of girls, the earning capacity and level of involvement of women in socio-economic activities is hampered. Addressing this will require considerable community sensitization – especially in rural areas where this problem is rife – to change perceptions of households and communities regarding girls. The success of community sensitization and advocacy programs that are geared towards improving girls' education outcomes will depend on leveraging traditional and religious institutions, given their influence.

MDG4: Child Mortality

• Reducing the number of infant and under-five deaths requires a comprehensive approach that takes into consideration health risks to mothers and children. Such a comprehensive approach will utilize both demand and supply-side considerations. For instance, equipping PHCs and recruiting qualified health workers should be accompanied with advocacy campaigns designed to increase uptake of reproductive health services by women and mothers, especially in rural areas where the problem is rife.

• Improved technical assistance to the Federal Ministry of Health is required to improve planning and effective implementation of health programmes and projects.

• Given the fact that demand for healthcare far exceeds supply (*i.e.* the availability of qualified healthcare workers), there is a need to leverage traditional structures to increase access to quality care, especially during childbirth. This may involve training Community Health Workers as volunteers to provide midwifery services to women. Some donor agencies active in Nigeria – such as DFID and the Bill and Melinda Gates Foundation – have tried this approach with significant results. This model can be replicated by the government in initiatives aimed at improving child and maternal health.

• The progress achieved under the under-five and infant mortality indicators, albeit below targets, is largely attributed to donor-funded interventions by multilateral and bilateral agencies. If this progress is to be sustained, the government – at the federal and state levels – must fulfil all of its outstanding counterpart obligations. A key way to achieve this is to advocate increased mainstreaming of development goals such as the SDGs in the development of their budgets.

MDG5: Maternal Health

• Considerable investment is required as a foundation for improving maternal and child health outcomes in Nigeria. This may require increasing the national budget allocation to the health sector. The African Union has recommended that countries spend 15% of their budget on the health sector to improve health outcomes in Africa. This is a useful starting point for achieving desired maternal and health outcomes under the SDGs.

• The Community Health Workers (CHWs) programme, which has proved effective in Angola, should be replicated in Nigeria. Training midwives as skilled birth attendants should improve access to basic obstetric services (*i.e.* pre- and post-natal care) in rural areas, where most of the maternal deaths occur. A nationwide CHWs programme is key to reducing underlying inequalities in access to quality care in Nigeria. A ready supply of health providers with basic midwifery skills, complemented by referral services for birth-related complications, is key to preventing or reducing maternal deaths in Nigeria.

MDG6: HIV/AIDS, Malaria and Tuberculosis

• Resources should be committed to HIV prevention with a view to reducing new cases of the disease. Preventive interventions will help reduce the amount of funds necessary to treat the disease. PMTCT initiatives should form the core of preventive interventions as a way of reducing new cases. Furthermore, increased use by patients of anti-retroviral (ARV) prophylaxis is a key to reducing the HIV burden in Nigeria. This should also be complemented by making ARV prohylaxis readily available for patients or persons infected with HIV. This requires significant investment by the government through the Federal Ministry of Health. Furthermore, there is a need for the government to invest in research and development with a view to improving the effectiveness of PMTCT initiatives and improving the treatment of people infected with the disease.

• Managing the malaria burden requires sufficient investment in the provision of insecticide-treated nets and Artemisinin-based combination therapy to effectively treat those affected. This should also reduce malaria-related deaths in Nigeria. In addition, preventive sensitization campaigns should be intensified, especially in rural areas, to increase knowledge and education among communities about effective ways of combating the spread of the disease.

• Interventions to control the burden or spread of tuberculosis should be combined with interventions aimed at controlling the spread of HIV/AIDS, considering the positive correlation between HIV prevalence and TB prevalence. Furthermore, TB is treatable; however, effective treatment is largely dependent on early detection. Hence, the spread of TB can be controlled by advocacy measures designed to encourage people to screen themselves for TB.

MDG7: Environmental Sustainability

• The government at both the federal and state levels should scale up WASH information management systems across the six geopolitical regions of the country with added emphasis on identifying and efficiently allocating resources to improve coverage in rural areas. This should reduce the problem of duplication in WASH interventions by development partners. Furthermore, there is a need to strengthen coordination and institutional collaboration in the WASH sector to sustain gains of the past and maximize the benefits of contributions by sector partners.

• Government, as a driver of change, should improve the capacity of local authorities, including municipal councils, to enable them to meet their WASH obligations to the citizenry. This should bridge the water coverage deficit between urban and rural areas.

• The government should establish a joint learning and monitoring secretariat – consisting of CSOs, NGOs and the Federal Ministry of Water Resources – to monitor the implementation of WASH projects. This should address the problem of corruption in the awarding and implementation of contracts by the Ministry. Furthermore, there is a need for increased collaboration between the government and development partners with a view to reducing or preventing duplication in WASH interventions across the six geopolitical regions.

MDG8: Global Partnership for Development

• Concerns remain about Nigeria's rising debt profile. Consequently, there is need for the Federal Ministry of Finance to implement the Fiscal Responsibility Act of 2007. This legislation provides the legal framework to implement the required controls on domestic and foreign borrowing, especially at the state level. Failure to stem the country's rising debt profile may limit ODA inflows and, as such, jeopardize the economic well-being of the majority of the citizenry, especially those living below the poverty line.

• Nigeria has demonstrated improved potential to leverage the benefits of ICT. In fact, ICT presents a viable alternative for diversifying its economy from dependence on crude oil exports. Data costs remain very high and out of reach of the majority of the population, especially those who reside in rural areas. To this end, the Nigeria Communications Commission (NCC) must support mobile telecoms service providers in expanding coverage to rural areas. Furthermore, the NCC should utilize its Universal Service Provision Fund to subsidize data costs and improve telecoms service coverage with a view to deepening internet penetration in Nigeria.

Outlook: Transitioning from the MDGs to the SDGs

Achieving the SDGs in Nigeria hinges on addressing inherent gaps identified under the 2015 Development Agenda, broadening the focus of the MDGs to new activities and sectors, and deepening any successes achieved to ensure that targets for the 17 goals are realized. The achievement of the SDGs depends on a political commitment and its integration into national and sectoral policy frameworks. Realizing desired development outcomes through the SDGs and bringing about change will be challenging, considering that Nigeria grossly underperformed in some of the indicators – especially in the areas of health and education – for the MDGs. There are three main risks that threaten Nigeria's capacity to realize the SDGs: weak institutions and vested interests; an inability to retain and harness the institutional knowledge gained from the implementation of the MDGs; and policy uncertainty.[570]

If existing institutions and individuals with vested interests are not challenged, the status quo will persist. Essentially, public institutions responsible for implementing projects that support the realization of the SDGs are likely to frustrate collective development interests if effective accountability mechanisms are absent. The political elite are the biggest culprits here, as rent-seeking and individual interests only serve to derail progress and contribute to the mismanagement of resources. With respect to the inability to retain and harness the institutional knowledge gained from the implementation of the MDGs, the loss of this knowledge that has accompanied Nigeria's improving development trajectory over the last ten years weakens the foundation for the realization of the SDGs. Relevant authorities must develop a mechanism for collecting and conceptualizing knowledge and experiences gained from the MDGs with a view to preventing a situation where individuals attempt to reinvent the wheel without due consideration for what has worked in the past. With respect to policy uncertainty, any strategy developed for the SDGs must fit into the overall development framework of the new administration without threatening or

---

[570] United Nations Development Programme, "Nigeria's road to the SDGs: Country transition strategy". Working Paper (2015).

conflicting with the institutional structures and mandates of this larger agenda. Considering the breadth of goals identified for the Post-2015 Development Agenda (17 goals, as opposed to just eight for the MDGs), which encompass a significant portion of government activities, the risks of conflict are much greater than with the MDGs and inherent tensions will be most exposed during the transitional period when the SDGs are being integrated into new sectors, organizations and practices.

As inherent gaps were identified under the MDGs, there are also opportunities for improvement under the SDGs. One of these opportunities is Nigeria's past leadership and institutional capacity on the MDGs. These invaluable resources are critical to a rapid and effective transition. Another opportunity is the consistency of the SDGs with Nigeria's domestic political agenda and development priorities, *i.e.* Vision 20:2020, ERGP, etc. The development discourse in Nigeria is already focused on issues such as poverty reduction, social inclusion, environmental sustainability, etc., which are at the core of the SDGs. Consequently, the SDGs should provide more impetus as opposed to necessitating a large scale shift. Again, the timing of the SDGs coincides with a new government – the election of President Muhammadu Buhari – and this provides a unique opportunity for political commitment and reducing policy uncertainty risk.

Building strong institutions, especially those tasked with implementing the SDGs, is key to improving on any achievements recorded under the MDGs. Consequently, there is a need to formulate institutional frameworks – especially at the federal and state levels – that inform seamless coordination between the institutions tasked with implementing and monitoring actions towards the SDGs. The local governments cannot be left out of this discourse, as they are closer to the rural areas where the impacts of SDG-driven initiatives should be most felt. However, capacity at the local government level remains weak and this makes meaningful engagement challenging. Consequently, building capacity – including promoting autonomy – among local governments is key to successfully adapting actions towards the SDGs.

Whilst analysing Nigeria's performance under the MDGs, weak collaboration with the private sector was identified as one of the factors responsible for underperformance in some of the goals. The government alone cannot handle the burden of development and, as such, the relationship between the public and private sectors must be strengthened and made more systematic. The government and development partners can leverage the National Economic Council to ensure that the broader economic growth agenda – such as the Economic Recovery and Growth Plan of the current administration – is reconciled with the required social and environmental investments.

Finally, formulating an institutional framework to strengthen coordination between government MDAs at both the federal and state levels will benefit from including institutional arrangements for monitoring and evaluation (M&E). The current fragmentation of M&E responsibilities across the different MDAs hinders coherent reporting and will need to be significantly expanded to encompass all of the dimensions of the SDGs. Ideally, the National Planning Commission, also referred to as the Ministry of Budget and Planning, should drive the M&E institutionalization process.

BIBLIOGRAPHY

AbdulQadir, I., "The Almajiri system of education today". Paper presented Bayero University, Kano State (2003). Accessed from: http://www.gamji.com/article5000/NEWS5956.htm [5 January 2017].

Abdulraheem, N.M., "Rights of women in pre and post-colonial era in Nigeria: Challenges for today", *Journal of Public Law*, 3 (2010): 83-93.

Action Aid, "Floods in Nigeria: Revisiting state accountability on emergency response/preparedness and disaster risk reduction in Nigeria". Policy Brief (2012). Accessed from: https://reliefweb.int/sites/reliefweb.int/files/resources/POLICY%20BRIEF-2012.pdf [11 November 2017].

Action Aid Nigeria, *Corruption and Poverty in Nigeria: A Report* (Abuja: Action Aid, 2015).

Adedeji, T.O., and Oboh, C.S., "An empirical analysis of tax leakages and economic growth in Nigeria", *European Journal of Economics, Finance & Administrative Sciences*, 48 (2012).

Adeniyi, J.P., "Poor quality of rural life in Nigeria: Implication for a policy". *Rural Development in Nigeria*, 1 (1984).

Adetoro, G.W., and Awoo, E.O., "A statistical analysis of child mortality: Evidence from Nigeria", *Journal of Demography & Social Statistics*, 1 (2014): 110-120. Accessed from: http://eprints.covenantuniversity.edu.ng/4262/1/A%20Statistical%20Analysis%20of%20Child%20Mortality%20-%20Gbemi%20%26%20Amoo.pdf [18 March 2017].

Africa Check, "Education for the Girl Child in Northern Nigeria: Girl Education in Nigeria", August 2007. Accessed from: https://africacheck.org/wp-content/uploads/2017/03/July-info-graphic.pdf [21 December 2017].

Africa Progress Panel, "Maternal Health: Investing in a Lifeline of Healthy Societies & Economies", Policy Brief (2010). Accessed from: http://www.who.int/pmnch/topics/maternal/app_maternal_health_english.pdf.

African Economic Outlook, *Promoting Youth Unemployment* (OECD, UNDP and UNECA, 2012).

Agbodike, F.C., Igbokwe-Ibeto, C.J., and Nkah, B.C., "Local government administration and the challenges of sustainable development in Nigeria", *Review of Public Administration & Management*, 3 (2014): 95-105.

Aidelunuoghene, O., "The Paradox of Poverty in Nigeria". *Research Journal of Finance and Accounting*, 5 (2014): 116-122.

Aina, O., "How corruption contributes to poverty". Paper presented at the International Conference on Development of Social Enterprise and Social Business for Eradication of Extreme Poverty and Street Begging, Chittagong, Bangladesh, 19-20 December 2014.

Aina, T. "The Shanty Town Economy". In Datta, S. (ed), *Third World Industrialization: Reappraisals and Perspectives* (Uppsala: Ord & Form, 1990).

Ajaga, K.B., "Problems of evaluation in Nigeria's secondary school". *Education Studies*, 4 (2002): 70-79.

Amaza, M., "Nomadic conflict: Nigeria's next security challenge is at a tipping point and could be as deadly as Boko Haram". Special Report, April 2016. Accessed from: https://qz.com/670768/nigerias-next-security-challenge-is-at-a-tipping-point-and-could-be-as-deadly-as-boko-haram/ [14 November 2017].

Amis, P., and Rakodi, C., "Urban Poverty: Issues for Research and Policy". *Journal of International Development*, 6 (1994).

Amos, E, *Education in Northern Nigeria* (London: George Allyn University Press: 1996).

Anaduaka, U., "The Universal Basic Education (UBE) Programme in Nigeria: Problems and Prospects". *Journal of Research in Development*, 11 (2013): 152-157. Accessed from: http://www.transcampus.org/JORINDV11Jun2013/Jorind%20Vol11%20No1%20Jun%20Chapter20.pdf [3 January 2017].

Antai, D., "Regional inequalities in under-5 mortality in Nigeria: A population-based analysis of individual and community-level determinants". *Population Health Metrics*, 9 (2011).

Anyanwu, J.C., "President Babangida's Structural Adjustment Programme and Inflation in Nigeria". *Journal of Social Development in Africa*, 7 (1992): 5-24.

Arowolo, T., *Ending Malaria in Nigeria: The WHO Agenda* (Abuja: Malaria Containment Programme, 2016).

Asia Development Bank, "Introduction to the Millennium Development Goals: Key Indicators for Asia and the Pacific 2009". Accessed from: https://www.adb.org/sites/default/files/publication/27727/mdg-introduction.pdf [15 February 2017].

Asodike, J.D., and Ikpitibo, C.L., "Basic Issues in Primary Education Delivery in Nigeria". *European Scientific Journal*, 8 (2010): 150-164.

Augustus, A., "An evaluation of transport infrastructure in Lagos State, Nigeria". *Journal of Alternative Perspectives in the Social Sciences*, 5 (2013): 477-494. Accessed from: http://www.japss.org/upload/2.%20Atubi.pdf [18 October 2017].

Awe, B., "Women political participation: Why the barrier?" *Daily Times*, 31 October 1995.

Aworemi, J.R., Abdul-Azeez, I.A., ane Opoola, N.A., "An appraisal of the factors influencing rural-urban migration in some selected local government areas of Lagos State, Nigeria". *Journal of Sustainable Development*, 4 (2011): 137-141.

Ayuba, K.A., "Environmental impacts of oil exploration and exploitation in the Niger Delta region of Nigeria". *Global Journal of Science Frontier Research in Environment & Earth Sciences* 12 (2012): 18-28.

Bagheera, "The Asian and African Elephant: An Endangered Species". Discussion Paper (2009). Accessed from: http://www.bagheera.com/inthewild/van_anim_elephant.htm [19 November 2017].

Baiyewu, L., "Senate probes codeine abuse in the North". *Punch Newspapers* [online], 11 October 2017. Accessed from: http://punchng.com/senate-probes-codeine-abuse-in-north/ [22 December 2017].

Balakrishnan, R., and Heintz, J., "Making the International Monetary Fund Accountable to Human Rights". Accessed from: https://www.huffingtonpost.com/radhika-balakrishnan/making-the-international_b_549976.html [20 September 2017].

Bauer, S., Brandi, C., Chan, S., and Mathis, O.L., "Take urgent action to combat climate change and its impact". OECD Discussion Paper, October 2016. Accessed from: https://www.oecd.org/pcd/DIE__Comments__on__SDG__proposals__150226.pdf [22 October 2017].

Belgian Federal Public Service, Foreign Affairs, Foreign Trade & Development Cooperation, "Global Partnership for Development: Millennium Development Goal 8" (Directorate General of Development Cooperation, 2005).

Benjamin, A.D., Michael, H.K., Pratima, L.R., Athalia, C., Kevin, M.D., Frank, M., Sarah, D.B., Sara, H., and Oliver, W.M., "CDC's response to the 2014-2016 Ebola Epidemic-Guinea, Liberia, and Sierra Leone". *Morbidity & Mortality Weekly Report* (2016): 12-20.

Bill & Melinda Gates Foundation, "Supporting Nigeria's Progress." Accessed from: http://www.gatesfoundation.org/Where-We-Work/Africa-Office/Focus-Countries/Nigeria.

Birdsall, N., Ross, D., and Sabot, R., "Inequality and growth reconsidered: Lessons from East Asia". *World Bank Economic Review*, 9 (1995).

Bisssessar, N, "Does corruption persist in Sub-Saharan Africa?" *International Advances in Economic Research*, 15 (2009): 336-350.

Bobadoye, S., and Fakere, A., "Slum prevalence in Nigeria: What role for architects?" *World Environment Journal*, 3 (2013): 45-51. Accessed from: http://article.sapub.org/pdf/10.5923.j.env.20130302.02.pdf [22 October 2017].

Brandi, C., "Conserve and sustainably use the oceans, seas and marine resources for sustainable development". OECD Discussion Paper (2016). Accessed from: https://www.oecd.org/pcd/DIE__Comments__on__SDG__proposals__150226.pdf [October 2017].

Braunvan, J., "Towards a renewed focus on rural development". *Journal of Agriculture and Development*, 11 (2004): 4-6.

Brazil Ministry of Planning, Development and Management, "Voluntary National Review on the Sustainable Development Goals" (2017). Accessed from: https://sustainabledevelopment.un.org/content/documents/15806Brazil_English.pdf [27 October 2017].

"Brent Crude falls under US$100, lowest in 14 months", Financial Post, 8 September 2014.

British Broadcasting Corporation, "Nigeria has 'largest number of out-of-school children' in the world". Africa Report, 25 July 2017. Accessed from: http://www.bbc.com/news/world-africa-40715305 [13 September 2017].

British Broadcasting Corporation, "Rohingya Crisis: UN Rights Chief Cannot Rule Out Genocide". Special Report, 5 December 2017. Accessed from: http://www.bbc.com/news/world-asia-42234469 [22 October 2017].

British Council, *Gender in Nigeria Report: Improving the Lives of Girls*, 2nd ed. (Abuja: British Council Nigeria, 2012).

British Council, "Girls' Education in Nigeria: Issues, Influencers, and Actions". Policy Report, 2014. Accessed from: https://www.britishcouncil.org/sites/default/files/british-council-girls-education-nigeria-report.pdf [24 September 2017].

Building Nigeria's Response to Climate Change Project, "National Adaptation Strategy and Plan of Action on Climate Change for Nigeria". Technical Report (2011). Accessed from: http://csdevnet.org/wp-content/uploads/NATIONAL-ADAPTATION-STRATEGY-AND-PLAN-OF-ACTION.pdf [12 October 2017].

Burnside, C., and Dollar, D., "Aid, policies and growth". World Bank Policy Research Working Paper No. 1777 (1997).

Cameron, J., "The Economic Benefits of Increased Literacy". Paper prepared for the Education for All Global Monitoring Report 'Literacy for Life', 2006.

Campos, N., Dimova, R., and Ahmed, S., "Whither corruption? A quantitative survey of the literature on corruption and growth". *CEPR Discussion* 8140 (2010).

Canada International Development Agency, *Gender and Politics in Nigeria.* (Ottawa: Policy Department, 1996).

Catholic International Development Charity, "Sustainable Development Goals: Action towards 2030" (2015). Accessed from: https://cafod.org.uk/content/download/27011/266522/version/2/file/CAFOD_SDG_Action_Towards_2030_%20Single.pdf [13 October 2017].

Center on International Cooperation, "Goals in a post-2015 development framework: Options and strategic choices". Working Report (2013). Accessed from: http://cic.nyu.edu/sites/default/files/cic_goals_in_a_post-2015_development_framework_a4_2.pdf [27 August 2017].

Civil Liberties Organization, "Blood trail: Repression and resistance in the Niger Delta". Country Analysis Brief (2002), 4. Accessed from: http://www.eia.doe.gov/cab/index.html.pds [15 January 2017].

Collis, J., and Hussey, R., *Business Research: A practical guide for undergraduate and postgraduate students*, 3rd ed. (London: Palgrave Macmillan, 2005).

Connected Development, "An examination of girls' education policies in Nigeria with a focus on the North East." *Policy Brief*, February 2017. Accessed from: http://connecteddevelopment.org/wp-content/uploads/2017/02/Girl-Child-Education-Policies-in-Nigeria-and-Its-North-Eastern-Part...pdf [12 September 2017].

Dangote, A., "Rice Importation Costs Nigeria US$2bn Annually," *Vanguard Newspapers*, 15 February 2015. Accessed from: https://www.vanguardngr.com/2017/02/rice-importation-costs-nigeria-2bn-annually-dangote/ [12 October 2017].

Dawaki, S., Al-Mekhlafi, H., Ithoi, I., Ibrahim, J., Atroosh, W., Abdusalam, A., Sady, H., Elyana, F., Adamu, A., Yelwa, S., Al-Areeqi, M., Subramaniam, L., Nasr, N., and Lau, Y., "Is Nigeria winning the battle against malaria? Prevalence, risk factors and KAP assessment among Hausa communities in Kano state". *Malaria Journal*, 15 (2016): 351-355.

DAWN, *Breaking through the development silos: SRHR, MDGs and Gender Equity: Experiences from Mexico, India and Nigeria*, (e-book, 2013). Accessed from: http://issuu.com/dawnfeminist/docs/breakingsilos [11 September 2017].

Decentralization and Local Governance (DeLoG), "Post-2015 Global Development Agenda: Making the Case for Decentralization and Local Governance". Working Paper 2, February 2013.

Desai, V.S., "Importance of Literacy in India's Economic Growth". *International Journal of Economic Research*, 32 (2012): 112-124.

Doreo Partners, "The Nigerian Unemployment Challenge". Africa Report Features (2013).

Economic and Social Commission for Western Asia, "The 2030 Agenda for Sustainable Development: A new roadmap to achieve gender equality and the empowerment of women and girls". Committee on Women 7th Session 20-21 January 2016. Accessed from: https://sustainabledevelopment.un.org/content/documents/9783ESCWA_2030%20Agenda%20for%20Sustainable%20Development-Gender%20Equality.pdf

Edoh, T., "Poverty and the survival of democracy in Nigeria". *Nigeria Journal of Political & Administrative Studies*, 1 (2003).

Effiong, S.A., and Etowa, U.E., "Oil spillage cost, gas flaring cost and life expectancy rate of the Niger Delta people of Nigeria". *Advances in Management & Applied Economics*, 2 (2012): 211-228.

Ekpe, D., Eja, A.E., and John, E.I., "Women's gender equality in Nigeria: A critical analysis of socio-economic and political (gender issues)". *Journal of Research in Gender & Development* 4 (2014): 15-20.

El-Rufai, N.A., and Okolo, J., "What is restructuring and does Nigeria need it?" Chatham House, Africa Programme Meeting, 21 September 2017.

Enhancing Financial Innovation and Access, "Access to Financial Services in Nigeria (A2F) 2016 Survey", October 2016. Accessed from: http://www.efina.org.ng/assets/A2F/2016/Key-Findings-A2F-2016.pdf [19 November 2017].

Ezeh, O.K., Agho, K.E., Dibley, M.J., Hall, J., and Page, A.N., "The impact of water & sanitation on childhood mortality in Nigeria: Evidence from demographic and health surveys, 2003-2013". *International Journal of Environmental Research & Public Health*, 11 (2014): 9256-9272.

Federal Government, *National Education Development Plan* (Abuja: Federal Ministry of Education, 2004).

Federal Ministry of Agriculture, "Positioning the Agriculture Sector to support export-oriented growth". Policy Brief (2014).

Federal Ministry of Environment, Nigerian Conservation Foundation, WWF UK and CEESP-IUCN Commission on Environmental, Economic, and Social Policy, "Niger Delta Resource Damage Assessment and Restoration Project" (2006).

Federal Ministry of Finance, *National Capacity Assessment Report of Nigeria* (Abuja: Federal Ministry of Finance, 2012).

Federal Ministry of Health, *National Health Management: Revised Policy Programme and Strategic Plan of Action* (Abuja: Department of Health Planning & Research, 2006).

Federal Ministry of Health, *National HIV Sero-Prevalence Sentinel Survey 2008* (Abuja: Federal Ministry of Health, 2012).

Federal Ministry of Health, *National Malaria Control Programme*, (Abuja: Department of Public Health, 2014).

Federal Ministry of Health, "National Strategic Health Development Framework 2009-2015". Accessed from: http://www.internationalhealthpartnership.net/fileadmin/uploads/ihp/Documents/Country_Pages/Nigeria/Nigeria%20National%20Strategic%20Health%20Development%20Plan%20Framework%202009-2015.pdf [3 January 2017].

Federal Ministry of Health, *National Tuberculosis and Leprosy Control Programme* (Abuja: Department of Public Health, 2010).

Federal Ministry of Health, *Revised National Policy* (Abuja: Federal Ministry of Health, 2012).

Federal Ministry of Health, *Strategic Plan for Tuberculosis Control: Towards Universal Access to Prevention, Diagnosis, and Treatment 2015-2020* Abuja: Department of Public Health, 2015).

Federal Ministry of Power, "Investment opportunities in the Nigerian power sector". Presentation at an Investment Summit organized by the Ministry (2014). Accessed from: http://www.power.gov.ng/download/Investment%20Opportunities%20in%20the%20Nigerian%20Power%20Sector.pdf [22 September 2015].

Federal Ministry of Water Resources, "National Water Resources Policy (2016-2030)". Accessed from: http://www.waterresources.ng/wp-content/uploads/2017/02/Download.pdf [15 October 2017].

Federal Republic of Nigeria, *National Policy on Education*, (Abuja: Federal Government Nigeria Publications, 2004).

Federal Republic of Nigeria, World Bank, EU, UN, et al., "Nigeria: Post-Disaster Needs Assessment of the 2012 Floods". PDNA Report 2013. Accessed from: https://www.gfdrr.org/sites/gfdrr/files/NIGERIA_PDNA_PRINT_05_29_2013_WEB.pdf [27 October 2017].

Ferreira, F.H.G., and Ravallion, M., "Global Poverty and Inequality: A review of evidence". World Bank Policy Research Working Paper 4623 (2008).

Feyehun, O.A, "Household environmental health hazards and child survival in Sub-Saharan Africa". DHS Working Papers, *Demographic & Health Research* 74 (2010). Accessed from: http://dhsprogram.com/pubs/pdf/WP74/WP74.pdf [11 August 2017].

Fleurbaey, M., "Beyond GDP: The quest for a measure of social welfare". *Journal of Economic Literature*, 47 (2009): 1029-1075.

Food and Agriculture Organization, *The state of food insecurity in the world*, (Rome: United Nations, 2014).

Food and Agriculture Organization, *The state of food security in the world: economic growth is necessary but not sufficient to accelerate reduction of hunger and malnutrition* (Rome: FAO, 2012).

Friends of the Earth, "Gas Flaring in Nigeria, 2004". Accessed from: http://www.foe.co.uk [14 January 2017].

Gboyega, A., *Democracy and development: The imperative of local governance* (Ibadan: University of Ibadan, 2003), 6-7.

George, T., "Lethal violence against women". IFRA Working Paper Series, 15 January 2015. Accessed from: http://www.nigeriawatch.org/media/html/WP7George.pdf [22 September 2017].

Giugliani, C., Duncan, B.B., Harzheim, E., Lavor, A.C., Lavor, M.C., Machado, M.M.T., Barbosa, M.I., Bornstein, V.J., Pontes, A.L., and Knauth, D.R., "Community Health Workers Programme in Luanda, Angola: An Evaluation of the Implementation Process". *Human Resources for Health* (2014): 26-58.

Global Financial Integrity, "Illicit financial flows from Africa: Hidden resource for development. Working Paper (2008). Accessed from: http://www.gfintegrity.org/storage/gfip/documents/reports/gfi_africa report_web.pdf [2 December 2017].

Goodland G., "The Concept of Environmental Sustainability". *Annual Review of Ecology and Systematics*, 26 (1995): 1-24.

Graduate Women International, "Challenges and achievements in the implementation of the Millennium Development Goals for gaps and lessons learned, March 2016". Accessed from: http://www.graduatewomen.org/challenges-achievements-implementation-millennium-development-goals-women-girls-gaps-lessons-learned-csw-58/ [13 September 2017].

Greenwood, B.M., Bojang, K., Whitty, C.J.M., and Targett, G.A.T., "Malaria". *The Lancet*, 265 (9469): 1474-1480.

Harding, A., "The Private Health Sector: A key to reaching women with maternal health programmes". Women Deliver Conference 2010.

Harrison, K.A., "The struggle to reduce high maternal mortality in Nigeria". *African Journal of Reproductive Health*, 13 (2009).

High-Level Panel of Eminent Persons on the Post-2015 Development Agenda, *A New Global Partnership: Eradicate Poverty and Transform Economies through Sustainable Development* (New York: United Nations Publications, 2013).

House of Commons International Development Committee, "DFID's programme in Nigeria, Second Report of Session 2016-17".

Ibrahim, A., "The role of private sector in implementing the Sustainable Development Goals (SDGs) in Bangladesh". Presentation at the Workshop "Realization of the SDGs" organized by the Metropolitan Chamber of Commerce & Industry, Dhaka, and the Citizens Platform for SDGs, Bangladesh, 2 October 2016. Accessed from: http://cpd.org.bd/wp-content/uploads/2016/10/Role-of-Private-Sector-in-SDGs-Implementation.pdf [12 November 2017].

Idowu, A.E., Osinaike, M.O., and Ajayi, M.P., "Maternal health challenges and prospects for national development: a case study of Badagry local government, Lagos State". *African Journals*, 9 (2011).

Ifemeje, S., and Ikpeze, O., "Global trend towards gender equality: Nigeria's experience in focus". *Kuwait Chapter of Arabian Journal of Business & Management Review*, 2 (2012): 51-63.

Igbuzor, O., "Review of Nigeria Millennium Development Goals: 2005 report". Paper presented at the MDG/CAP Nigeria planning meeting, Abuja, 2006.

Igbuzor, O, "The Millennium Development Goals: Can Nigeria meet the goals in 2015?" Paper presented at the Symposium on the Millennium Development Goals and Nigeria, Institute of Chartered Accountants of Nigeria, Abuja, 2015.

Ijeoma, O., "Access to primary healthcare services and child mortality in Orumba North Local Government Area, Anambra State". Thesis, Faculty of Social Sciences, University of Nigeria, Nsukka, 2009.

Ijeoma, S., "Nigeria & Climate Change Adaptation". *ISSP Insight*, May 2012. Accessed from: https://www.sustainabilityprofessionals.org/system/files/May%202012-Nigeria%20and%20Climate%20Change%20Adaptation.pdf.

International Monetary Fund, "Nigeria's economy will contract by 1.8%" (2016). Accessed from: https://www.ft.com/content/ab4f9ce6-4dc9-11e6-88c5-db83e98a590a [14 January 2017].

Institute for Women's Policy Research, "The gender wage gap 2016: earnings differences by gender, race, and ethnicity". Research Report. Accessed from: https://iwpr.org/publications/gender-wage-gap-2016-earnings-differences-gender-race-ethnicity/ [12 November 2017].

Institute of Chartered Accountants of Nigeria, "Growth without development in Nigeria: confronting the paradox". Paper presented at the 43rd Annual ICAN Conference, Abuja, 10 October 2013. Accessed from: http://www.icanig.org/speeches/inventory_images/26.pdf [4 March 2017].

International Centre for Energy, Environment & Development, "Nigeria adopts climate change policy document". Accessed from: http://iceednigeria.org/ic/nigeria-adopts-climate-change-policy-document/ [12 September 2017].

International Fund for Agricultural Development, *New realities, new challenges: new opportunities for tomorrow's generation* (Rome: IFAD, 2010).

International Labour Office, *Global Employment Trends for Women* (Geneva: ILO, 2009).

International Telecommunication Union, "Telecommunication/ICT markets and trends in Africa, October 2017". Accessed from: https://www.itu.int/ITU-D/ict/statistics/material/af_report07.pdf [14 October 2017].

Iredale, R., "Luring overeas trained doctors to Australia: Issues of training, regulating and trading". *International Migration Journal*, 47 (2009): 31-65.

Jisse, S.R., "The dropout crisis in Nigeria's education". *Education Studies*, 5 (2010): 56-70.

Joseph, R.A., *Democracy and prebendal politics in Nigeria* (Cambridge: Cambridge University Press, 2014).

Kabeer, N., "Gender Equality, poverty eradication and the MDGs: Promoting women's capabilities and participation". *Gender & Development Series*, 13. Economic & Social Commission in Asia & the Pacific (2003).

Kanayo, O., "Poverty Incidence and Reduction Strategies in Nigeria: Challenges of Meeting 2015 MDG Targets". *Journal of Economics*, 5 (2014): 201-217.

Kingsley, P., "What caused the refugee crisis?" *The Guardian*, 9 December 2015. Accessed from: https://www.theguardian.com/commentisfree/2015/dec/09/what-caused-the-refugee-crisis-google [24 October 2017].

Kolawole, T.O., Adeigbe Y.K., Zaggi, Y.H., and Owonibi, E., "Millennium Development Goals (MDGs) in Nigeria: Issues and Problems". *Global Journal of Human Social Science*, 14 (2014).

Koopman, J.S., "Diarrhea and school toilet hygiene in Cali, Colombia". *American Journal of Epidemiology*, 107 (1978): 412-420.

Kosemani, J.M., "The ethnic factor in educational disparity in Nigeria". In *Educational Disparity: The Nigeria Situation* (Lagos State: Africa Heritage Research & Publications, 1992).

Kristof, N.D., "The hidden hunger", *New York Times*, 23 May 2009. Accessed from: http://www.nytimes.com/2009/05/24/opin ion/24kristof.html [15 February 2017].

Lagos Bureau of Statistics, *Abstract of Local Government Statistics*, (Ikeja: Ministry of Economic Planning & Budget, 2012).

Lagos State Government/United Nations Centre for Human Settlements, "Identification of Urban Renewal Areas in Metropolitan Lagos". Urban and Regional Planning Division: United Nations Development Programme UNCHS Habitat N1R 82/00/Implementation (1984).

Legal Defense & Assistance Project, *Gender Issues*, 2 (2003).
Leon, T., "The State of Liberal Democracy in Africa: Resurgence or retreat". *Development Policy Analysis*, 12 (2010).
Loewe, M., and Rippin, N., "The Sustainable Development Goals (SDGs) of the Post-2015 Development Agenda: Comments on the OWG and SDSN Proposals, 26 February 2015". Accessed from: https://www.oecd.org/pcd/DIE__Comments__on__SDG__proposals__150226.pdf [21 August 2017].
Lukpata, V.I., "Revenue Allocation Formulae in Nigeria: A Continuous Search". *International Journal of Public Administration & Management Research*, 2 (2013).
MacArthur, J.W., "The Origins of the Millennium Development Goals". *SAIS Review*, 2 (2014): 5-24. Accessed from: http://johnmcarthur.com/wp-content/uploads/2015/01/SAISreview2014mcarthur.pdf [4 January 2017].
Maduagwu, S., *Development of education in Nigeria: Past, present and future* (Port Harcourt: Japan Foundation, 1999).
Majekodunmi, A., "Federalism in Nigeria: The past, current peril and future hopes". *Journal of Policy and Development Studies*, 9 (2015): 107-120.
Manby, B., *The price of oil: Corporate responsibility and human rights violations in Nigeria's oil producing communities* (New York: Human Rights Watch, 1999).
Metcalfe-Hough, V., *The migration crisis? Facts, challenges and possible solutions* (London: Overseas Development Institute, 2015).
Mills, G., "Why is Africa Poor?" Center for Global Liberty & Prosperity, Briefing Paper (2010). Accessed from: http://www.thebrenthurstfoundation.org/workspace/files/dbp6.pdf [2 September 2017].
Moja, T., "Nigeria Education Sector Analysis: An Analytical Synthesis of Performance and Main Issues". World Bank, January 2000.
Mojekwu, J.N., "Maternal mortality: Natural risk to women". *Ghana Journal of Development Studies*, 2 (2005): 129-141.
Momoh, M., "World Bank commits US$500mn to Nigeria's social protection programme". *Africa Review* [online] 30 March 2016. Accessed from: http://www.africareview.com/business-finance/World-Bank-supports-Nigeria-social-protection-programme/979184-3139066-g2fwnkz/index.html.
Naomi, O., "Towards an integrated view of human rights". *Hunger Teach Net*, 6 (1995): 6-7.
Nasidi, A., and Harry, T.O., "The Epidemiology of HIV/AIDS in Nigeria". Accessed from: http://www.apin.harvard.edu/Chapter2.pdf.
National Bureau of Statistics, "Annual Abstract of Statistics, 2012". Accessed from: http://www.nigerianstat.gov.ng [22 January 2016].

National Bureau of Statistics, "Electricity supply and demand: Briefing Document" [online] (2015). Accessed from: http://www.nigerianstat.gov.ng/pdfuploads/ELECTRICITY%20SUPPLY%20AND%20DEMAND.pdf [22 October 2017].

National Bureau of Statistics, "Nigerians living in poverty grows to 61%". Accessed from: http://www.bbc.com/news/world-africa-17015873 [14 December 2016].

National Bureau of Statistics, *National School Census*, (Abuja: NBS, 2006).

National Bureau of Statistics, *Nigeria Telecommunications (Services) Sector Report* (Abuja: NBS, 2016).

National Bureau of Statistics, *The Nigerian Poverty Profile 2010 Report* (Abuja, FCT: 2012).

National Planning Commission, "Transparency and accountability in governance". *Vanguard Newspapers*, 22 March 2005.

National Population Commission and ICF Macro, *Nigerian Demographic and Health Survey 2008* (Abuja: ICF Macro and Calverton, 2009).

National Population Commission, *Population Data for Nigeria* (Abuja: National Population Commission, 2009).

Ndubuisi, A. L., and Asia, I.O., "Environmental pollution in oil producing areas of the Niger Delta Basin, Nigeria: Empirical assessment of trends and people's perception". *Environmental Research Journal* (2007): 18-26. Accessed from: https://www.scholar.google.com [12 January 2017].

Nigeria Bureau of Statistics, *Labour Market Assessment Report*, (Abuja: NBS, 2012).

Nigeria Bureau of Statistics, "Unemployment in Nigeria". *Vanguard Newspaper*, 23 December 2017. Accessed from: https://www.vanguardngr.com/2017/12/nigerias-unemployment-rate-rises-14-2-18-8/ [27 December 2017].

Nigeria Sovereign Investment Authority, "Reversing Medical Toursim in Nigeria". In PricewaterhouseCoopers, "Restoring trust to Nigeria's Healthcare System", Working Report 2016. Accessed from: https://www.pwc.com/ng/en/assets/pdf/restoring-trust-to-nigeria-healthcare-system.pdf.

Norman, C., "Utilizing incentives for global family planning and reproductive health services uptake: Altruistic or a euphemism for population control?" Master's thesis, Graduate School of Arts & Sciences, Brandeis University, 2013.

Nwagwu, E.J., "Unemployment and poverty in Nigeria: A link to national insecurity". *Global Journal of Politics and Law Research*, 2 (2014): 19-35.

Obi, P., "Nigeria: Health Sector's Hidden Crisis". *This Day*, June 2013. Accessed from: http://www.allafrica.com/stories/201309260109.html?viewall=1 [2 January 2017].

Obong, J.O., "The state of basic education in Nigeria: The way forward". Paper presented at the 47th annual conference of science teachers, Calabar, 13-19 August 2006.

Odion, W.E., *Millennium Development Goals (MDGs) and the Poverty Questions in Nigeria* (Abuja: Panaf Publishing, 2009).

OECD, "Nigeria: Economic Overview, 2012". Accessed from: http://www.oecd.org/swac/publications/Nigeria_e-version_en_light.pdf [11 December 2016].

Office of the High Commissioner for Human Rights, *Addressing gender equality in the Post-2015 Development Framework: The Contribution of the United Nations Human Rights System* (Geneva: OHCHR, 2012).

Ogoko, G., *Baseline Survey Report* (Enugu State: South Saharan Social Development Organization, 2016).

Ogundipe, S., and Oluwole, J., "Nigeria loses US$14bn annually to herdsmen-farmers clashes". Special Report, 15 April 2016. Accessed from: https://www.premiumtimesng.com/news/headlines/201829-nigeria-loses-14-billion-annually-herdsmen-farmers-clashes-report.html [29 November 2016].

Ogundipe, S., Obinna, C., and Olwale, G., "Global Fund uncovers fraud in malaria, tuberculosis, HIV/AIDS grants to Nigeria". *Vanguard Newspapers*, 6 May 2016. Accessed from: https://www.vanguardngr.com/2016/05/global-fund-uncovers-fraud-malaria-tb-hivaids-grants-nigeria/ [22 November 2017].

Ogunjimi, L.O., Ibe, R., and Ikorok, M.M., "Curbing maternal and child mortality: The Nigerian experience". *International Journal of Nursing & Midwifery*, 4 (2012): 33-39.

Ogunsanmi, J.O., and Ibimiluyi, F.O., "From the Universal Primary Education (UPE) to Universal Education (UBE): Implications for Counselling in primary and junior secondary schools in Nigeria". *International Journal of Psychology & Counselling*, 6 (2014): 89-93.

Okakwu, E., "Despite challenges, EFCC making progress in anti-corruption war". *Premium Times*, 30 August 2017.

Okunmadewa, F., "Nigeria Poverty Reduction, Growth, Strategies and Options in Nigeria: Prospects for Development". University of Ibadan, 1996.

Olurode, L., "State and Political Participation: Women in Nigeria's 2011 Elections". Discussion Paper (2013). Accessed from: http://library.fes.de/pdf-files/bueros/nigeria/10192.pdf [25 September 2017].

Omoluabi, E., *Needs assessment of the health sector* (Abuja: International Organization for Migration, 2013).

Omonubi, M.M., *Gender inequality in Nigeria* (Ibadan: Spectrum Books, 2002).

Omoruyi, G., "Causes of maternal mortality in Nigeria". *Sunday Observer*, 24 May 2008.

Organization for Economic Cooperation and Development, "Adoption of technologies for sustainable farming systems". Wageningen Workshop Proceedings, 2001. Accessed from: http://www.oecd.org/greengrowth/sustainable-agriculture/2739771.pdf [15 October 2017].

Ortiz, I., and Cummins, M., "Global inequality: Beyond the bottom billion: A rapid review of income distribution in 141 countries". UNICEF Policy & Practice, April 2011. Accessed from: https://www.unicef.org/socialpolicy/files/Global_Inequality.pdf [18 October 2017].

Osita-Njoku, A., and Chikere, P., "Consequences of Boko Haram Terrorism on Women in Northern Nigeria". *Applied Research Journal*, 1 (2015): 101-107. Accessed from: http://arjournal.org/files/2015/05/ARJ-V.1n.3.101-107.pdf [16 September 2017].

Overseas Development Institute, "Universal Primary Education: Uganda". Policy Brief, February 2006. Accessed from: https://www.odi.org/sites/odi.org.uk/files/odi-assets/publications-opinion-files/4072.pdf [24 February 2017].

Ovie, F., and Akpomuview, B. "An appraisal of poverty alleviation programmes in Nigeria". *Journal of Research in Development*, 9 (2011): 296-304.

Oxfam, "Inequality in Nigeria: Exploring the drivers." Oxfam International Working Report, May 2017. Accessed from: https://www.oxfam.org/sites/www.oxfam.org/files/file_attachments/cr-inequality-in-nigeria-170517-en.pdf [15 September 2017].

Oxfam, *Measuring Poverty in Nigeria* (Abuja: Oxfam, 2003)

Oxford Institute for Energy Studies, "The significance of the US withdrawal from the Paris Agreement on Climate Change". Discussion Paper, June 2017. Accessed from: https://www.oxfordenergy.org/wpcms/wp-content/uploads/2017/06/The-Significance-of-the-US-Withdrawal-from-the-Paris-Agreement-on-Climate-Change.pdf [12 November 2017].

PBL Netherlands Environmental Assessment Agency, *Trends in Global CO2 Emissions: 2016 Report* (Department of Environment: the Hague, 2016).

Peil, M., *Nigerian politics: The people's view* (London, Cassel, 1976).

Pew Research Center, "Wealth gaps rise to record highs between whites, blacks, Hispanics". Accessed from: http://www.pewsocialtrends.org/2011/07/26/wealth-gaps-rise-to-record-highs-between-whites-blacks-hispanics/.

Proshare, "Nigeria as an import-dependent economy: Outlook for commodities and impact on ordinary people". Working Paper, January 2017. Accessed from: https://www.proshareng.com/news/NIGERIA%20ECONOMY/Nigeria-As-An-Import-Dependent-Economy---Outlook-for-Commodities-and-Impact-on-Ordinary-People-/33432 [11 July 2017].

Provost, C., "Everything you need to know about UK aid and the 0.7% spending pledge". *The Guardian*, 13 June 2016.

Sharma, P., Dwivedi, S., and Singh, D., "Global Poverty, Hunger, and Malnutrition: A Situational Analysis". DFID Study (2016).

PricewaterhouseCoopers, "What next for Nigeria's economy? Navigating the rocky road ahead". Technical Report (2016). Accessed from: http://www.pwc.com/ng/en/assets/pdf/economy-watch-may-2015.pdf [8 December 2016].

PricewaterhouseCoopers, "The Economic Recovery & Growth Plan (ERGP): 2017-2020". Policy Brief (2017). Accessed from: https://www.pwc.com/ng/en/assets/pdf/economy-alert-april-2017.pdf.

Philips, A.O., "A general overview of the Structural Adjustment Programme". In Philips, A.C., and Ndekwu, E.C. (eds.), *Structural Adjustment Programme in a Developing Economy: The Case of Nigeria* (Ibadan: NISER, 1987).

Ranis, G., *Human Development and Economic Growth* (New Haven: Yale University Economic Growth Center, 2004).

Reci, A., "Advantages and disadvantages of foreign assistance in Albania", *Forum Scientiae Oeconomia*, 2 (2014): 124-132.

Rippin, N., Keijzer, N., Loewe, M., and Schraven, B., "Goal 10: Reduce inequality within and among countries". SDG Working Report (2016). Acessed from: https://www.oecd.org/pcd/DIE__Comments__on__SDG__proposals__150226.pdf [22 November 2017].

Saker, L., Lee, K., Cannito, B., Gilmore, A., and Campbell-Lendrum, D., "Globalization & Infectious Diseases: A Review of the Linkages". *WHO Special Topics* 3 (2004).

Salami, C.G.E,, "Youth employment in Nigeria: A Time for Creative Intervention", *International Journal of Business & Marketing Management*, 1 (2013): 18-26.

Sanitation for All, "Nigeria overview: Water, sanitation and hygiene." Briefing Note [online] (2017). Accessed from: http://sanitationandwaterforall.org/wp-content/uploads/download-manager-files/2017%20Nigeria%20Overview_final.pdf.

Saunders, M., Lewis, P., and Thornhill, A., *Research Methods for Business Students*, 3rd ed. (Harlow, Essex: Financial Times Prentice Hall, 2005).

SDG Compass, "Take urgent action to combat climate change and its impacts". Policy Brief (2016). Accessed from: https://sdgcompass.org/wp-content/uploads/2016/04/Goal_13.pdf [13 November 2017].

Sen, A., *Development as Freedom* (Oxford: Oxford University Press).

Shay, I.H., and Say, L., "Maternal mortality and maternity care from 1990-2005: Uneven but important gains". *Reproductive Health Matters*, 15 (2005): 17-27.

Sklar, R.L., Onwudiwe, E., and Kew, D., "Nigeria: Completing Obasanjo's Legacy". *Journal of Democracy*, 17 (2006): 100-115.

Tahir, G., "The Universal Basic Education Programme: Issues and Challenges". Lecture delivered at the Federal College of Education, Kano State.

Taiwo, O., Asuzu, D., and Alade, B., "Economic and fiscal implications of Nigeria's rebased GDP". Accessed from: http://www.pwc.com/ng/en/publications/gross-domestic-product-does-size-really-matter.html [17 February 2017].

Transparency International, "Nigeria Country Overview: Corruption Perception Index 2016". Accessed from: https://www.transparency.org/country/NGA [12 August 2017].

Uhunmwuangho, S.O., and Epelle, A., "Corruption and the Nigerian state: The relevance of ICPC and EFCC in the war against the scourge". *Babcock Journal of Management & Social Sciences*, 6 (2007).

UK Department for International Development, *Eliminating hunger: strategy for achieving the Millennium Development Goal on Hunger* (London: DFID, 2003).

Ukaigwe, G.A., "Evolving an Ideal Revenue Sharing Formula In Nigerian Issues, Problems and Prospects". Master's Thesis: University of Nigeria Nsukka, 2012.

Ukoji, V.N., "Trends and patterns of fatal road accidents in Nigeria (2006-2014)". *Nigeria Watch* [online] 28 November 2014. Accessed from: http://www.nigeriawatch.org/media/html/WP6VitusV6Final.pdf [16 October 2017].

UN Women, *A Transformative Stand-Alone Goal on Achieving Gender Equality, Women's Rights and Women's Empowerment: Imperatives and Key Components* (New York: UN Women, 2013).

UN Women, "Accelerating gender equality through the Post-2015 Development Agenda". Accessed from: https://unwomen.org.au/wp-content/uploads/2015/10/Accelerating-Gender-Equality-through-the-Post-2015-Development-Agenda.pdf [2 September 2017].

UNECA, AU, AFDB, & UNDP, "Food security in Africa: Issues, challenges, and lessons". MDG Report (2013). Accessed from: https://www.afdb.org/fileadmin/uploads/afdb/Documents/Publications/Millennium_Development_Goals__MDGs__Report_2013.pdf.

UNESCO, "World Conference on Higher Education Framework and Action" (2001). Accessed from: http://www.jyu.tilunesco2001/conference.html [23 February 2017].

UNFPA. "Nigeria: Child marriage country profile, 2012".

UN-Habitat, "Development Context and the Millennium Agenda: The Challenge of Slums". Accessed from: https://unhabitat.org/wp-content/uploads/2003/07/GRHS_2003_Chapter_01_Revised_2010.pdf.

UN-Habitat, *Emerging futures in urbanization and development, World Cities Report* (Nairobi: UN Habitat, 2016).

UNICEF, "400,000 children in North-East Nigeria at risk of severe acute malnutrition". Briefing Note 31, January 2017. Accessed from: https://www.unicef.org/nutrition/nigeria_94178.html [10 November 2017].

UNICEF, "At a Glance: Nigeria 2008-2012". Accessed from: https://www.unicef.org/infobycountry/nigeria_statistics.html.

UNICEF, "General Facts: Mother, Newborn and Child Health and Mortality in Nigeria". Fact Sheet, September 2012. Accessed from: https://www.unicef.org/nigeria/ng_publications_advocacybrochure.pdf [13 March 2017].

UNICEF, "Maternal and newborn health in Nigeria: Developing strategies to accelerate progress". Policy Brief, June 2010. Accessed from: https://www.unicef.org/sowc09/docs/SOWC09-Panel-1.3-EN.pdf [11 March 2017].

UNICEF, "Nigeria: Female Genital Mutilation". FactSheet May 2007. Accessed from: https://www.unicef.org/nigeria/FGM_.pdf [9 October 2017].

UNICEF, "Nigeria: WaSH Country Summary Sheet 2008". Accessed from: https://www.unicef.org/nigeria/NG_resources_washsummary.pdf.

UNICEF, "Nutrition: Malnutrition rates in Under-5 children in Nigeria". Factsheet, Accessed from: https://www.unicef.org/nigeria/factsheets_NUTRITION_low.pdf [20 September 2017].

UNICEF, *Promoting Gender Equality: An Equity-Focused Approach to Programming* (New York: UNICEF, 2011).

UNICEF, "WaSH in Schools in Angola". Accessed from: https://issuu.com/unicefangola/docs/wash_schools_angola_2016.

UNICEF and Federal Ministry of Water Resources, "Making Nigeria Open Defecation-free by 2025". Strategy Document, February 2015. Accessed from: https://www.unicef.org/nigeria/NATIONAL_ROAD_MAP_FOR_ELIMINATING_OPEN_DEFECATION_IN_NIGERIA.pdf [4 September 2017].

UNICEF and World Health Organization, "Achieving the Malaria MDG Target: Reversing the incidence of Malaria 2000-2015" (2015). Accessed from: http://apps.who.int/iris/bitstream/10665/184521/1/9789241509442_eng.pdf [18 March 2017].

United Nations, "Achieving Equality, Women's Empowerment and Strengthening Development Cooperation" (2010). Accessed from: http://www.un.org/en/ecosoc/docs/pdfs/10-50143_(e)_(desa)dialogues_ecosoc_achieving_gender_equality_women_empowerment.pdf [23 February 2017].

United Nations, "Challenges in raising private sector resources for financing sustainable development". Working Paper (2016). Accessed from: https://sustainabledevelopment.un.org/content/documents/2106Chapter%203-challenges%20in%20raising%20private%20sector%20resources.pdf [22 November 2017].

United Nations, "Goal 4: Reduce Child Mortality". Fact Sheet (2010). Accessed from: http://www.un.org/millenniumgoals/pdf/MDG_FS_4_EN.pdf [12 March 2017].

United Nations, "Goal 6: Combat HIV/AIDS, Malaria and Other Diseases". Fact sheet (2010).

United Nations, "Goal 7: Environmental Sustainability". Fact Sheet (2008). Accessed from: http://www.un.org/millenniumgoals/2008highlevel/pdf/newsroom/Goal%207%20FINAL.pdf [19 February 2017].

United Nations, "MDGs Fact Sheet" (2010).

United Nations, "Millennium Project: what they are", (2000). Accessed from: http://www.unmillenniumproject.org/goals/ [3 January 2017].

United Nations, "Nigeria: Humanitarian Response Plan (HRP) for the North East". Policy Brief (2016). Accessed from: https://reliefweb.int/sites/reliefweb.int/files/resources/nigeria_2016_hrp_11012016.pdf [22 October 2017].

United Nations, "Realizing the future we want. UN System Task Team on the Post-2015 Development Agenda: Report to the Secretary General" (2012).

United Nations, "Sustainable cities: Why they matter". Working Paper (2017). Accessed from: http://www.un.org/sustainabledevelopment/wp-content/uploads/2016/08/16-00055K_Why-it-Matters_Goal-11_Cities_2p.pdf [22 October 2017].

United Nations, "Towards sustainable cities". Working Paper (2013). Accessed from: http://www.un.org/en/development/desa/policy/wess/wess_current/wess2013/Chapter3.pdf [13 November 2017].

United Nations, "Transforming our world: The 2030 Agenda for Sustainable Development". Working Paper A/RES/70/1 (2016). Accessed from: https://sustainabledevelopment.un.org/content/documents/21252030%20Agenda%20for%20Sustainable%20Development%20web.pdf [28 September 2017].

United Nations, *The Millennium Development Goals Report* (New York: UN, 2010).

United Nations, *The Millennium Development Goals Report* (New York: UN, 2013).

United Nations, "The United Nations Development Agenda: Development for All" (2007). Accessed from: http://www.un.org/esa/devagenda/UNDA_BW5_Final.pdf [4 January 2017].

United Nations, "UN Summit, Goal 8: Develop a Global Partnership for Development, Fact Sheet, September 2010". Accessed from: http://www.un.org/millenniumgoals/pdf/MDG_FS_8_EN.pdf [21 March 2017].

United Nations, "UN Systems Task Team on the Post-2015 UN Development Agenda: Science, Technology and Innovation for Sustainable Development in the Global Partnership for Development Beyond 2015" (2015). Accessed from: http://www.un.org/en/development/desa/policy/untaskteam_undf/thinkpieces/28_thinkpiece_science.pdf [22 October 2017].

United Nations Association-UK, *Global Development Goals: Partnership for Progress* (London: UNA-UK, 2016).

United Nations Development Group, "Socio-economic Impact of Ebola Virus Disease in West African Countries: A call for national and regional containment, recovery and protection" (2015). Accessed from: https://reliefweb.int/sites/reliefweb.int/files/resources/ebola-west-africa.pdf.

United Nations Development Programme, "Human Development Report 2007, Country Fact Sheet: Nigeria". Accessed from: http://hdrstatsundp.org/countries/countryfactsheets/ctyfsMGA.html.

United Nations Development Programme, *Human Development Report: Work for Human Development* (New York: UNDP, 2015).

United Nations Development Programme, "Human Development for All: Human Development Report 2016". Accessed from: http://hdr.undp.org/sites/all/themes/hdr_theme/country-notes/NGA.pdf [3 March 2017].

United Nations Development Programme, "Human Development Report 2004". Accessed from: www.hdr.undp.org [3 January 2017].

United Nations Development Programme, *Niger Delta Human Development Report* (Abuja: UNDP, 2006).

United Nations Development Programme, "Nigeria: The Human Development Index: Going Beyond Income, Human Development Report 2009". Accessed from: http://www.http://hdstats.undp.org/en/countries/country_fact_sheets/cty_fs_NGA.html [22 March 2017].

United Nations Development Programme, *Partners in Development: How Donors Can Better Engage the Private Sector for Development in LDCs* (New York: UN Global Impact, 2011).

United Nations Development Programme, "Sustainable Development Goals" (2016). Accessed from: http://www.undp.org/content/dam/undp/library/corporate/brochure/SDGs_Booklet_Web_En.pdf [22 September 2017].

United Nations Development Programme, OSSAP-MDGs and DFID, "Millennium Development Goals: End-point Report for Nigeria, September 2015". Accessed from: http://www.ng.undp.org/content/dam/nigeria/docs/MDGs/Nigeria_MDG_Report%202015%20Full%20Report.pdf [22 August2017].

United Nations Environment Programme, *Environmental Assessment of Ogoniland* (Nairobi: UNEP, 2011).

United Nations Environment Programme, "Sustainable consumption and production indicators for the future SDGs" (2015). Accessed from: https://sustainabledevelopment.un.org/content/documents/2301SCP%20indicators.pdf [23 August 2017].

United Nations Office of the Coordinator Humanitarian Affairs, "Nigeria: Humanitarian Response Plan for North East Nigeria" (2017). Accessed from: http://reliefweb.int/sites/reliefweb.int/files/resources/ocha_nga_hrp_2017_summary_16122016.pdf.

Universal Basic Education Commission, "Universal Basic Education Act of 2004". Accessed from: https://ubeconline.com/ [23 October 2017].

Universal Basic Education Commission, *Universal Basic Education Programme, Annual Report 2006* (Abuja: UBEC, 2006).

Universal Basic Education Commission, *Standard Action Plan Based on the UBE Act* (Abuja: UBEC, 2004).

US Agency for International Development, "Angola: Water and Sanitation Profile". (2014). Accessed from: http://pdf.usaid.gov/pdf_docs/Pnado925.pdf [21 October 2017].

US Agency for International Development, *HIV/AIDS in Nigeria* (Abuja: USAID, 2005).

US Agency for International Development-Nigeria, "Strengthening Integrated Delivery of HIV/AIDS Services (SIDHAS) Project: Mid-term Evaluation Final Report, May 2015". Accessed from: http://pdf.usaid.gov/pdf_docs/PA00KNBT.pdf.

US Agency for International Development, "Urban Profile: 'Nigeria making cities work" (2002). Available from: http//www.makingcitieswork.org/files/pdf/Africa/Nigeria

US Central Intelligence Agency, "World Factbook: Nigeria" (2016). Accessed from: https://www.cia.gov/library/publications/resources/the-world-factbook/geos/ni.html [21 January 2017].

US Embassy in Nigeria, "Education Fact Sheet 2012". Accessed from: https://photos.state.gov/libraries/nigeria/487468/pdfs/JanuaryEducationFactSheet.pdf.

US Embassy in Nigeria, "Malaria Fact Sheet" (2011). Accessed from: http://photos.state.gov/libraries/nigeria/231771/Public/December-MalariaFactSheet2.pdf [22 March 2017].

US Embassy in Nigeria, "Malaria Fact Sheet" (2012).

US Embassy in Nigeria, "Nigeria Tuberculosis Fact Sheet" (2012).

US$321mn Abacha loot: Nigeria concludes negotiation with Switzerland". *Premium Times*, 26 October 2017. Accessed from: https://www.premiumtimesng.com/news/top-news/247432-321-million-abacha-loot-nigeria-concludes-negotiation-switzerland.html [10 November 2017].

Vandemoortele, J., "Advancing the global development agenda post-2015: Some thoughts, ideas, and practical suggestions. Paper presented by the UN System Task Team on the Post-2015 Development Agenda. Accessed from http://www.un.org/millenniumgoals/pdf/jan_vandemoortele_Aug.pdf.

Wichterich, C., *The future we want: A feminist perspective* (Berlin: Heinrich Boll Stiftung, 2013).

"Women, gender equality in Nigeria: A critical analysis of socio-economic and political gender issues". *Journal of Research in Peace, Gender and Development*, 4 (2014): 15-20. Accessed from: http://www.interesjournals.org/full-articles/women-gender-equality-in-nigeria-a-critical-analysis-of-socio-economic-and-political-gender-issues.pdf?view=inline [11 January 2017].

Women's Environment and Development Organization, "Women's Action Agenda 21". Advocacy Paper (1991). Accessed from: http://www.wedo.org [28 August 2017].

World Bank, *Achieving Universal Primary Education by 2015: A Chance for Every Child* (Washington: IBRD, 2003).

World Bank, "Country Partnership Strategy for the Federal Republic of Nigeria: FY2014-2017". Report No. 82501-NG. Accessed from: http://documents.worldbank.org/curated/en/214371468098983763/pdf/825010CAS0P133040Box385166B00OUO090.pdf.

World Bank, *Education for All: Assessing the level of progress made by the Nigerian Government* (Abuja: IBRD, 2014).

World Bank, "From agriculture to nutrition: Pathways, synergies, and outcomes". Report No. 40196-GLB (2007).

World Bank, "Nigeria: Access to improved sanitation facilities". Accessed from: https://data.worldbank.org/indicator/SH.STA.ACSN?locations=NG [11 October 2017].

World Bank, "Nigeria: Economic Profile". *Quarterly Report*, July 2013. Accessed from: http://www.worlbank.org [17 July 2017].

World Bank, "Nigeria: Poverty in the Midst of Plenty – The challenge of growth with inclusion". Report No. 14733-UNI. Accessed from: http://documents.worldbank.org/curated/en/582991468759320261/pdf/multi0page.pdf [11 January 2017].

World Bank, *Poverty and Shared Prosperity: Talking on Inequality* (Washington: IBRD/World Bank, 2016).

World Bank, *Poverty: World Development Report* (Washington: World Bank, 2001).

World Bank, *Voices for the Poor* (Washington: World Bank, 2003).

World Bank, *World Development Indicators 2013* (Washington: World Bank, 2013).

World Economic Forum, "The Global Risks Report 2015". Accessed from: http://www3.weforum.org/docs/WEF_Global_Risks_2015_Report.pdf.

World Health Organization, *Factsheet: Maternal Mortality* (Geneva: WHO, 2011).

World Health Organization, "Global Aids Response Progress Reporting, 2016". Accessed from: https://aidsreportingtool.unaids.org/static/docs/GARPR_Guidelines_2016_EN.pdf.

World Health Organization, "Global HIV/AIDS Response: Epidemic Update and Health Sector Progress towards Universal Access". Progress Report 2012. Accessed from: http://www.who.int/hiv/pub/progress_report2011/hiv_full_report_2011.pdf [7 March 2017].

World Health Organization, "Malaria Report". Working Paper (2012).
World Health Organization, *Maternal Mortality: Fact Sheet* (Geneva: WHO, 2016).
World Health Organization, "Nutritional challenges". Working Report (2013). Accessed from: http://www.who.int/nutrition/challenges/en/index.html [13 September 2017].
World Health Organization, "Positioning health in the post-2015 development agenda". Discussion paper (2012). Accessed from: http://www.who.int/topics/millennium_development_goals/post2015/WHOdiscussionpaper_October2012.pdf.
World Health Organization, *Proportion of Births Attended by a Skilled Health Worker: Factsheet* (Geneva: WHO, 2008).
World Health Organization, "Surgical workforce in Nigeria: Stock and flow of medical and dental practioners in Nigeria, with special focus on health workforce training in Cross River States. Case Study (2015). Accessed from: http://www.who.int/workforcealliance/031616NigeriaCaseStudyweb.pdf [22 September 2017].
World Health Organization, "The World Health Report: Reducing Risks, Promoting Healthy Life" (2002). Accessed from: http://www.who.int/whr/2002/en/whr02_en.pdf [16 September 2017].
World Health Organization, "Violence against women". Factsheet (2016). Accessed from: http://www.who.int/mediacentre/factsheets/fs239/en/ [5 March 2017].
World Health Organization, "Water & Sanitation Challenges in Nigeria". Working Paper (2014).
World Health Organization. *Working together for health: The world health report 2006* (Geneva: WHO, 2006). Accessed from: http://www.who.int/whr/2006/whr06_en.pdf [1 January 2017].
World Health Organization, "World Health Statistics, 2011". Accessed from: http://www.who.int/whosis/whostat/EN_WHS2011_full.pdf [7 March 2017].
World Health Organization and UNICEF, *Trends in Maternal Mortality: 1990 to 2015* (Abuja: WHO, 2015).
World Health Organization and UNICEF, "WHO/UNICEF Joint Monitoring Programme for Water Supply and Sanitation (JMP)" (2008).
World Health Organization, UNICEF and UNAIDS, *A guide on indicators for the monitoring and reporting on health sector response to HIV/AIDS* (Geneva: WHO, 2011).

Structures éditoriales du groupe L'Harmattan

L'Harmattan Italie
Via degli Artisti, 15
10124 Torino
harmattan.italia@gmail.com

L'Harmattan Hongrie
Kossuth l. u. 14-16.
1053 Budapest
harmattan@harmattan.hu

L'Harmattan Sénégal
10 VDN en face Mermoz
BP 45034 Dakar-Fann
senharmattan@gmail.com

L'Harmattan Cameroun
TSINGA/FECAFOOT
BP 11486 Yaoundé
inkoukam@gmail.com

L'Harmattan Burkina Faso
Achille Somé – tengnule@hotmail.fr

L'Harmattan Guinée
Almamya, rue KA 028 OKB Agency
BP 3470 Conakry
harmattanguinee@yahoo.fr

L'Harmattan RDC
185, avenue Nyangwe
Commune de Lingwala – Kinshasa
matangilamusadila@yahoo.fr

L'Harmattan Congo
67, boulevard Denis-Sassou-N'Guesso
BP 2874 Brazzaville
harmattan.congo@yahoo.fr

L'Harmattan Mali
Sirakoro-Meguetana V31
Bamako
syllaka@yahoo.fr

L'Harmattan Togo
Djidjole – Lomé
Maison Amela
face EPP BATOME
ddamela@aol.com

L'Harmattan Côte d'Ivoire
Résidence Karl – Cité des Arts
Abidjan-Cocody
03 BP 1588 Abidjan
espace_harmattan.ci@hotmail.fr

L'Harmattan Algérie
22, rue Moulay-Mohamed
31000 Oran
info2@harmattan-algerie.com

L'Harmattan Maroc
5, rue Ferrane-Kouicha, Talaâ-Elkbira
Chrableyine, Fès-Médine
30000 Fès
harmattan.maroc@gmail.com

Nos librairies en France

Librairie internationale
16, rue des Écoles – 75005 Paris
librairie.internationale@harmattan.fr
01 40 46 79 11
www.librairieharmattan.com

Librairie l'Espace Harmattan
21 bis, rue des Écoles – 75005 Paris
librairie.espace@harmattan.fr
01 43 29 49 42

Lib. sciences humaines & histoire
21, rue des Écoles – 75005 Paris
librairie.sh@harmattan.fr
01 46 34 13 71
www.librairieharmattansh.com

Lib. Méditerranée & Moyen-Orient
7, rue des Carmes – 75005 Paris
librairie.mediterranee@harmattan.fr
01 43 29 71 15

Librairie Le Lucernaire
53, rue Notre-Dame-des-Champs – 75006 Paris
librairie@lucernaire.fr
01 42 22 67 13

www.ingramcontent.com/pod-product-compliance
Lightning Source LLC
Chambersburg PA
CBHW071434230926
51846CB00001B/224